ARE YOU AN OSTRICH OR A LLAMA?

ESSAYS IN HOSPITALITY MARKETING AND
MANAGEMENT

LARRY MOGELONSKY

authorHOUSE®

AuthorHouse™
1663 Liberty Drive
Bloomington, IN 47403
www.authorhouse.com
Phone: 1-800-839-8640

Published by AuthorHouse   07/10/2012

ISBN: 978-1-4772-4012-0 (sc)
ISBN: 978-1-4772-4013-7 (hc)

Library of Congress Control Number: 2012912243

Any people depicted in stock imagery provided by Thinkstock are models, and such images are being used for illustrative purposes only.
Certain stock imagery © *Thinkstock.*

This book is printed on acid-free paper.

Because of the dynamic nature of the Internet, any web addresses or links contained in this book may have changed since publication and may no longer be valid. The views expressed in this work are solely those of the author and do not necessarily reflect the views of the publisher, and the publisher hereby disclaims any responsibility for them.

Reviews of Are You an Ostrich or a Llama

The most important element of the hotel experience is the interaction between guest and employee. Larry's book offers a comprehensive review of how to achieve success as a hotel manager in a changing world, while maintaining an all-important focus on customer service. "Are you an Ostrich or a Llama?" will help managers navigate the latest technologies while providing the utmost in hospitality.

Isadore Sharp
Chairman
Four Seasons Hotels & Resorts

Leave it to Larry Mogelonsky, one of the industry's most prolific visionaries, to write a book that examines every minute detail of how hospitality should be run—LIKE CLOCKWORK. His unique personal experiences combined with his professionalism give readers a hands-on approach to the issues affecting today's hotelier. This book should be a permanent addition to the library of every hotel operator and management team.

Benedict Cummins
Publisher
HotelExecutive.com

If you are looking for a self-gloating book by some hotel executive, telling you how wonderful they conduct business, this book is not for you. With his precise, often humorous and enjoyable writing style, Larry's book is a breath of fresh air, in an industry that was able somehow to portray itself as sophisticated and cutting edge and that is instead paying the price for a decade of self-inflicted wounds. Through a series of poignant articles, Larry looks at the hospitality world with an inquisitive eye, paying attention to the smallest of details and trends as well as questioning the industry to its core and often-misleading beliefs. A must read for any hotel executive.

Renato Alesiani
President and COO
Wave Crest Hotels & Resorts

As a long time fan, I always look forward to Larry Mogelonsky's business savvy articles and insights on hospitality marketing, which I excitedly share with the managers of the Library Hotel Collection. Larry's thought process is so logical and perceptive, readers will find themselves saying. "Yes! How true!" but more importantly, "I am going to do that, too!" because it is thick with practical ideas on how to make your business prosper. I highly recommend this book to anyone who wants to elevate the business acumen of their company and find a wealth of opportunities to please customers and maximize profitability.

Adele Gutman
Vice President of Marketing
Library Hotel Collection

A wonderful read. Insightful, intelligent and fun to read and identify with.

Janis Clapoff
Managing Director (former)
Ojai Valley Inn & Spa

Larry is one of those rare individuals that will provide you with an outsider's perspective from an insider's point of view. You may not agree with everything Larry has to say, but I'm willing to bet that most of it will ring true when you take the time to think about it.

Chuck Kelley
Principal
G7 Hospitality Group Inc.

Larry takes what we hoteliers often think is difficult and simplifies it in a way that makes perfect sense. A must read for hoteliers to understand that excellent guest service leads to greater profitability.

Gordon Carncross
Principal
G7 Hospitality Group Inc.

Larry nails some of the critical issues facing hoteliers today and gives them a 'velvet hammer' approach to solutions. Throughout the book, I couldn't help but see immediate parallels with many of the property situations encountered on a day-to-day basis. A great read.

Marshall Calder
President-Americas
Great Hotels of the World

The complexities of hotel operations and marketing are rarely found in a single book. Yet, Larry is able to intertwine these two core elements of hospitality management in a single edition, and present these in an easy-to-read approach. The use of real live experiences and interviews with leaders in the field brings these topics to life, and prompts further debate amongst practitioners. Read it, then reflect upon how these examples can enhance your operations.

Kuno W. Fasel
Chief Operating Officer
COMO Hotels & Resorts

From the first article to the end, Larry provides a wealth of information for hotel managers to wrestle with, to question their strategies and operational plans. There is learning in every chapter.

Fred Grapstein
President
New York's Hotel Pennsylvania

You can run but you can't hide from the truths in this book: Wishy-washy it's not. Hopefully, you'll read these words of advice carefully and more than once—until you can truly see the ostrich in the mirror. This is solid advice, but offered with great humor. I found myself saying "Yes!" and chuckling at the same time. Good stuff!

William J. Callnin
Chairman & Managing Director
Cayuga Hospitality Advisors

For Maureen

Table of Contents

Reviews of Are You an Ostrich or a Llama

Guest Services

Social Media

Branding

Operations and Human Resources

Traditional Marketing

Internet Marketing

Conclusion

Preface Part One

The hotel world is full of obstinacy and opportunities. But that could be any industry. Whether by experience or sheer luck, I happen to have a knack for hotels. That's what I've come to know.

Call it indulgent, but I enjoy travel, delighted by the different experiences that each new city and new property gives me. With my marketing background and a love for hotels, a book blending the two is only natural.

Working as an advertising consultant for hotels can be frustrating. I'm the guy that's called in to tell them what's wrong and offer a solution. Sometimes they listen. Other times they don't, insist I'm wrong and, on rare occasions, let me go. Sometimes my ideas are radical. Other times my ideas are so straightforward they're impossible to refute.

Yet, some managers still do. Nowadays, the industry is marred by numerous redundancies and assumptions that are all bubbling to the surface in many different and interesting ways by the rapid spread of information thanks to the Internet.

Turning 60, I wanted to start giving back. Out of altruism and a dash of frustration, I started publishing short articles on various hospitality topics in early 2011. The following pages were compiled from several different online and print hospitality editorials, reworked to form a cohesive argument.

The overarching theme of these articles is to highlight some of the key differences between what we as hoteliers perceive as important and what is actually important for driving occupancy. That's what it's all about, right? No matter the average rate or the F&B sales, if there are no guests, then the hotel is a bust.

So, what drives occupancy? There seems to be a rather large gap between the answer taught in schools and what occurs in reality. Hospitality theory would have you studying through daily metrics, juggling channel distribution opportunities and fine-tuning revenue management figures. Hotels and resorts can be much simpler than micromanaging every number that stacks up on your desk.

Hotels are about the experience. Give your guests something unique and care for them like you would your own family and friends. It's my core belief that superior guest services override any gaps in property features or room amenities. Advertising and promotions will get you new business, as will a renovation, big event or new facility. Repeat business, however, is based on a positive, emotional experience, and the marketing costs for this are always much lower. You will not retain your customers without a personality both warm and attentive.

The Internet has rewritten how the hospitality game is played. It's faster. There are scores of new channels to promote your inventory. Guests can broadcast their complaint to thousands of people before you'd had a chance to take corrective action. When it comes to social media, there's managing, monitoring, posting, replying, sharing, tweeting, pinning, commenting, bookmarking and dozens more. For hotel managers, the apt word is overwhelming.

But it doesn't have to be. Technological developments may be moving at a cheetah's pace, but human nature is still more or less status quo. We all still respond to the same civility and face-to-face compassion to which our grandfathers and our grandfather's grandfathers responded. It all boils down to guest services and your ability to keep visitors happy.

That's why I assembled these articles into a book; a guide to instill this fundamental sense of what's important; to fill in the gaps between where classroom analysis ends and real, 21st century hospitality begins. No matter what new problems come your way, if your guest services are solid then you'll survive. After all, only satisfied guests will give you that coveted word of mouth—recommendations often more powerful than the most influential of advertisements or social media campaigns.

So, how did I end up with this opinion? Why do I feel as though my intuition is better aligned with where the market is headed? Well, it all started at a very young age . . .

My First Hotel Job

Everyone has to start somewhere. For most of us in the hotel business, that first job in the industry can often define the best couple decades. It is your opportunity to prove to yourself that you have made the correct career decision. It is a validation exercise.

My first hotel job was strictly unintentional. High school was ending for the year and my father coerced me to earn some of my own money for the summer.

With my birthday in September, I was approaching sixteen years old. I took the city bus downtown, not really knowing how to go about getting a position nor what I would be doing. The day was extremely muggy for late June in Montreal and my brief bus journey ended at the Journey's Inn. (Thank goodness, the property has been re-flagged!) A relatively new property at the time, the building included two restaurants, several meeting rooms and four floors of underground parking.

In one of the buried, sub-basement offices, I met with the human resources manager named Marcel (name changed). His weight, I estimated well in excess of 300 pounds, and wearing a short sleeve white shirt and thin dark tie, he sweated profusely; the air-conditioning being no match for the hotel's laundry easily heard next door. Marcel was pleasant enough, and, judging from the job applications sorted into a shoulder high pile on his desk, he seemed rather enthused to meet an applicant, or anyone for that matter, in person.

Marcel advised me that, unfortunately, there were no jobs currently available for dishwashers, bus boys, stewarding, convention services, custodians, maintenance, bellmen, laundry, front desk or even housekeeping which he described as a 'job for the ladies.' Naturally, I was disappointed. Half out the door, he asked, "(Attendez une minute.) Oh, wait. Do you drive?"

Drive? Me, an adolescent asked to operate a vehicle? Now, I ask you, how could any fifteen-year-old, self-respecting male teenager respond with anything but an affirmative, I responded, "Of course (Mes, certainment!)."

"Great," said Marcel, "The summer season brings a lot of tourists from New York and Boston. We'll need extra car valet staff starting this holiday weekend. So, come back next Friday. Be here no later than 8AM. Pay is ninety cents an hour plus tips." With that, Marcel dug back into his paperwork, leaving me in a stunned elation before running back to catch another bus home.

Recognizing that I had been living on a five-dollar weekly allowance, the prospect of making close to forty bucks, or more with tips, a week was exhilarating. Somewhat daunting, however, was the task of learning how to drive over the next week and a half!

Unlike most of our neighbors at the time, my family didn't own a car. My father's eyesight precluded him from driving. My mother had no real need to drive; everything we needed was within a short walk away.

A friend of mine had an older brother, who had recently attained that coveted 'age of majority' in the teenage world, acquiring his learner's permit at the age of sixteen and a half. Done in secret, my driving lessons consisted of several trips around the local shopping center parking lot and the unpaved, winding golf course road at the base of our street. A lofty estimate would put me at four or five hours of total training behind the wheel or the front passenger seat.

Arriving for my first day on the job, my uniform was an ill-fitting polyester jacket, name badge and a shiny, thin black tie, styled after Marcel no doubt. And the training was non-existent. Looking back at this, many years later, this was a liability nightmare.

But my few hours behind the wheel served me proud. Within a day or so, I was negotiating the up and down ramps of the garage, and backing cars into their appropriate parking positions with relative ease. Relative, of course, being the key word.

The days rolled by and the summer was progressing well for our small car jockey team. One of our pastimes was to accelerate cars through the garage then brake aggressively before the next down ramp, trying to see how fast we could nudge the speedometer forward. My colleagues were quite adept at this even though I never seemed to match their finesse. Perhaps the fact that I was about five to seven years younger and far less experienced might have had somewhat of a bearing on this proficiency.

One sunny Friday afternoon, a guest arrived in a magnificent Chrysler New Yorker, a forest green, four-door hardtop with a black vinyl roof. If you remember, or are familiar with, the late 1960s, these cars were true land barges. Exceptionally comfortable, the New Yorker offered ample room for three passengers in both the front and back seats, not to mention a humongous trunk. While this car had outstanding power from its 440 cubic inch, high compression, V-8 engine, I was soon to learn that its drum brakes were not of equal caliber.

Steering onto the down ramp, I could feel the incredible torque and seemingly endless horsepower. I stabbed the gas pedal and the car literally roared ahead. Impressive, I thought for a fleeting second or two. The surprise came when I needed the brakes. Slamming them down with full force, the New Yorker acquainted itself with the concrete foundation wall at about ten to fifteen miles an hour, sufficient to knock the engine practically off its mounts and sandwich the radiator into where the engine was supposed to be.

I was not hurt, but everyone easily heard the sound of the impact. One of the first to appear on the scene was my good friend Marcel. As panic immediately obfuscated his logic centers, he held it together long enough to inquire about my driver's license, for insurance purposes, no doubt. Stammering out that I didn't have one, with a not-so-subtle mention that I was still only fifteen years old, Marcel's mood turned from bad to oblivion with a quintessential beet red complexion. Using words in French whose translation would be obvious to any person from Asia or Africa, I was asked impolitely to vacate the premises, and fast.

Getting canned was fine, and before leaving, I asked for my pay for the past week. Audacious with a dab of teenage naiveté, perhaps? Marcel grabbed a fifty-dollar bill from his wallet, and slammed it into my hand, warning me never to show up at his hotel again. For the time being, my short-lived career in the hospitality industry reached an abrupt conclusion.

Sadly, I didn't renew my love for the industry until I started working as the advertising agency at the Four Seasons, Inn on the Park Hotel in Toronto some twenty years later. Moving from the guest services side to the behind-the-scenes strategic planning, I found the hotel world to be increasingly intriguing. Plus, by this point I was an MBA graduate and was more than keen towards issues larger than parking lot bumper cars.

I am sure that everyone has his or her own unique "entry" experience. Think back to what you've learned in the past ten, twenty, even thirty years. Now, determine how you are going to make this profession better for those who are just starting out on your team. Make their first experience memorable for all the right reasons.

Hotels 2020: A Scenario

(Note: All names in this essay are imaginary and any resemblance to individuals or corporations is not to be construed as having any bearing in reality.)

Jimmy Smitherson, the director of revenue, marketing and sales of the Rebellion Hotel, has a problem. It's not one of occupancy. The hotel has long since passed all FIT sales onto RoomSteady, an OTA management liaison that meticulously manages occupancy to meet a stated target. Rather, it was a new decree from TravelOrx, the leading OTA formed after several years of ravenous mergers and acquisitions. Between all the boilerplate banter, Jimmy read the punch line, "As of October 1, 2020, the Rebellion Hotel will no longer be considered a part of our combined distribution systems."

The OTA was firing the hotel! How could this have happened? How did the power reverse so quickly from supplier to distributor? Just ten years earlier, OTAs only represented roughly 10% of total sales, hardly enough to cause any real panic. Hotel management, eager to build occupancy levels and smooth the peaks and valleys in their businesses, embraced these Internet distribution systems. It was easy; just assign the inventory and let the revenue manager sort out the delivery. In doing so, there was no need to advertise or even promote. After all, that was the OTAs' responsibility, wasn't it?

Like any good thing, hotels continued to lap at the bowl of OTA volume offers. What was once 10% or 20% of FIT sales soon became 35% and then well over half of total sales. OTA advertising on television, online, newspapers and even movie theaters was smart, sticky and very persuasive. Winning numerous CLIO awards, the OTAs had the financial clout to hire savvy Hollywood producers and Madison Avenue's finest ad agencies. Needless to say, their "share of mind" (an advertising term designed to determine top-of-mind awareness) was well above any of the hotel chains.

Once the 50% share of business threshold was breached, hotel management recognized that their revenue manager was the pivotal position in their business. Why keep directors of marketing around when marketing was reduced to paltry local ads, the odd web site update, keeping wedding planners happy and the annual incentive shows? Even the sales people had more to do, managing group business. With so much leverage, the revenue manager assumed the senior directorial position in planning committees, incorporating both marketing and sales disciplines.

After all, the revenue director was a position cemented by hard data. Every decision inferred a direct and time-stamped return on investment. Advertising? You best ensure the ad has a set offer rate and expiry date so its potency could be measured, and only somewhat at that. What about advertising that focused on brand building and imagery? Forget it. Not quantifiable. As such, director of marketing titles became misnomers; carryovers from the hotel's glory days when marketing budgets were actually a significant figure and creative branding decisions were essential.

For a while, the world was perfect. With occupancy delivered through the OTAs, general managers were happy and operations were streamlined. However, profit margins remained mediocre as the OTAs continued to expand their commissions to offset their own ever-growing advertising and promotion costs. And here was the festering tapeworm in every hotel's belly. By controlling the airwaves, the OTAs controlled the loyalty of the customer base, winning over the younger generations as the baby boomers ebbed from the market.

The pivotal year was 2019. Early in the year, TravelOrx boldly acquired the omnipresent All-Americas Hotel Group and its 16,000 worldwide properties. At first, the industry just shrugged it off. The price TravelOrx paid was nearly double All-America's current market share price, irking some eyebrows on Wall Street, but quickly sealing the deal.

Within three months, All-America properties consistently appeared at the #1 and #2 spots on the TravelOrx web site. By month six, TravelOrx installed a built-in loyalty program aligning purchases of All-America properties with airlines and car rentals. The reward incentives were exceedingly consumer friendly. Not to be outdone, the remaining OTAs moved to acquire other major hotel chains. This series of rapid acquisitions were touted by Wall Street gurus as a 'synergistic coming of age' for the hospitality industry.

A conglomerate turf war also became natural. Each of the OTA powerhouses built effective marketing programs to galvanize their respective franchises and sign on new hotel allegiances. Independent properties, like the Rebellion Hotel, were left with the scraps—low rankings, reduced prices and ever-higher OTA commission rates—until even those became undesirable and were cut off all together.

Jimmy was stuck. His general manager needed a plan. The Rebellion Hotel had not done any real marketing in over four years. Their advertising agency, if you could call it that, was in reality a part-time freelancer with a fast Mac computer whose 'creative' consisted of a mix between local F&B and spa ads, but not really much else. Jimmy's college education and business background were both fully in line with the OTA-evolved industry: all finance and statistics, with only limited introductory-level marketing courses. Good as he was with numbers, he had no real experience in brand strategies, creative planning and ad purchases, tools of a bygone era.

Losing the entire fourth quarter was a disaster beyond anything he could think of. It was also the only real blip in occupancy he had ever encountered in his eight-year hospitality career. Jimmy tiptoed into the weekly planning committee, cool sweat drenching his undershirt. Was it his fault the property was in this predicament, or was he merely a pawn in a much larger game?

His solution shocked the room. Provocative and bold, he proposed to move the hotel away from the FIT business. Jimmy's plan reflected the core dynamic in the marketplace—aging boomers. Essentially, his strategy was not one of renewed competition, but surrender. In essence, Jimmy's proposal called for the Rebellion Hotel to give up on the hotel industry.

Now predominantly in their 70s, the demographic sought downsized accommodations; not quite ready for nursing homes, but often without sufficient funds to acquire high-priced condos. By appealing to these long-term customers, the Rebellion Hotel effectively shielded itself from the volatile FIT turf war currently underway. With fewer boomers traveling each quarter, the independent traveler market was now completely dominated by younger consumers—people who after years of exposure to alluring OTA advertising campaigns and online reservation systems were all in the OTAs' pockets with no alliances to any one hotel brand in particular. Moreover, the net rate from long-term residences wasn't that much different than the previous year's yield after factoring those high OTA commissions.

Given all that the hotel industry has been through in the past twenty years, how did the general manager and the rest of the room react to this proposal? What would you recommend in Jimmy's place? How do you think the FIT market will shift as the baby boomer generation continues to age? Can you foresee the OTAs moving into the hotel business or will anti-trust prevent such actions? What are your thoughts on the future of hospitality distribution channels? All are good questions to ask yourself and discuss with your colleagues.

Preface Part Two

The 'Hotels 2020' article gets to the core of why I decided to publish this book. It's not just a rant against the OTAs or WiFi surcharges. It's a message of hope for our industry. And the foundation for this lies in the attitude of individual managers.

Are you an ostrich with your 'head in the sand', forcefully pecking your way around for every morsel of food? Or, are you a llama with a docile, attentive behavior and a soft coat of fur? Think of these two animals as a metaphor for the two encompassing styles of management. As in all aspects of life, it's all too easy to obstinately push ahead on your path and insist that others follow. Instead, soften your resolve by listening, accepting and accommodating new suggestions.

Technology is here to stay. We, as hoteliers, will forever be trying to integrate new electronic tools, get on the bandwagon with new social media networks and play catch up with the world at large. What you can, and should, trust are the fundamentals of human interaction.

Remove the gadgetry, remove the software that's streamlining your hotel processes, remove the amenities used to sell your property, and then what do you have? You have people interacting with people. Presenting yourself as endlessly courteous, being attentive to requests and working towards flawless services are all forms of enhancing your staff-to-guest interactions. Those interactions coalesce into an overall positive guest experience and animated word of mouth.

This is the core of the guest experience, and if you can focus your operations and marketing through this perspective, then it'll be clear skies ahead. What bothers me about the OTAs is that their layout and booking methodology focuses primarily on price, and in turn neglects the guest services aspects that build real loyalty.

You have to take the good with the bad, though. The OTAs are an excellent source of honest feedback on your operations, but only if you know how to measure the strings of qualitative data and read between the lines. All the technology advancements in the past decade promote short-term thinking and short-term solutions. A negative reviewer posted on TripAdvisor claiming their room was dirty, so you reprimand the custodial managers. Your occupancy is low for the rest of the month, so you panic and release the leftover rooms onto a flash sale web site. Stop before you press the panic button!

You have to remain conscious of long-term strategy and how technology will fit around your core objectives, instead of resorting to defensive tactics. Don't become a 'weather vane' hotel marketer, constantly responding to technological changes. Be open to new electronic tools, but think about how they can work to enhance or display your sophisticated operations and superior guest services. Unless you are a techno-oriented hotel, you do not need to be the first on the block to have every new gadget, but you shouldn't be the last either.

I've grouped the articles in this book to get you thinking about this 'human factor' in the right way, starting with the core—guest services—then looking at how this can be applied to aspects of social media, branding, operations and lastly marketing. The end purpose is to make your guests happy and ensure that they leave your hotel on a positive note. Yes, be tech savvy and embrace social media, just don't let it get in the way of what's really important.

Guest Services

ARC The.Hotel is located in downtown Ottawa, Canada's capital city. An office building conversion, the hotel allures guests with modern furnishings and superlative service.

Introduction to Guest Services

Superior guest services conquer all. I can't stress this enough. Each visitor is unique and each will have a particular set of tastes. Some will complain, and when they do, it's your responsibility to compensate them in order to live up to the guest experience your brand promises. Ideally though, guests will be singing your praises because their experiences have already lived up to and gone beyond what they were expecting.

This grouping of articles isn't meant to be an introduction to the diverse range of topics that 'guest services' entails. Rather, I'm going to assume you already know what this term tacitly implies from the classroom, on-property training, or simply through countless human interactions over the years. My intentions are to help spark your guest services imagination, to introduce some new hotel-oriented terminology, to open your eyes to some of the underlying contributors to poor guest service, to make you think about some of the finer nuances involved in this process, and to get you back on track.

A caveat. On the verge of what might be called my 'golden years', I've been blessed to have stayed at some very luxurious properties, but this wasn't always the case. When I first started out, many of the hotels I slept in were questionable at best. But as I progressed through my career, the rooms improved (as did my salary!). Thus, I'm not so much blessed as I've earned my stripes. Rest assured, despite having ascended through the many stratospheres of opulence, I am confident that these inferences are directly applicable for lower tier, economy hotels.

Lastly, a large part of this section deals with how guest services integrate with social media and how these forms of communications tie into the bigger picture of branding. Guest services and branding have always been wholly entwined towards the overall goal of driving occupancy and giving guests an exceptional vacation or business stay over. As it stands today, however, social media is rapidly coalescing with the mechanisms of what makes guest services function effectively.

I want to emphasize that service should always be considered as a brand distinguisher, a tool of differentiation. Remember that the more things change the more they stay the same. No matter how technology advances, if you apply the fundamentals of proper guest services and guest interactions then occupancy will be a nonissue.

Qualifying Guest Services One Interaction at a Time

A weekend getaway to Miami was inspirational in understanding hotels and service. My thirty years of extensive travel around the world translates into tens of thousands of employee-to-guest transactions of various dimensions, and this is the experience I now bring to the table each time I check in. Service has been on the back of my mind throughout my tenure in the industry, and it was while relaxing on the beach that I had my true 'eureka' moment.

Let me first reflect on some of the interactions I had while vacationing in South Beach. The flight was a breeze, and after a short taxi ride, we arrived at our accommodations. We checked in and went to lunch as our room was not quite ready. So from the beginning of our stay, here is what I experienced in rapid succession:

- Doorman greeting
- Bellman to take bags and providing bag tags
- Front desk to confirm reservation and credit card
- Concierge to provide in-house restaurant options
- Restaurant reception
- Server (multiple times)
- Bus staff (multiple times)
- Uninterested and somewhat disgruntled front desk receptionist to pick up room keys
- Bell captain to request bags
- Another member of the bell staff to bring our bags to the room
- Room service staff to drop off a welcome amenity
- Telephone call from guest services to see if everything was in order

Notice that of all those human contacts, I attributed no explicitly positive adjectives. Friendliness was my expectation for the norm amongst this four-star hotel staff. It was only when I returned to the front desk after lunch that I came across a surly fellow, someone who was rather apathetic about his work. The weekend excursion is still fresh in my mind, pleasant as it was with all the palm trees and brilliant sunshine. Yet, this one brusque encounter is what I remember the most about the otherwise outstanding service received.

All egos aside, I pride myself as being a fairly humble traveler. If that one front desk staff member had not been so indifferent, my vacation would have been flawless. With nothing to complain about, the hotel would have received a perfect score. When it came to my review on TripAdvisor, I overlooked this one individual and wrote some genuine words of praise. Others might not have been as generous.

Reflecting on my South Beach mini-vacation generated three powerful inferences. First, congeniality from hotel employees is not a bonus, but rather the assumed standard of service at a luxury property, and for that matter, any hotel. Moreover, it is only when this standard is broken that guests really take notice, for good or for bad. Finally, the attitude of staff was more important for my experience than the quality of the facilities, which were indeed excellent.

This is something I pick up on when I read through online reviews. One guest might boast about how great the property is, but they still feel at a loss due to a few less-than-agreeable staff encounters. On the flip side, a critic who is willing to admit that the room or spa accommodations were a few notches below perfect might nonetheless write a positive review based on the gregarious nature of the employees. My conclusion is that regardless of room price or amenities, the innermost kernel of guest services is the compassion of your front line staff.

The proliferation of the revenue manager (RM) offers a good illustration for one large shortcoming in the industry. RMs are able to justify their actions and successes because they have direct metrics to prove their worth towards fueling revenue. They have been instrumental in modernizing some of the financial aspects of hospitality operations.

But how do you quantify guest service? Just as every human is unique, so too is every human experience. Even with online rating aggregates and customer feedback forms, you'll never get the concrete numbers that an RM can extract. Without these intricate statistics, how can you determine with precision where you need to improve?

A quick exercise should help clarify this problem. Look at your property's 'big picture' for a moment, with its diverse operations, daily tasks and all other pizzazz. Then, remove the front desk, restaurant, spa and all other amenities from your mind and think only about the individuals—people talking to other people. At its core, customer service is about being respectful, attentive and courteous at all times—all the qualities you'd regularly look for in another human being. If your staff can embody this, then everything else becomes second nature.

So to figure out how to quantify service, perhaps what each property needs is a new management position dedicated to educating all employees about the fundamental importance of treating the guests right at all times. Call the position director of guest services, or the manager of guest satisfaction. Maybe it is human resources, or the training manager's duty to uphold this policy. But don't minimize the importance: this is planning committee level stuff!

True, this still doesn't directly equate to a numerical methodology, but it lends itself toward cleansing your hotel of negative experiences. The quantification will come through happier guests, better third-party reviews and more return visits. A roaming arbitrator on the lookout for ways to improve the friendliness of your staff will heighten your customer loyalty and brand reputation—it's all linked to this basic human practice.

This is perhaps the simplest, and yet possibly the hardest, concept to master. Staff oversight and continual training in this area will do wonders for everything else down the road. Treat every customer like your best friend and you can't go wrong.

Inverting the Organizational Pyramid
to Build Service Reputation

Adapting your organizational structure for today's rapid communications is a hot topic amongst hoteliers. We all know it's a necessity, and we're all curious about how best to initiate this change. But when it comes to the fine print, however, we are often left in the dark. Managers are bombarded with so much work they seldom have the opportunity to investigate all the technological resources at their disposal.

In the past, a firm pyramidal structure of information distribution provided adequate time for senior managers to review and respond. As well, it insulated executives from trivial data, letting them focus on the big picture. Decision-making occurred at a steady pace, flowing from the GM to the planning committee, then to their line managers. The results reached the guests.

Remember the notion of delivery 'in a New York minute'? Forget it. It's too slow when it comes to guest services nowadays. Ditto for next week's executive planning committee meeting. Information has to move faster to keep up with the latest postings on your social media outlets and online review sites. Your response to any sort of mishap has to be instantaneous.

In other industries, one prevalent technique is a 'flattening' of the pyramid, where the ranks of middle management are slashed to heighten team initiatives and the sharing of ideas. But this isn't directly applicable to hotels, as each department has such a unique set of skills. What I am proposing as an alternative to this is an inversion of the classic hierarchical organization pyramid in order for positive guest relations to be maintained even as new technologies work to erode patience and leniency for staff errors.

Think of the water works. Water flows downhill not uphill. Communications work the same way. It is much easier for information to move down the chain of command to the line staff than for it to percolate back up to the executive team.

A compact pyramid will hasten this transmission, but not in a manner significant enough to make a difference by the time a disgruntled guest leaves your hotel or posts a diatribe online. Instead, visualize inverting the pyramid. Put your guests at the top of the chart and next to them are those in direct contact with guests—your line staff.

The importance of this communications model cannot be underestimated. Social media and rating sites like TripAdvisor allow guests to re-tell their on-property experiences in real time, both good and bad. They do not wait for the weekly planning committee before they wreak havoc based on a distasteful room, spa or restaurant experience. The future of your hotel rests in their hands (quite literally given that customers will likely use their iPhone, Blackberry or Android smartphones to voice concerns).

So, how do you go about inverting your communications? The answer is empowerment. Line staff can no longer simply follow orders and react to unfamiliar situations by first seeking the wisdom of their immediate supervisors. They must learn to adapt and respond on their own. It's no longer just about data flowing downstream to the executive team, but making sure the upper strata of the pyramid—the guests—are well fed.

There are two steps to this change in methodology. First, you must foster a culture of independent action. Front line staff must be given the opportunity to answer guest requests without the 'silo thinking' attitude of clearing every action by their manager. Even better, meld the principles of traditional data filtering and pyramid flattening into codependent action so that the manager and line staff work to address the problem. That is, building an organizational structure with strong interdepartmental sharing. Tandem action will assure that no loss in response time and, as well, the line staff will be learning through doing.

Now for an example. Let's say a guest felt his or her meal at the hotel's restaurant was displeasing. The normal lines of communication would prompt the waiter, busboy or host who noted the grievance to tell a supervisor and that supervisor would coordinate the eventual response. The key word here is eventual. Managers are increasingly rushed for time and a request like this may not illicit a pressing reaction.

Empowerment in this scenario means that a staff member has the ability to alleviate the troubled guest on the spot with simple yet elegant actions such as complimentary desserts, coffees or drinks. Taking this one step further, that employee should then be able to initiate feedback with staff in other departments; all within reason, of course.

Imagine complaining about a meal, receiving a free confection as a result, but then, upon returning to your room, there's a gift from the spa along with a handwritten apology. Now that's customer service! I don't know about you, but I would be ecstatic if this happened to me, fully negating any of my previous objections. What's important to infer from this case is how little the manager has to be involved in the play-by-play as well as the tremendous impact of a prompt reply.

Sure, you 'comped' some F&B, but all for the noble cause of protecting your brand image. The consequences of failing to directly mitigate could far outweigh any minor revenue loss. Remember, all a guest needs is a smartphone and a smidgen of free time for an endorsement or a denigration to appear online. Your line staff should be able to help decide which of these two conclusions is posted.

Empowering your team to delegate ensures that your property is keeping pace with the rapidity of web communications. Line staff should know that this sort of discourse is sensible, even if it takes months, or the better part of a year, for them to master all the nuances of immediate guest satisfaction. So, leave decision-making to those at the top of the organizational structure, but think of ways where this pyramid can be inverted to better serve your customers.

Double Deviations:
Two Wrongs Never Makes a Right

When does a service issue become an outright problem instead of just a temporary inconvenience? What is the 'tipping point' that provokes a guest to write a comment in, say, TripAdvisor, or worse, speak ill words about you to their friends and never return to your property? And, most importantly, once you find this threshold, how do you ensure that things never reach this point?

A new age definition for this process is 'Double Deviation'; a term you might have heard in passing, and yet, it's one you should have on the back of your mind at all times. Customer complaints follow an initiation and propagation couplet. That is, an issue only becomes a bona fide problem when guests are not adequately compensated for the initial error, or when a second error occurs.

I will use a trip to Philadelphia last year as an example. My wife and I spent the weekend at a downtown luxury property. To avoid embarrassment, I'll leave out the name of this well-known chain establishment.

The first morning we chose to dine at the hotel's minimally-crowded restaurant and were not impressed in the least. We waited a full ten minutes for our simple order of bacon and eggs to be taken and another twenty for it to arrive; cold and no forthcoming apology. Having a table near the kitchen, we could hear the staff chatting it up all throughout our half hour hang-up. Unacceptable. We left without touching our food and complained to the front desk, then went offsite for real food and activities.

Returning that evening, we found a rather contrite note and a fruit basket in our room. Apology accepted. In our mind, the issue was fully resolved by the positive response by the staff. We chalked this up as a once-in-a-blue-moon sort of fault. It did not impede our travels and we are not above thinking that there may have been other extenuating circumstances outside of the staff's control.

Then came the coup de grace. Housekeeping had cleaned the bathroom without leaving any towels. A minor grievance, negligible even, but it set off a flood of bad memories from that morning. The subdued breakfast mishap roared back into our heads and solidified a negative impression of the hotel.

Once was okay, but twice was utterly deplorable, despite the adequate compensation for the first wrongdoing. Needless to say, we're never staying there again. And when asked about our trip to Philly, a foremost topic of discussion was always the horrible service, conferred ahead of any other experience involving the hotel. This property not only lost a customer, but many other prospects via our justifiably unenthusiastic word of mouth.

The nature of 'Double Deviations' means you understanding that perfection is not an absolute requirement. After all, no property can be perfect all the time. Even the best of us have slip ups.

The challenge is to handle slip-ups in a capacity sufficient to prevent a double deviation. That is, if you do make a mistake, educate your staff on the importance of not making another. I was willing to look past one hefty fault, especially given the admission of guilt from a manager. But two faults proved in my mind that the hotel just didn't value us as customers.

Everyone has a slightly different comprehension of double deviations. For guests like me, the fact that they made the effort to acknowledge their error was enough to quell my doubts. However, had they not granted reparation, then that act, or failure to act, would have counted as the second strike. From all accounts, it would appear as though baseball is even more lenient than hospitality—three strikes the deathblow instead of two.

Others may not be so lenient. A more audacious guest might deem a letter of apology and evening fruit tray as unsatisfactory, expecting compensation immediately following the incident. Although I like to think these people are in the minority, it should nonetheless be the responsibility of the front desk to coordinate an urgent response in order to suppress even the most unforgiving of clientele.

The correct interpretation and anticipation of personal reactions to gaps in service is a critical tool to prevent double deviations and bolster your property's reputation. Here are some questions to ask yourself:

- How are your line managers made aware of problems that arise out of service complaints or other direct contact with guests?
- Are team members in direct contact with guests empowered to rectify situations immediately without their manager's approval?
- Are grievances and their effective resolutions documented and shared with the team for further learning?
- Does your training program identify immediate problem solving strategies?
- Do you monitor online rating sites and social media to identify unresolved issues as a lesson for improving services?
- Is all of this written down, or codified in some way, into a policy statement?

Double deviations are almost never a one-strike policy; guests will give you another chance to demonstrate your clemency. Whenever a guest complains, you should 'red flag' that individual to ensure that they cannot find reason for a second reprimand.

Immediacy is the critical factor here. Simply put: the sooner you identify the issue, the sooner a resolution plan can be initiated. Take advantage of the modern communication tools that are available to you—phones, text messages and the Internet. My experience indicates that you have to address the problem the day of, and at the latest before the guest leaves your hotel. Learning about such mistakes at or after check out is simply too late, and your brand and business will suffer.

Lessons Learned from the Film Casablanca

There probably isn't a single person over forty who can't remember the incredible 100 minutes of film history entitled *Casablanca* (1942), revolving around the gin joint dubbed Rick's Café Américain. If you haven't seen this Oscar winner, it's been re-mastered and definitely worth the watch. As a fun exercise in hospitality, let's use this cinema classic as a template to see how you can improve your accommodations.

1. **Be visible.** Rick Blaine (Humphrey Bogart) not only has his name in lights above the door, but he makes an appearance every night. He mingles with his guests freely, acknowledging the VIPs and regulars. He has an easy rapport with the staff, who all instinctively know when and when not to approach him. How often does your General Manager drop in to visit guests at your restaurant, bar or pool? Does your team, at any level of employment, feel comfortable speaking with the GM directly? (Note: the GMs name does not need to be on the door!)

2. **As an owner, don't act like Major Heinrich Strasser.** This proverbial bad guy doesn't just walk through Rick's, he struts and makes demands of everyone on staff. The Major wants everyone to know that he's in charge, even though it's under Rick's care. Owners must respect their GMs' decisions, even when there's disagreement. An owner's presence on property should be low profile; no one wants a Strasser!

3. **VIPs should be respected and given privacy.** When Victor Laszlo and Ilsa Lund enter Rick's, they are discreetly ushered to a private table. Staff is quickly summoned to make them comfortable. Several patrons approach them, but are turned away. Despite a romantic entanglement with Ilsa, Rick is nevertheless professional and calm.

4. **You need security.** People like Signor Ferrari and Ugarte are not savory characters. You see them, and you just know that trouble is brewing. Take the same approach at your property. Ensure that

your Loss Prevention Team is well versed on all aspects of security and any potential for lawsuits. Have a crisis communications plan, and review it on a frequent basis.

5. **Make friends with your local sheriff or police force.** In the movie, Rick has an outstanding relationship with Captain Louis Renault and relies upon Renault's creative rule bending to keep the café open, despite the war setting. At the film's conclusion, when they watch Victor and Ilsa fly off the tarmac, Rick once again relies on his friendship to save him from the firing squad. While I am not advocating anything illicit, a close relationship with the police in your area is a wise and strategic long term move.

6. **Live music beats a DJ anytime.** True, not everyone is Sam—a piano player with an eternally humble mood as the lyrics of 'As Time Goes By' flow angelically from his lips. Live music makes Rick's both exciting and romantic. A piano can easily be overlooked in favor of electronic lounge music as a way to enhance the ambiance of a lobby, bar or restaurant. So if you have one, why not put it to good use?

7. **Not everyone likes Karaoke.** At one point, a group begins to sing 'Die Wacht am Rhein,' ('The Watch on the Rhine') a German patriotic song. Infuriated, Laszlo asks the band to play 'La Marseillaise,' with authorization from Rick. In doing so, everyone bursts out in unison, so much so that the Germans end up being washed out. In retaliation, Strasser orders Renault to close the café. The implications for modern hotel management are that you have to respect all patrons, as the results can be detrimental to your business, even if only a minority is displeased.

8. **Above all, a full house is a happy house.** In every scene, the café is alive with hardly an empty table and staff constantly rushing to satisfy orders. Profits must surely be flowing. This boils down to a fundamental aspect of human behavior. Have you ever been to an empty nightclub and felt out of place? Would you feel the same way if the place was jammed with patrons? Crowds of people feed one another and amplify a given atmosphere, leading more often than

not to higher overall per-person sales at a bar or restaurant. I always advocate occupancy ahead of rate, and Rick's Café Américain is certainly a great example of why.

Of course, all these hotelier takeaways are layered underneath a timeless love story that I'd recommend to anyone. Casablanca isn't the only film to debut an embroiled innkeeper, and I'm sure you have your own favorites to draw comparisons to the industry.

What's Important to Today's C-Suite Traveler

Beyond a quiet, comfortable night's sleep, what does the senior business executive traveler need? I posed this question to hundreds of CEOs, COOs, CFOs, CMOs and CIOs in a survey conducted in the first quarter of 2011. The results are straightforward, and provide a head's up for any hotelier wishing to adequately cater to this demographic.

Insofar as methodology, I used a mailed survey with the selection of candidates chosen from directories of corporations with sales in excess of $100 million, and no more than one billion dollars. The questions were distributed amongst C-suite holders in North America (78% of those polled resided in the USA, 22% were Canadian), asking only of their requirements for domestic travel. Inferences about overseas travel or European/Asian travel habits should not be implied. Respondents who completed the survey received a financial donation to their specified charity with no additional compensation.

A 30% response rate was received, equating to 59 useable surveys, 53 of which were male. Given the limited female sample size, they were not deemed statistically significant to be included in the final analysis. The average age of the respondents was reported as 47. Income level was not asked, nor was marital status.

The average executive canvassed spent 26 nights in hotels for business purposes through 2010 (this excludes stays in corporate owned apartments). Over half of those polled worked for companies that had corporate rate programs with major hotel chains. While half of the respondents had a member of their staff arrange the hotel booking for them, interestingly, over 90% either specified, or provided input on the hotel selection for their stay.

First Question: "In addition to getting a good night's sleep (comfortable bed, quiet room, excellent HVAC) and the hotel's location relative to your needs, what other factors are important in your selection of a hotel room for a business stay?"

There were 30 different items listed. For each one, the respondent rated them from 0 (not at all important) to 5 (critical). The individual scores were then summed for each item and averaged to provide an overall score out of five, adjusted for no response. The results clustered into three distinct groups: Top (4.1-4.8), Middle (1.7-3.7), and Bottom (0.4-1.3), with no statistical significance within each group. Here are the results:

Items with a total average score of 4.1 to 4.8, ranked in descending order.

- High speed Internet access
- Friendly, courteous service at check-in
- Bottled water available
- Being recognized at check-in
- Express check-out
- National newspaper delivered in the morning
- High quality towels
- Check-in early and check-out late capabilities
- Prompt room service breakfast available
- Coffee and coffee maker available in room
- Welcome amenity
- Easily accessible power outlet to recharge cell phone or mobile device
- Accurate, timely wakeup call

Items that scored an average of 1.7 to 3.7, ranked in descending order.

- News channels available on television
- Working desk with ergonomic chair and good lighting
- Bathrobe
- Iron and ironing board
- All day room service menu
- Voice mail
- Room security
- Top quality toiletries
- Map of jogging trails available

Items that scored an average of 0.4 to 1.3, ranked in descending order.

- Turn down amenity
- Promotions or events/activities displayed in room
- Pay movies
- CD, radio or iPhone player
- Mini-bar
- Hotel store catalog and/or order form
- In-room magazines (Note: ranked the lowest with a 0.4 score!)

Second Question: "What is the average tip that you leave, per night, for the housekeeping staff?" Interestingly, 19% of those polled reported zero, with the average of all 53 respondents being $5.74 per night.

Third Question: "What single charge added to your folio on check-out is the most frustrating?" This was an open-ended question without any prompting. Over half of the answers had to do with paying for Internet services. A close second was paying for bottled water.

Fourth Question: "What could hotels do better?" Again, this was an open-ended question without any prompting. The answers were broad ranging, with many of the surveys giving multiple responses. Here are the ones that were mentioned by at least four respondents:

- Stop charging for extras
- Free Internet and/or higher speed Internet services
- Free bottled water by the bed or for the road
- Faster car valet service
- Check-in and check-out via mobile devices
- Larger television

Before drawing any conclusions, you should remember that senior executives, when on business, are no-nonsense travelers. Their requirements should be easily manageable by all properties. It also became quite evident that Internet connectivity, both price as well as service speed, area a premier pet peeve.

Of note, the primary question stated 'in addition to a good night's sleep'. Hence, this survey makes the somewhat naïve assumption that this can, and should, be accomplished.

So, if all senior executives need is a good night's sleep, fast Internet connectivity and free bottled water, what differentiates your property from the others? Is it how your property is found through advertising or Internet searches? Is it your frequent flyer programs, or loyalty cards? Although these are more branding-type questions, it's still important to consider them in tandem with guest services.

And this short survey indeed raises a host of further questions. However, the takeaway message is simple. If these basic, high-priority service needs are consistently met, then it will help with customer retention and free up resources to better plan the next steps.

The Power of a Personalized Handwritten Note

Communication is too easy these days. With the trifecta of a computer, a cell phone and a printer, there's no need to write out personal correspondence anymore. That is, unless you want to make an impact.

Take hotel welcome cards for example. You arrive at your room and a colorful tray of fruit is waiting there ready to serve; a nice touch in and of itself. But then you notice the greeting letter is a printed note. It could have been made just for you or it could have been made from a template built years ago. You don't know.

Now suppose that same greeting letter is a handwritten note with your name on it. Regardless of length or what's said, you know that someone had to physically take the time to write that note, and that it probably hasn't been sitting around for too long either. It sends a persuasive subliminal message.

Consider spam. How often do you get junk email personally addressed to you? Despite very strong filtering, I nonetheless get dozens every day. And for each one, I'm able to categorize it as real or junk within seconds. If it's the latter, then the spam is in the trash well before the time it takes to read the author or title, let alone the opening sentence.

For almost three decades now, it's become all too easy to set up a template in Microsoft Word and print off a hundred letters to different people then mail them out within the hour. We are satiated with electronically generated mass messages wherever we are, so much so that the process has taken on an aura of effortlessness.

As a result, when you do pick up the pen, you're not only expressing what is written, but communicating on a whole different wavelength. Whether you copy off a template or not, the recipient knows that someone had to spend the time to write out each individual word. Moreover, people appreciate the effort required to write with a legible and stylish cursive.

One of our former clients, Ojai Valley Inn & Spa in Ojai, California, was the master of personal notes. Each and every guest arrival included a warm, friendly handwritten note from the managing director or a senior staff member. These letters took time to write, but the impressions reinforced their well-deserved five-diamond reputation.

To me, receiving a handwritten letter comes along with an inherent quality of friendship and a greater understanding of one another. It's as if the sender and I have this subconscious bond, and an electronic version will never suffice. But it doesn't stop there.

Picture arriving at your room again, but this time, instead of just a written draft with your name on it, there's also a little message attached relating to who you are. This could be a reference to a past stay or even a reply to something said on Twitter. As the hotelier, you must view each guest as an individual with specific needs, and not just a dollar sign.

Compare the rush you get when you open a personalized gift to when you receive paltry cash or a gift certificate. Friends give gifts, bosses give cash. It's the same feeling with handwritten notes, only to a lesser magnitude. Think of it as just one more elegant touch in your arsenal. Now throw in the element of surprise and the guest is yours for life!

I realize this is probably old news for many senior managers, but the problem is I don't see handwritten notes often enough. It's a subtle element that can easily be overlooked when you reevaluate your property's guest service mandate. The peculiar nature of this trend, however, is that the more obsolete the pen-to-paper method becomes, the more effective it will be. So ask yourself: when was the last time you sent out a handwritten correspondence to a guest?

Meet the Managers: A One-Two Punch
of Social Media and Face Time

Here's a marketing creed that was scribed into textbooks well over thirty years ago, back when I was a mere MBA student: People connect with other people, and not necessarily with businesses. For a long time, this wasn't exactly feasible. Even in the hospitality world, where personality is king, managers meeting customers on a one-to-one basis wasn't always in the cards.

Nowadays though, sites like Twitter and LinkedIn are paving the way for resurgence of quality communication from management directly down to the consumer. But look closely at this practice: nothing has really changed. Even with the leaps and bounds of electronic messaging systems, people still crave that personal touch.

Hence the title of this section! Whenever, or wherever, you can get your guests to 'meet the managers,' you're not only giving your hotel a real face, but as well, drastically enhancing client retention. With this in mind, social media presents both a challenge and opportunity to accomplish this task.

The challenge is that managers have to commit themselves to a role in the public eye, albeit even when reluctant. People are the new brand, no longer just the hotel logo and top brass. What managers say on their personal online accounts is now intrinsically linked to their respective properties, whether for good or for bad. Luckily, many have already found the opportunity within this trend, harnessing these new channels to build stronger personal connections and grow their businesses.

Obvious from the introduction, embracing social media is imperative for this process, but a first step should always involve a trip to HR to see whose job descriptions might curtail social media responsibilities. From there the devil is in the details, so let's go through a few choice techniques I've seen work in recent years.

When it comes to LinkedIn, every manager should have an account and join your company group. Although the site is chiefly for professional networking, it will open your staff to a worldwide forum for business ideas, emerging trends and potential partnerships.

Twitter offers a host of options for building these bridges. For your generic company account, only one or two people should be tasked with posting material, giving them space to add some zest and initialize direct messages. Next, talk to your managers about their own profiles and how they would use the site to converse with guests. The idea here is to develop person-to-person relationships; something much harder to accomplish when a guest converses with a faceless corporate account.

The prospects are good for Facebook, too. You can easily design a tab to introduce each manager with a picture, or build a custom fan page for each department and link them all to the main page. Managers should also be active participants on the wall, commenting on what fans are saying as well as providing original insights.

Blogging is the fourth big one here. Most blog content management systems allow you to designate regular columns authored by specific staff members. You'd be surprised how far the phrase 'By XX Manager' goes when at the end of an entry. Or, you could even run a 'Manager of the Month' editorial to highlight your team's characters and fun stories.

The online possibilities are aplenty, even including video, and a commensurate YouTube channel, which I did not previously discuss. But to me, however, these are just a launch pad. You still have to find ways to squeeze in some face-to-face time for maximal efficacy.

To start, personalized greeting letters should be in every room; the power of a handwritten note working its charm. Seeing managers in the lobby welcoming guests is another powerful statement, especially when it comes to a VIP arrival or a group coordinator. A sharp uniform can exacerbate appearances as well. Beyond that, you have to get creative.

Look to what your hotel offers and to where your line staff might interact with customers. If you run a golf resort, consider a tournament, or even some foursomes, where guests are paired with managers. Perhaps your managers could greet and eat with patrons at the lobby bar, making their jovial presence felt, but also indicating that the F&B are top notch. How about a follow-up phone call after a guest has departed? Not only are these personal, but as well, they're great avenues for constructive feedback.

An excellent reference is the work done chain-wide by the Kimpton Hotel Group. In all of their properties, they host a Managers' Reception happy hour where guests could partake in an informal wine tasting while they mingled with the staff. It is unintimidating, casual fun and there was incentive beyond simple introductions to get people through the door. Plus, it was a chance for the managers to unwind, boosting team morale in the process. Kudos to Kimpton!

So, what I suggest is you sit down with your fellow managers and discuss your strategy for heightening interactions with guests, both online and face-to-face in a winning combination. Have a plan and stick to it. Sure, it's a lot of effort, but the rewards are definitely worth it.

Leveraging the Communications Hierarchy

Have you ever thought of your communications in terms of a hierarchial order based upon its ability to effectively reach the recipient? With so many options available for you, your sales team and your staff, the topic merits further investigation.

I'd like to outline thirteen different communications methods based on the level of personality and effectiveness conveyed of each in ascending order. I'm sure there are more, but this list covers a pretty wide spectrum. This ranking is based upon my own personal experiences and may not be exactly the same for everyone. Nor can it be deemed the same for a decade down the road, especially given the way social media continues to alter the ways in which we talk.

Even with these limitations, the broad strokes will ring true. Ranked from lowest to highest, they are:

- Twitter Message (lowest)
- Facebook Message
- LinkedIn Message
- Bulk Text Message
- Personalized Text Message
- Group Email
- Personalized Email
- Cell/Noisy Phone Call
- Typed Letter, Hand-Signed
- Office/Quiet Phone Call
- Handwritten Note
- Group Meeting
- Individual, One-On-One Meeting (highest)

What is clearly identified here is that the closer the personal interaction, the better the quality of influence. Any opportunity you have to meet your customer or business partner face-to-face far exceeds the influence of lesser and more impersonal modes of communications. In fact, sometimes using a lower communication channel can be considered insulting and detract from your business goals.

In 1964, Marshall McLuhan coined the phrase, 'The Medium is the Message' meaning that the form of a medium embeds itself in the message. While social media and electronic communications had yet to be invented, the symbiotic relationship by which the medium influences how the message is perceived remains true to this day, and you'd be wise to analyze how you can best utilize your channels.

It is important to understand the relative significance of items within the hierarchy and how you and your team manage your own business communications process. To maximize your return on relationships, I've developed the following axioms to adhere to:

1. **The more important the situation, the higher the communications level that must be initiated.** This is quintessentially demonstrated in the world of politics, where one-on-one summits between leaders are oftentimes the only route for resolving serious conflicts. Use the same approach when situations requiring this type of intervention are necessary in your business, but also seek them out wherever possible, time permitting of course. Face-to-face meetings convey far more than the words themselves—emotions, character and friendship. Meeting with someone is more memorable than a phone call, and thus your customer will be much more likely to act on your behalf following a personal meeting than a chat or the telephone.

2. **Respond to inquiries in kind, and never with a lower level of communication.** If a customer telephones you, you should telephone your response. Or, an even better option could be to elevate the level of communications and seek out a meeting. A personalized email might be acceptable in some cases, but only if you acknowledge the initial telephone inquiry and offer an explanation where why you are emailing instead of phoning them back. And in this instance, if the recipient doesn't reply to your email promptly, then you should take the initiative and pick up the telephone.

   Furthermore, responding to a phone call or an email with a text message or social media message is outright unacceptable. It shows an unwillingness to openly grow the relationship, shading you in a negative, cowardly light. Frankly, this is a big problem with the millennial generation, and it's your job as responsible managers to discourage this from progressing under your care.

3. **Elevating communications by too many levels brings a sense of urgency and is excellent way of demonstrating superior service.** This communicates instantly to your consumers that they are a priority. Imagine the positive feelings that such a customer experiences when their email inquiry generates a telephone call—and not just a telephone call a week later, but within a day or two.

   Responding too many levels higher, however, can generate a sense of unease. For example, a potential customer might not yet be ready to commit, and increasing the level of communications could be seen as an act of desperation or that you have too much time on your hands. Use your discretion.

4. **Don't forget the value of a handwritten note.** In these days of electronic communications and mail merge, a hand written piece has increased in value. People understand how laborious this process is versus typing something out. Used sparingly, it can become a very powerful tool in your communications arsenal.

5. **Avoid personal communications based purely upon social media.** This does not at all mean to eradicate social media from your agenda. Rather, look at social media less as a means of effectively communicating directly with any individual, and more of an information and awareness generation vehicle. You should not really expect a consumer to respond to a Tweet or Facebook note as a sales closing vehicle. Instead, think of these low tier mediums as 'foot in the door' tactics; a starting point from which to open higher, more personal channels.

6. **Encourage your staff to stop hiding behind their voice mail.** Telephone communications is important. Answer your phone and have your staff do the same. It is amazing to me how CEOs will answer their phone line personally, yet many sales managers are just 'too busy' to lift up their own telephone. After awhile, I no

longer want to deal with these 'harried' individuals and will seek out others who are more respectful of my time.

7. **Train your junior staff to move their communications 'up' the hierarchy.** Too often, I've seen junior staff frustrated by their own use of communications; emailing a client when they should be using the telephone, sending out a group note, or using text messages for information release. Barring a few exceptions, moving up the communication hierarchy will bear fruit. As well, not knowing how is almost as bad as not knowing altogether.

Be sure to train your junior staff on an action plan and procedure for effectively prompting an upward shift. Even though it might seem counterproductive, using higher channels actually saves time, as it is easier to reach definitive conclusions and make decisions as a group. Ten emails back and forth over several days oftentimes accomplish the same as one twenty minute phone call.

Hitchcock and Hotels

Whether it's a straight-laced caper or psychological thriller, the late Sir Alfred Hitchcock certainly had a lot to say about human behavior and the medium of film. But after catching *North by Northwest* (1959) on late night reruns—specifically, Cary Grant roaming the lavishly decorated Plaza Hotel in New York City—I had a revelation.

As a top tier Hollywood director, Hitchcock was blessed with decades of location scouting and overnight stays at some of the world's best hotels. As such, he likely developed a keen eye for what they had in common and what makes a classy joint. Whether he intended to or not, Hitchcock translated this tacit understanding onto the screen, imbuing some firm teachings for hoteliers. So let's dig through some of his masterpieces and see what lessons we can find.

One of the reasons Hitchcock's thrillers worked so well was that he understood the importance of bringing his audiences into the proper mindset for a thriller, starting right from the opening credits, which were often accompanied by frightful, percussive scores. The director also knew that in order for people to fully appreciate the rigorous chase scenes and showdowns at the climax of each film, he'd first have to contrast this with some sense of normalcy at the onset.

What better way to establish this precursory repose than by setting the mood with a few scenes at a hotel in the opening half? A grand ballroom lounge with soft piano jazz in the background. Opulent suites furnished in rich woods and polished leather. Fashionable and good-looking people bustling through marble-clad lobbies. More often than not, the check-in counter wasn't merely a place to pay but one for socializing and positive interactions. All are far from where you'd expect a crime to take place. By their very nature, these hotel settings exude an air of calm, but also pique our curiosity. Such stylish locales are places we all want to visit.

Nowhere is this more apparent than in *To Catch a Thief* (1955). The film opens at the Carlton Hotel overlooking Cannes, drawing the audience into the foreign allure of French Riviera. Audience members want to travel here, and they do, albeit vicariously, by watching the film. Thematically adhering to this ultra-posh atmosphere, the story revolves around a group of jewel thieves. Brilliant sunny days along the crystalline waters of the Mediterranean amplify the tense nights of burglaries, police chases and forbidden romance.

The takeaway here pertains to how you set the mood for your guests. Know the feeling you want to evoke and make it apparent from the moment they first step inside. You want to transport your guests to fantastical place built around a given theme.

So, what are you after? Is it an ultra-modern, and slightly futuristic, enchantment? Or maybe your hotel is better suited to the gothic charm of some classic metropolitan properties? The key is to match every physical aspect to this theme, from the large-scale lobby centerpieces and bellhop uniforms all the way down to the font chosen for the web site and brochures.

Next comes color and light to amplify this mood. Employing some very clever tricks, whenever a hotel was geared to be a comfortable setting for the protagonist, Hitchcock would fill the screen with bright colors to confirm this feeling. This went far beyond clear blue skies and well-lit sets. Alongside the expertise of a sharp cinematographer and production design team, such shots were filled with reflective props and active backdrops. That is, not just a wall, but objects throughout to add textural depth.

Now consider *Psycho* (1960) where the first-world locales of New York City or the South of France are swapped for the dingy Bates Motel in an isolated part of rural Southwestern America. The rooms are cramped to induce a subtle claustrophobia. The colors are muted to augment shadows and our fear of the unknown. As well, revisit *The Birds* (1963) where the jovial palette of San Francisco in the opening act is gradually transformed into the overcast grayscale of Bodega Bay to clue us in for danger.

Obvious inferences from the above examples should suggest that when it comes to light and color, make sure your hotel is as vibrant as possible, and be very cautious when designing a darker, tighter space. The proper use of color will bring out your guests' senses and ease them into the magic of the experience.

Painting the walls in a new hue is only the start of converting your hotel into a cinematic gem. Incite positive moods by allowing as much natural light in as possible, even if it means replacing those thick drapes. Fill the negative spaces in your common areas with wholesome décor to round out the theme and nix any dreary feelings.

Lastly, use formality to solidify the mood. Hitchcock readily made use of hotel staff to advance the story; only he did so in some very unambiguous ways. First, his staff members were always depicted in clearly identifiable uniforms that never edged towards casual attire. They were all distinctively well-dressed in solid colors and fabrics, so much so that even without a character introduction you'd instantly know their role.

The director's hotel staff aired towards formality in their presentation and mannerisms. Always dependable with a, "Yes, Sir!" here, followed by a, "My pleasure, Sir!" or a, "Thank you, Madame!" there, this air of geniality established that they were trustworthy and respectful of their guests, as well as reaffirming the feel of an upscale hotel. True, Hitchcock oftentimes used this pretense to trick the audience later by revealing a staff member to be in cahoots with the main villain, but these were intentional plot devices building on our previously conceived notions of the setting and this stylized formality.

Hitchcock was a master of bringing us into his vision, and you should think about any parallels to your hotel. For instance, part of the fantasy of a hotel is that a guest is catered to. So, when it comes to your staff, instruct them to be as chivalrous as possible. Open the doors and pull out the chairs. Combine this with a brightly colored and well-suited theme, and then with any luck, your guests will leave your hotel and say, "It's like being in a movie!"

Lessons Learned from Top Asian Hotels

A tour of five Asian cities opened my eyes to how hospitality products and services should be managed. I was really taken aback. Backed by strong national economies, continuously growing ADR and occupancy levels are the norm on this continent. Coming from North America, I see Asian hotels as true leaders in guest service, and there's a lot that can be learned.

Mind you, my stay encompassed four luxury chains, including InterContinental, Shangri-La, COMO and Four Seasons, but none appeared to be too voracious in their profit taking. Rather, all were reinvesting in their businesses and actively setting new standards. Instead of singling out any individual property or chain, I will attempt to cover some of the differentiating elements of these Asian hotels as a single entity.

1. **It's All About Service.** By and large, the service levels experienced in all properties were at a palpably superior level than that previously witnessed in similar quality level North American hotels and luxury properties in Europe. This was accomplished not just through the anticipated higher staff levels, but as well, by what appears to be a stronger and more adroit commitment to service. None of the haughty, only-work-for-a-tip attitude! Instead, little touches in areas like valet, room service, housekeeping, F&B, front desk and concierge accumulated into something far greater. In fact, try as I might, in three weeks of travel, only one service deficiency was noted, and it was trivial.

2. **Paying Attention to the Details.** Every luxury hotel guest expects comfortable and elegant accommodations, a broad array of food choices, and service efficiencies. What set these Asian properties apart are details normally not seen stateside. Some examples include: newspapers delivered with gloves to avoid ink stains on your hands; rather than pillow-chocolates, a small cake at turndown service; notes handed out in leather, personalized folders; multiple bathroom amenity packages, including full shaving and dental kits; padded and sectioned jewelry boxes inside the room safe; a

stationery kit of goodies to help handle minor business requirements; in-room espresso maker (not just a coffeemaker); multiple lighting configurations for various times of day and ambiance; a unique two-piece martini glass set; contribution envelopes to support local charities as a deposit for your coin change; and proper folios for your departure invoice. I could go on, but these are just a few top-of-mind examples.

3. **Continuous Innovation.** These properties continue to test new ways of improving their guest relationships through product enhancements. In one hotel, they were experimenting with a dedicated floor for couples. Another property was testing new menus. Another was testing iPads as a control tool in guest rooms. Still another was encouraging customers to test and modify wild, new drink combinations.

4. **Expert Maintenance to Support Quality Construction.** As expected, the wood, marble and granite used for room furnishings were all immaculate. While the properties ranged in age from seven to over 20 years old, they all had the feeling of a newly opened hotel. This was largely a result of superb maintenance levels. No visible marks or scuffs were noted on doorframes or hallway corners. Soft goods and upholstery was always fresh, both in look and smell. All electronics were up-to-date and far beyond what is the norm for North America. Somehow, even working in many languages, I could actually figure out the television remote control, and all offered seamless, free Internet connectivity with exceptional bandwidth.

5. **Visible Leadership.** Without exception, it was commonplace to see a member of senior property management in the reception area each morning, and often in the evening as well. While the primary role appeared to be greeting guests, they also served as a reassurance that the team was performing its duties. One evening, I met a general manager in the restaurant after 10PM because he was waiting for a VIP guest to arrive from a delayed flight. Of note, he was telephoned from the arriving limousine a few minutes in advance to efficiently orchestrate the meet and greet.

While you may look at this list and check things off for your property as 'done that', it is the simple fact that all of these properties are accomplishing these tasks 365 days of the year, and everyone still has a smile on their face. My trip to Asia was enlightening and I encourage all North American hospitality managers to find the time to travel there for a firsthand experience.

The Butler Did It

Unless you were born into royalty or lived abroad at some wealthy uncle's residence, chances are you've had limited experience with the latest rapidly growing luxury hotel service accoutrement—the butler. A recent article in the New York Times discussed several new concierge-style amenities, all designed to take the place of meager service components in the travel sector. Whereas airlines continue to siphon every dollar out of guest services, hotels are stepping in with programs of their own, filling in the disparage in an adept and highly creative manner.

Browsing Wikipedia, the word 'butler' derives from the Old French bouteleur (cup bearer) and from bouteille (bottle). The role of the butler, for centuries, has been that of the chief steward of a household; the attendant entrusted with the care and serving of alcoholic beverages. As well, they managed the rest of the staff and liaised matters between the patron family and cooks, maids, groundskeepers and any other tenants.

Peaking in the 1920s, there were approximately 30,000 butlers in Great Britain. Today, even with resurgences amongst wealthy households, there are still only about 5,000 trained butlers in the UK. The introduction of a butler service in luxury hotels can be a logical extension of asserting elite status and creating an opulent ambiance akin to what was felt in the 1920s. For instance, butlers and butler-style training programs have long been associated with Ritz-Carlton, undoubtedly reinforcing the hotel chain's already outstanding reputation.

My first personal experience with a butler occurred when staying at the Lanesborough Hotel in London, shortly after its opening in early 1992. This property, among the finest in the world, was known for assigning a butler to each of its guests; a practice it still does today twenty years later. I had no knowledge of what a butler could do for a traveler and although this unexpected luxury greatly enhanced my hotel experience, I still felt at a loss. I would have appreciated knowing about the butler service in advance so that I could prepare and fully maximize my usage of the amenity.

Subsequently, I have had experiences with butlers at the St. Regis in Rome, COMO Shambhala Estate in Bali, and the COMO Metropolitan in Bangkok. In each location, the butler served not only to enhance our stay, but also as the perfect ambassador for the property and the brand. Some examples of how I utilized the amenity include:

- Dinner reservations, both on and off property
- Securing theatre tickets, probably in concert with the Concierge, but also printing out theatre reviews and providing ideas for post-theatre entertainment
- Airport departure and transfers and luggage packing
- Facility utilization including spa appointments, personal trainers and dry cleaning
- Planning a last-minute surprise birthday party that included decorations and cakes, and all done with total secrecy from my spouse
- Procuring emergency luggage when shopping selections just couldn't fit
- Arranging for artwork purchased at auction to be shipped home at a later date

Butler services are not cheap, however; the costs involved in offering this service mandate a significantly higher ADR. Moreover, the decision to initiate a butler program should be tempered by the availability of appropriate staff, as properly trained butlers are both expensive and rare. Expanding your concierge services to imitate what butlers accomplish might be another avenue to consider.

Not to be confused with concierge services already in place, butlers are truly personalized for guests, servicing one or a few, rather than the entire hotel. This allows them the flexibility to move throughout the environs, without being stationed at a desk within the lobby.

As the luxury hotel segment becomes increasingly competitive, each brand strives to outdo one another with the latest spa amenity upgrades, trendy décor and other expensive upgrades like the installation of new gym facilities or an infinity pool. This is almost becoming a war of attrition.

Instead, I view guest services as the ultimate means of differentiation. Adding a premium butler service marks a clear method to distinguish your hotel at a fraction of the cost of physical renovations. The butler is a concept directly attuned to the modern ideals of luxury of luxury guest services.

Furthermore, I expect that most guests still have no idea how much a butler can enhance their stays. Teaching such consumers on how to use a butler and explicitly advertising this new amenity are both essential steps to implementation. Especially when considering that the number of properties offering butler services is limited at this time, most aging baby boomers, myself included, are only now starting to recognize the advantages of such lavish hotel pampering. With this in mind, 'better butlering' will likely be a hot topic for the next few years.

Food & Beverage: Role Play Reversal

When your reputation as one of the finest properties in the world is at stake, the need for continuous reinvention is not just a concept, but also a necessity. Visiting Los Angeles, I had the opportunity to experience exceptional service and a top-quality product. But what stood out most at the Montage Beverly Hills were several unique aspects of the food and beverage operation.

For those who have never toured this operation, the primary restaurant is an outpost of the Scarpetta franchise. With outlets in Las Vegas, Toronto and several other centers, the eatery offers modern, chic Italian food at prices that make your local pasta joint seem like fast food. No question, the service, food, décor and ambiance were absolutely flawless. As the guidebooks would say, this restaurant is worth an extra visit.

But what is perhaps most intriguing about this restaurant is the kitchen. Designed not only for efficiency, this is truly a case where the back of the house takes center stage. Stainless steel counters are replaced with exceptional quality granite or marble surfaces with chrome inserts. With large picture windows, the kitchen looks out onto a busy local street at ground level. Chefs, sous-chefs, saucier and others all work in symphonic concert under the watchful eyes of not only the executive chef, but also customers who choose to eat at a kitchen counter. And this is not just some 'chef's table' in the corner of a large commercial kitchen. Rather, diners are positioned in the center of the action.

In effect, the Montage has turned the world of food preparation into the forefront of guest entertainment. They give their customers a fun experience, rather than just expensive, and probably very tasty, food. It's an exercise both in customer loyalty and generating positive word of mouth. And from what I could tell, the staff seemed to enjoy the limelight, too.

Not to be outdone, the bar has taken its role as a front-of-house draw and moved to a back-of-house speakeasy status. The Montage's latest rendition is a throwback to the Prohibition Era. Named '£10' after the distillery engraving on the back of a Scottish banknote, there was no instantly recognizable signage. Key access required, the bar's decor is a virtual sea of Lalique crystal and features an incredible range of rare and exotic Scotch single malts, many from the Macallan Distillery.

By moving a seemingly accessible product to the realm of inaccessibility, the Montage further differentiates itself from other competitors through exclusivity. The personal service also goes beyond the expected with the bartender/mixologist/Scotch guru bringing selected spirits directly to the table to pour, discuss and complete the order.

There is no question that the Montage Beverly Hills needed to take these proactive steps to differentiate itself. Competition in the über-luxury segment from Four Seasons, Peninsula, the renewed Bel-Air and others is fierce. Customers accustomed to paying ADRs in the nosebleed range are fickle. Local "1%" diners are equally demanding. I wholly applaud Montage's approach and innovative leadership.

But new ideas in hotels need not be restricted to the top of the food chain. All hoteliers have the opportunity to have their own 'Montage' victory story. Give Montage full credit. All it takes is the commitment to succeed and a good dose of creativity. What's holding you back?

Is It Okay to Fire a Guest?

Hoteliers are bound by the code of customer service. Like doctors' Hippocratic Oath, hoteliers are sworn to uphold the safety, comfort and needs of their guests, treating them as if they were friends invited into their home. I've experienced this level of customer respect, going above and beyond the call of duty. It is impressive.

As Manager-on-Duty (MOD), I've also suffered abuse from inebriated guests, dealt with impossible demands and cleaned up messes with descriptions that defy the written word. When does this end? And does it break the unwritten code of hospitality to say no to a guest?

Let's start from a legal perspective. You have no right to discriminate or bar service to anyone on the basis of race, religion, color, sex, sexual preference, or nationality. That's a given for all hoteliers.

But what about individuals who are known to be difficult such as, for example, those who drink to excess? In a similar vein, what about groups that are known to be troublesome? Should you bar them from your establishment? Airlines have a 'No Fly List' and perhaps it is high time that hoteliers take a similar approach towards malfeasant behavior. It would not be difficult to do. Today's computer systems allow for sharing of information, at the least throughout a hotel chain. Of course, there is an inherent risk in this approach. This proverbial 'no stay list' could quickly become a hotbed of discriminatory practice.

So, setting this list idea aside, what can an hotelier do to gain the respect necessary to ensure that his or her hotel does not bear the brunt of every guest's frustration? Furthermore, consider this argument not only from a damage control perspective, but also from the point of view of other guests who might share in your discomfort. Sometimes a utilitarian approach truly is best. After all, you don't want your inability to remove a surly visitor to impact how other guests perceive your service levels when it comes time for an online appraisal.

Quick Ways to Improve Your Guest Welcome

Over the past thirty years of business travel, I've checked into hundreds of different hotels. You would think that by now the process would be fairly boring and routine. Yet, with each trip there comes a moment of anticipation and excitement as my eyes breath in the exceptional features and layout of each new setting.

To me, the check-in is one of the most important elements of the guest experience. While some may believe that the reservation process is the first opportunity for guest interaction, in today's interactive world, it pales in comparison to the physical visitor arrival. With this in mind, here are some suggestions (and questions you can ask yourself) to make your guests feel special when they reach your property.

1. **A Sense of Arrival: The Walk Through (Part One Exterior).** When was the last time you checked in at your own property? I mean, really checked in, with suitcases and even kids in tow. What does the motor court look like? Is the first impression one of oil stains or floral arrangements? First impressions count—huge! What is that critical initial look to your property?

2. **The Doorman.** One of the best doormen I know is Robbie at Hotel Pennsylvania. This is a 1,700-room property, yet he seems to know just about everyone by name. He's always smiling and his gregarious demeanor is contagious. Don't underestimate the importance of your doorman. His or her positive outlook can set the tone for a great guest experience. How do you treat your doormen?

3. **The Bell Staff.** Like a well-orchestrated tag team wrestling match, your bell staff are the connectors between the doorman and the front desk. They should move your guest seamlessly from one to the other with the highest level of efficiency. Good bell staff manages to get your guest's entire luggage onto a single cart effortlessly. Great bell staff is also trained to learn about guest needs and, somehow, communicate this to the front desk staff or concierge without the

guest even knowing. Remarkably, great bell staff is a rarity, and if you are fortunate to have a solid team, take steps to protect them.

4. **The Walk Through (Part Two Interior).** In the less-than-one-minute that it takes for the guest to walk from the portico to the front desk, critical impressions of your property are made. I like to think of this as the 'wow' moment. What does your guest see? Make sure there is at least one item that cues them to relax and be at ease, such as a grand floral arrangement. Take the walk yourself and see if you can identify the 'wow' factors within your property.

5. **The Greeting.** How does your front desk staff greet your guests? Are they consistent in their approach? Is there a script they follow? I expect front desk staff to be warm, attentive and informative. They should not be distracted by the telephone or any other minor task. This is your true front line staff. Make sure they are your best.

6. **Value-Added Up-Sell.** Positive interactions with your guests at check-in afford you the opportunity to explain some of the features of your property. Here is your chance to sell dinner reservations, spa appointments or extended concierge services. Consider adding tablet computers to your front desk arsenal as a slide show style of selling tool.

7. **The Hand Off.** As a guest leaves your front desk, check to see that they have all of the necessary paperwork. This should include, room key (or keys if requested), a copy of all of their reservations, valet parking receipt, a map of the property (the accordion-fold pocket maps are a few pennies each and a real useful item for guests), plus any additional literature. Depending on your approach, this may be given to the bellman, or to another representative of the property who escorts the guest to the room. Ideally, this paperwork need not be given to the guest, unless they have indicated that they don't want to have bell service. If it's being given to the guest, make sure they are collected in an envelope or folder. Too often I've been given a batch of loose papers and had trouble keeping it all in order.

8. **The Elevator.** For most visitors the next step is a trip in one of your elevators. When was the last time you looked at this small interaction critically? What does the advertising panel communicate? What's the topic of discussion? Is there music? Ensure the flooring and carpets are flawless. And remember, an out of service elevator is a telltale sign of weak property maintenance.

9. **The Room.** The first glance at the guest room is an important greeting component. Make a good first impression—lights aimed, a minimum number of tent cards and special offer flyers, flawless housekeeping, spa samples, local magazines, welcome notes, rose petals for the romantics, complementary fruit platters. Think of all the little details you can use to enhance that initial feeling.

I strongly encourage you to undertake your own check-in routine and see if your property meets your critical needs. It might be hard to get yourself out of your own headspace; especially your hotel that is like your second home and you've likely been spending several dozen hours on the floors each week. If necessary, hire an independent contractor who's knowledgeable in these critical areas to give you a third-party review and cover any aspects you may have overlooked.

Les Miserables: The Innkeeper Lives!

I always love going to see *Les Miserables*. It's easily my favorite play and I've seen it in Toronto, New York and London. Before I come to my point, let me digress for those unfamiliar.

Based on a novel written by Victor Hugo in 1862, the musical is set in the time leading up to the French Revolution. One of the more comical characters in this exceptional period piece was the Innkeeper, best known for the song 'Masters of the House' which jovially mocked the hotel industry at the time. I'll spare you my singing abilities, but a verse near the end definitely isn't pretty:

> "Charge 'em for the lice, extra for the mice
> Two percent for looking in the mirror twice
> Here a little slice, there a little cut
> Three percent for sleeping with the window shut
> When it comes to fixing prices
> There are a lot of tricks he knows
> How it all increases, all them bits and pieces"

Almost 250 years later after the novel's original publishing and how far has our industry moved? Not that far from what I have experienced. On a recent trip to a luxury chain property, our innkeeper was hard at work:

- $4.99 for a bottle of water
- $14.99 for Internet access
- $3.00 to receive a fax
- $5.00 to send a fax
- $35.00 for daily valet parking
- $1.00 for each 'toll free' long distance call outbound
- $14.99 for an in-room movie
- $5.00 for a soft drink from the mini-bar
- $5.00 for a small-sized Pringles (almost 20 cents per chip!)

The guest folio also included several different taxes, and local community improvement fees. The total for these extras, including room service breakfast, came to about a 50% surcharge versus the quoted room rate.

While the impetus for adding the Innkeeper character was mostly comic relief, the message nonetheless hits home. Service charges and extra fees are big business for hoteliers. My experience with numerous properties clearly identifies these areas as easy profit centers. What I propose will not sit well with those REVPAR-hungry property CFOs, so apologies in advance to my financial friends. In short, upper-scale properties need to recognize that many guests find this to be equivalent of petty larceny.

Several years ago, I stayed at a fantastic Relais & Chateaux property in the South of France called Les Mas Candille. The valet readily parked the car and there was bottled water in the room. I asked the general manager if I would be charged. Almost insulted, he replied, "Sir, you are in my home. Just as you would not ask me to pay if I stayed at your house, I would never consider charging you in mine."

Translate this bottled water example to other extraneous charges. I'm sure you recall the media turmoil when airlines heralded in the $25 checked baggage fees. An interesting note on this development is that the surcharges did not apply to business class travelers.

Perhaps what is needed in the hotel industry is a sense of differentiation whereby those who stay in suites and upgraded rooms will receive additional complimentary services such as those previously outlined. Promising one room rate with no extraneous charges may just be the cinch you need to distinguish your brand and launch a new marketing campaign. After all, lying to your guests is not the way towards a stellar service report card.

Conclusions

Did you notice any trends? Do you approach your guests with the disposition of an ostrich or a llama? Recall this comparative metaphor when assessing how you and your staff interact with guests. There are obviously many shades of gray to consider, but think broadly when forming your opinion.

Although it's near impossible to grasp these days, I like to consider guest services as independent of technology. Through this perspective, it becomes clear that guest interaction is of primary importance, and not the actual electronic know-how. Once you have this mastered, then integrating new technologies will be a breeze.

There are definitive ways to use technology to enhance the visitor experience while onsite, and your social media networks will be there to boost your brand while guests are offsite, both pre—and post-arrival. But whatever offsite work you do, the motivating factor for great online reviews and word of mouth will always be the experience that you deliver to guests while on property. You could be a technological 'dinosaur', completely oblivious to the plethora of online travel sites and social networks, and yet, if you treat people with the utmost of reverence, you'll nonetheless become known as a quality proprietor.

As I explore in later sections, it's becoming harder and harder for the average customer to identify with any one particular hotel brand name. Instead of solely relying on your marketing engine (although as an advertiser I would never suggest neglecting this venture), treat superior guest services as a point of brand differentiation. Your guests may not identify with your hotel name, but after a delightful meet-and-greet with a senior manager, perhaps they'll identify with your staff, with loyalty and positive word of mouth in tow.

Social Media

Spice Island Beach Resort continually ranks as one of the premier establishments in the Caribbean. Both the common areas and individual rooms display a magnificent sense of tropical relaxation and unique Grenadian culture.

Introduction to Social Media

Nowadays, it's impossible to discuss guest services without also considering your social network strategy. The two are inseparable. Treat social media as an extension of guest services. They are methods to not only entice visitors to stay with you, but to give them a flavor of how well they'll be treated once they arrive. Just as your brand is a promise of what will be delivered, your social networks can act as a preview of this promise.

A large part of a modern advertiser's job is devoted to assessing social media and seeing how it can be integrated with the overall marketing plan. The following chapters explore how to use various new channels that have arisen out of the 'social media gold rush' starting around 2007. Pay particular attention to the overriding themes and commonalities amongst the different networks.

Will social media stop with Facebook, Twitter, LinkedIn, Pinterest and YouTube? Most likely not. There will always be new entrants vying for your participation. As a hotelier, you must learn how to adapt and think proactively rather than reactively. My hope for you is to not only learn the ins and outs of these websites, but to develop thorough analytical skills to know their proper uses.

How Hotels Can Appeal to Travel Bloggers

If you haven't already realized, there's a very eager and knowledgeable community of writers ready to spread the good word about your hotel. The concept of the travel blogger is yet another to evolve from the Internet and their numbers have grown leaps and bounds within the travel world. If you look at how well they leverage the web and social media, you'll quickly grasp how making friends within this cluster can be beneficial.

Yet opinions on their true influence seem to be greatly divided. Many traditionalists adhere to courting only those writers who represent a major publication with sizeable reach. On the other hand, I've known hoteliers who hold them to the same esteem as journalists for prominent magazines, complete with comped rooms and free meals.

Which stance is right? Are travel bloggers just your typical guests who happen to write about their journeys from time to time? Or, should you go out of your way to give them the red carpet treatment?

I side with the latter through and through. Travel bloggers are a niche set of writers who can be a valuable asset to expand your market awareness to new sectors. But, let's first assess what these Internet writers actually do.

Acclaim from a travel blogger doesn't usually translate into a glossy four-page magazine spread, but rather a five to ten paragraph web editorial, often with handheld, homegrown photography. Such blog entries typically don't have as pervasive a reach, nor are they scribed with the same whimsical panache that underscores their printed ancestors. Such travel bloggers might not even grant you the opportunity to court them; they'll show up unannounced to soak in the natural vibe. As well, their articles will likely feature some not-too-heavily-Photoshopped images, bolstering the authentic feel of the prose.

And here's the kicker: travel bloggers love what they do. Starting a blog is relatively straightforward and inexpensive, but filling it with a constant flow of new articles requires commitment and passion; especially when dealing in travel, which can entail a lot of additional cash expenditures to voyage from spot to spot. Most of the bloggers I've met start with other jobs to sustain their hobby. They're a vocally positive group and very enthusiastic about any and every travel opportunity, even if it isn't attached to comps.

Building a support network for travel bloggers within your organization can be a powerful vessel to express your brand. Blogging also delivers the benefit of immediacy. Print has a lead time of three to six months, but blogging can be done on location or soon thereafter, affording your property an outlet for faster results if you know you're entering a lull in your media coverage.

Along these lines, travel bloggers are all fluent in social media, which will translate into more tweets, better cross-chatter and heightened SEO. Keep in mind that I have also experienced situations where negative bloggers describe their predicament in real-time from onsite!

The advantages are clear, so how then does one go about attracting these ambitious, and largely independent, writers to stay and endorse your property? Answers are aplenty.

Start by maintaining your existing relationships as you would for any other media contacts. Talk with your writer friends via social media and promote their blogs to your fans or followers. Reciprocation is all but a guarantee. Don't be afraid to ask them if they have any other press friends who might be willing to stay at your property. Or, perhaps consider opening a dialogue with their colleagues on Facebook.

Once you've reached out to your established contacts, extend your social media savvy out to other less-acquainted writers and build new relationships. Get involved in travel chats on Twitter and travel blogger groups that congregate on a monthly or semi-frequent basis.

Then comes the real meat of the courtship. Organize breakfast, lunch and dinner presentations in larger population centers to drum up some avid awareness. These always get a positive turnout, especially with due notice and avid preparation. Besides, who's going to say no to free food?

Next, offer specials or complimentary goods to bloggers when they are onsite, much like you would for other travel writers. Beyond this, consider hosting travel-blogger-focused media trips, or arrange to include at least one blogger on regular press visits.

There really are a variety of options here, and the key is to be proactive. Engage travel bloggers in the way that you want them to work for you. If you find one writer through his or her blog or twitter account, expect them to reply to you and to publish their support through this medium. Any way you cut it, garnering support and property buzz from travel bloggers is yet another way to gain that market edge, and it is crucial to build lasting relationships with this sect of people as their prominence is only going to grow.

Facebook for Hotels: Part One

Sorry to say, but this is not a freshman tips and tricks guide for those who just want a 'presence' on Facebook. This is a sophomore lesson on how to extend your Internet branding the right way; the way that will get you natural growth that actually translates into heightened loyalty and recognition. Especially now that the North American Facebook crowd has 'matured' towards how they perceive sponsored pages, you can't afford to be just another gimmick.

And the methodology here isn't actually all that heavy. In fact, it's quite easy for hoteliers to spread the word about their property. Here is the secret in a nutshell. Layer your informative message with a veneer of fun and warmth. Keeping this thought on the back of your mind will save you plenty of time and effort when it comes to using this networking goliath.

In this day and age, online users have rapidly become desensitized to all the advertising thrown at them. They can smell direct promotions a mile away, whether they crop up in text or graphics. People these days are so saturated with things to occupy their time that if you aren't fun, they will simply tune out. Facebook is no exception. If you're not relevant to what consumers want, they will cut you out of their newsfeed. Being fun means being entertaining. And people love entertainment.

For example, picture yourself in ancient Rome: you are the gladiator fighting for survival and all your fans are the Plebian mob cheering you on from the bleachers. You have but one choice. Give the people exactly what they want or face extinction. Times have changed, but the game remains the same.

Aha! But what does 'fun' mean in a modern sense? Therein lies the art of it all. Being fun means weaving a story around your hotel; a story with characters, adventure, mystery, and, above all, excitement.

Give the people photos or videos—not the glossy, professional (and costly!) works, but ones taken on the fly and in the moment. If you are the social media manager on property, you better have a smartphone or camera on hand at all times because you never know when that candid opportunity will present itself. But you can't be everywhere at once, and that is why you need to educate your fellow staff on the boon of being social and designate a company email to receive cool snapshots from avid guests.

Pictures and video clips tell stories, and stories get people talking. Whenever you post a neat little image about something—anything—that people could find interesting in three seconds or less, then fans will be much more inclined to press the 'like' button. And the beauty of this miniscule effort on their part is that when they 'like' something, it shows up in their newsfeed. Congratulations, you've just breached a new network for all of your fan's friends to see. Bonus marks for getting comments and responding to them. Regardless of the more complex metrics that Facebook offers, the 'like' is the ultimate vessel for increasing your exposure on this social media behemoth.

Obviously, what we are discussing here is brand awareness. If you are consistent with your amiable wall posts, fans will come to 'like' you even more, which means that their friends will see you multiple times and might even become your friends, especially if your interests align with theirs. And in-between all the quick notes, the true sense of what your hotel stands for will be told to them over a longer period of time, much the same way as chapters in a novel.

So just like the macabre analogy of the Roman Empire, let's give it an example. You are the public relations manager for a midsized property in Florida. Your resort has built its reputation around being an outstanding family getaway to soak in the sun and try out some beach or water related activities. You are looking to 'keep the good times rolling' by reaching out to your fan base via Facebook, and maybe get some extra sales.

The wrong way to go about it would be to post retouched images of that hired model couple windsurfing with perfect technique into the sunset, superimposed against a snappy headline and advertised booking deal. It isn't real, and the majority of people don't relate to what isn't authentic. Instead, what if you started taking 'in the moment' shots of guests or cool happenings around the resort? Whether it's water sports, reading a book at high noon or even a special dish that the chef made for an event, each one tells a story. A real story.

For instance, one day you go for an afternoon stroll along the beach and discover that two young siblings have just spent the last few hours constructing a sandcastle. You snap a picture and post it online. What does that say? Now layer that on top of last week's anecdote about a new dish offered at the restaurant and last month's album from the jazz festival held on the beach. Now you've got yourself a story; fun for the whole family with a dab of tropical flair.

Another crucial differentiating factor here is your lingo-vernacular for those literati out there. Every photo should have a caption, and not just some general description. Think about how you would talk to your friends and go from there. Let me repeat: don't write, talk. Save the precision syntax for press releases and news articles. When it comes to Facebook, feel free to break sentence structure, use a few ellipses or throw in some slang (non-derogatory, of course). This applies for regular wall posts as well as for taglines for albums, video or hot links.

But there are a few subtle nuances that are also worth mentioning. The big one is posting too often to the point of spam. I'd say a good middle ground is three to six times a week, especially you have something important to say or some very time sensitive material to disperse. The bottom line is you want to get your story across, but trim all the fat. Don't make a fan regret their commitment to you. Another such fallacy is to only post reminders about upcoming events without an engaging photo, link to the previous year's album or room for fan feedback. A couple lines of text sans color image will not attract anybody.

And thus, the proverbial keys to the kingdom lie with semi-consistent and engaging content. You need to portray the underlying message that you are committed to social media for the long haul without too much immediate inundation. Slow and steady wins the race.

Once your fans see that, they will want to connect with you via Facebook and be a part of all the action. The more you engage your fans with poignant information tidbits, the more your hotel will be in their thought stream. Mind share leads to word of mouth, which in turn leads to more prospective customers. And heck, once in a while, you can throw in a promotional offer and ask your fans to give it some thought. You already have an established, back-and-forth relationship, so they're likely to listen. Let the story of your hotel speak for itself.

Facebook for Hotels: Part Two

Here are more morsels about the big social media fish that should be on every hotelier's mind. We all know that Facebook is important and that you measure the number of fans or 'likes'. But what does this number really mean? Is having 10,000 fans versus just 2,000 directly correlated to the fiscal amount of business you do?

Fans range from people who have liked your page once to those who check-in from time to time or visit multiple times a week. Frequencies aside, how do you gauge which of your fans are spreading the good word? Are they consistently recommending your hotel to their friends? Are they going out of their way to help grow your business?

I don't mean to discount a large fan base, not in the least. Brand awareness is the first move toward sales, but there are still many steps in-between. Facebook page administration includes more in-depth follower metrics to give you a better sense of your true reach, but even then I am quite skeptical of the immediate effect of these types of statistics that reside purely within Facebook.

Instead of fans, what you really need are influencers—people who will actually bring guests to your hotel. Well, you're in luck! Where Facebook really shines is that it is possibly the best online route for nurturing your fans and turning them into influencers due to the specific ways in which it lets you talk with fans on a semi-personal basis. Think of the web site as an incubator; every fan has the potential to sing your praises, but you have to take full advantage of Facebook's capabilities to woo them over.

I'm a big believer that word-of-mouth hotel recommendations from friend to friend are still one of the most effective ways to get new customers. I'm old school like that, but that doesn't mean I don't embrace the voracious power of social media. Turning fans into influencers is like converting word of mouse back into word of mouth. This foot-in-the-door tactic is the easy part, and I'll assume that you're clear on it. If not, there are a multitude of articles and resources at your disposal on the web.

What I'm really talking about now is the next step: be in it for the long haul. Fans won't turn overnight. You will have to go out of your way on a one-to-one basis for any fan to return the favor. These types of connections take time; your real influencers won't all make themselves readily available at the drop of a hat. Think of the fun photos or interesting factoids you post as building blocks, each one a part of a bigger picture. The more you build, the more your influencers will emerge.

"But I monitor my page's insights," you may be thinking to yourself. True, this is beneficial and something I'd definitely advocate. But it won't tell you which individuals are repeatedly liking or commenting, or even more importantly, which of your fans are taking your message home. So, you have two options. Make a list of all the people who respond to each post and tally it up, or, trust the process and treat your page's fans like you would your guests. That's right; your Facebook page is an extension of your guest services policies.

There's a third option that I have to touch on briefly: software developments. The technological powers that be are swiftly catching up, and finding your online influencers is only going to get easier. Check out the work of companies like Klout.com. Soon enough, their class of web-based applications will be a staple for professional Facebook pages. Even with an electronic panacea like this, however, it'll still be hard to gauge word of mouth. That's why I insist: trust the process.

And definitely be on the lookout for constructive criticism. Compliment fans who post supportive comments. Answer questions fully and promptly. Address concerns with an honest explanation. And do so on a one-to-one basis. The buzz term for this is 'Online Concierge', which I had no part in designating but still love to throw around. As an online concierge, it's your job to be thoroughly knowledgeable about your property and the surrounding region, as well as to guide your fans with their inquiries.

When you help someone online, not only will they remember it, but others will also see you helping that person. If you can impress a fan with the substance of your answers, then they will impress you by casually talking about your hotel to their friends. A resourceful and courteous online reputation is a passive form of promotion in its own right.

On the flip side, are you willing to accept constructive criticism? Have you set up your Facebook page so there's a forum for fans to make suggestions? People love to be heard and be involved at the planning stage. Plus, you never know, there might be a gem or two out there to make it all worthwhile.

Next, become a hub of activity. Programmers at Facebook and third-party operators have done a wonderful job ensuring that the site is compatible with a host of extensions and custom-coded apps. Fans have adapted to expect these catchy additions, and fan pages have in turn adapted to their expectations. All this means there's a growing propensity to use the web site as a one-stop shop.

Analyze your competitive set. What tabs or fun little accessories have they added to customize their page? What can you emulate? Start by adding tabs that integrate all your other social media. Code for a reservation system or a newsletter signup tab. Any opportunity you have to engage more users with a fully-loaded page is one you should take.

Then the plan is to exceed their expectations. They should be proud to be your fans. Organize your photo albums and consistently add great content. Coupons, offers or Facebook-specific programs work well, too. Every upgrade you make will appeal to a slightly different subset of people within your gross fan base. Some people want candid photos of scenic beaches, others are looking for deals. Make your page exclusive by being inclusive.

Think of yourself as a community leader. This ties into the idea of being an online concierge as well as becoming a hub. Your posts don't always have to be about you. In fact, they shouldn't. Talk about that adorable small business a few blocks away from your property. Emphasize your commitment to sustainability. Share all local events. Publicly thank a generous supporter. Start to think of your fans as a part of your team then lead them accordingly.

And remember, your page isn't just for you. It's a place for fans to connect with one another, not just with your hotel. There are some amazing stories out there of friends finding each other on Facebook through mutual interests then they turn out to be neighbors in real life! And they'll remember who played matchmaker. You have the opportunity to brighten the lives of others, even if only for a couple seconds each day. Adhere to this mindset whenever you happen to log on.

Marketable Tweetables

As of mid-2011, Twitter became a firmly 'established' entity in the online world. Much like Facebook fan pages, the fair share of hotels have an online presence here and most people who want to be on Twitter are already using the application, and quite adroitly at that.

It's now a mature product, and as such, strategies have changed once more. Without that newcomer fervor, Twitter users are far less 'excitable'. Just being active for the sake of activity is the status quo—water under a vast digital bridge—and it won't sway consumers to action. So, how can hotels reinvigorate their online marketing campaign?

Here are four suggestions to keep your social media efforts alive and well, or help get you off the ground floor is you're a late entrant to the Twitter game:

1. **Quality of Followers.** Whenever someone evaluates a Twitter account, the first attribute they'll likely look at is the number of followers. It's a quantity that can be easily relayed up and down the management chain to track progress. There's also the crowd theory aspect at play—people will only listen to you if others are already listening.

    First, keep in mind that getting followers is easy. If you dedicate yourself to following industry leaders and other travel personalities, a fair amount will follow you back. Rinse and repeat until you're in the quadruple digits.

    Aside from increasing your followers from a pool of related users, you have look for quality followers—friends you actually talk with. These are the people who respond to your tweets and promote your material to their followers. Foster these Twitter relationships by replying to questions through public messages or reading your feed and retweeting interesting material to your followers. Make lists and form genuine relationships with these individuals. Twitter is, of course, just another avenue to find and connect with other people.

2. **Maintain Frequency.** Quality trumps quantity, but much like the number of followers, your daily number is important. With

so many tweets every hour and so many users generating content, you need frequency so that your followers will see your tweets when they login at various times throughout the day. Two or three tweets a week between Monday and Friday is the bare minimum to show that you are fully committed to using this online channel. Retweeting and quoting captivating messages from your quality followers will help fill the gaps. A good way to maintain frequency is to use Twitter management software to schedule your tweets for various times throughout the day. The key is to develop your message and be consistent with it.

3. **Vary Your Tweets.** Maintaining frequency and constantly rolling out interesting material requires foresight and a certain amount of variety to keep your audience engaged. Inundating Twitter users with the same type and style of tweets is boring. Their eyes will glaze over. For example, if all your tweets adhere to the format of text-hashtags-link, then it all appears the same in consumers' minds. Instead, thimblerig your words around with something like link-text-hashtags—subtle but it'll make a difference.

    Thinking long-term, organize a release schedule so your interesting factoids can be interspersed with promotional material, public messages and retweets. Build anticipation to future events through direct announcements and by appealing to your cabal of loyal Twitter friends. Write a few 'Did You Know?' blog articles then leave some click-through style tweets for people to find your blog. Variety is critical because you don't know exactly what will pique the interest of different people. As a hotel, some of your followers may be seeking deals or new offers, while others may be more entertainment focused. Cover all possible avenues and you'll end up engaging the largest audience.

4. **Online Concierge.** One of the best functions of Twitter is that the program is an easy, non-invasive way for people to contact you directly to inquire about your property. Treating this social media channel as an online concierge is a paramount virtue to uphold, because ultimately it's all about customer satisfaction.

    Start by announcing your followers that you are available to answer their questions through Twitter. Remind your audience to connect with you prior to arriving at your property. Stay up to date on fun activities and seasonal events in your area. Reply with links to more in-depth resources. Make sure all your social media channels are integrated with each other and with Twitter so any curious users can easily locate your Facebook fan page, blog, or any other site that may help. When potential guests contact you, respond fully and promptly. They'll remember your efforts and reward you in kind by talking about your property to their followers or to their friends in person.

How Hotels Can Use Yelp

Started as an online review channel seven years ago in San Francisco, Yelp is a top ranker in United States traffic, and has seen its share of global Internet page views, as well as overall usefulness, increase dramatically. The website distinguishes itself from the strictly travel-focused likes of TripAdvisor, Orbitz and Travelocity by serving up a local flair—think restaurants, bars, stores and spas, not just hotels.

Due to this key difference, Yelp doesn't just attract the vacation savvy crowd, but caters more wide-ranging and eclectic demographics including locals, avid shoppers, gourmands and bar hoppers. With nearly a decade's worth of accumulated listings and reviews, the site is now a leading third-party reference hub, so let's take a further look.

For starters, Yelp can do wonders for your SEO if you maintain up-to-date business descriptions, web site links and photos. Plus, you can monetize your involvement through special offers, announcements, pay-per-click ads and group buying services. It's these sorts of low-cost, easy-to-run promotional tools that can increase your presence amongst the emergent class of Yelp users and possibly generate a few new leads.

By far the most powerful facet is its reviews. Using similar tactics to what you might use for TripAdvisor, receptive and cooperative responses can go miles to reaffirm participants and build goodwill amongst potential customers surfing the digital landscape. Moreover, Yelp is another outlet to gather constructive feedback, and due to its key user contrasts from other online travel sites, you're bound to get a different scope of opinions about your operations.

I wouldn't recommend this system for everyone, however. A big problem is that the reviews are skewed towards those places with an already outstanding track record and posters don't seem to be as lenient as on TripAdvisor. So let's face it; if you manage a one star or two star property, your reviews won't be all that phenomenal and Yelp may only serve to highlight this mediocrity.

Next, I would caution against putting a 'Review Badge' on your property's website. Demonstrating credibility to your consumers through positive testimonials on Yelp is in itself a great idea. But why would you want to navigate traffic away from your web site, especially to a third-party domain which also lists the competition?

Make no mistake though, despite these potential drawbacks, I nonetheless believe that Yelp can be a handy tool for savvy hoteliers. The benefits of attracting a new set of customers, enhancing your SEO and having another outlet for constructive criticism are too good to ignore. The website should be considered as yet another critical aspect of your social media platform.

What I'd suggest is that you hit the ground running and join Yelp sooner rather than later. Last of note, Yelp allows users to write reviews for places not yet officially registered, so people might already be talking about your hotel without you knowing. All the more reason to sign up!

How Hotels Can Use FourSquare

Many companies already have a strong plan already in place for the big three: Facebook, Twitter and the corporate blog. On top of this, most savvy businesspeople are sufficiently acquainted with the ins and outs of social bookmarking sites. However, hoteliers should take note of mobile sign-in services. The big players as of this writing include the likes of FourSquare, Gowalla and Facebook Places. For the sake of not being overly complicated, let's focus the remainder of our attention on FourSquare—a company that grew substantially in 2010 and 2011—even though all three work by similar means.

Once a person has a FourSquare account, they 'check-in' to wherever they are via their phones and this serves as their online status. Fun, no? FourSquare uses GPS technology to verify where the cellular is in the world and to keep things honest. On top of this, people can be awarded 'Mayor' status by having the most check-ins for any given location, or earn specific 'Badges' by logging in from a given combination of places.

Sounds like fun, but how does it apply to hotels? Well, take Gap for instance. Last year, they launched a notorious FourSquare campaign where anyone who checked in at one of their locations received 25% off their purchase. Other large-scale corporations have followed suit, even offering additional discounts for holding mayoral status.

However, this doesn't exactly transfer to independent lodges or mid-sized chains that lack access to national advertising channels and the programming resources to seamlessly integrate these types of services into their operations. FourSquare boasts that they are universally applicable for small businesses and the hospitality industry, albeit with a word of caution. Like most of the contemporary social media tools, if you don't plan ahead and know your customers, then you might as well not even try.

First, there aren't enough people who understand FourSquare, let alone use it on a regular basis. The whole location-service trend in social media may just be a fad and may even fizzle into oblivion while some of the more straightforward networks maintain a consistent worldwide growth. The 3400% expansion (2009 to 2010) statistic for FourSquare is in itself a tad bloated as it encapsulates users who have made an account to try the novel software and have since lost interest.

Metrics for FourSquare's second full year (2011) on the market are more realistic in this regard, but the fact remains that the service still primarily caters to a younger, tech savvy demographic. The boomer and mature populations appear more aligned with Facebook, Twitter and LinkedIn, and it's likely that they won't be 'checking in' in any significant quantity. Additionally, FourSquare is more of an urban craze with only the big metropolises sharing in the excitement.

Nonetheless, there are some definitive strategies for hotels when it comes to these types of novel social networking concepts, especially if you are trying to reach the younger crowd. With many users forwarding their check-ins to Twitter or Facebook, incorporating FourSquare is an excellent way to garnish some free press across several networks. Usage can also be encouraged by placing a notice in the window or leaving a 'Please Check-In on FourSquare' sign by the entranceway.

Hoteliers seem to be an obvious benefactor of this new wave of social media as we already work at a place where you check-in (literally!). By extension, FourSquare could serve as yet another type of 'Online Concierge'. Of course, this is something that would need to be constantly monitored—something easier said than done. Gourmands have already largely gained from FourSquare's recent deals with third parties like the New York Times and Zagat, and so this could be great for promoting your in-house restaurants. The developers behind this location-based network appear to have a long-term plan for aiding their users and subscribing businesses alike, as noted by the site's recommendation system.

The question remains though, do you get on board or not? It's one thing to register your company on FourSquare; it's another entirely to maintain it and exploit it as a promotion vehicle. Judging its practicality on this level, most evidence points to no. Your time spent on this niche service would be better allocated to the bigger, content-oriented networks like Facebook, Twitter and your blog. In a broader sense, what's important here is to be a forward thinker and receptive to the ever-changing world of cyberspace.

How Hotels Can Use Hipmunk

If you think that online hotel queries start and stop at Expedia, then you'll be missing out on a neat little web site. Before I divulge on the nuances of this search engine, let me first digress and explain that the term 'to Hipmunk' describes bringing a new sense of simplicity and suave to an otherwise established industry, delighting customers in the process. And Hipmunk.com does just that for online hotel searches.

Starting first as an online fight search engine, Hipmunk promptly expanded to hotels, modeling their website on speed and ease. The creators don't want you to waste any time finding what hotel is right for you, and indeed, when you visit the site, this aspect becomes quite apparent. The only criteria for you to choose are the city, arrival and departure dates, and the number of rooms and guests.

"If it's so simple, why bother?" you might ask. Well, this type of clean, efficient layout is just what the smartphone ordered. With the ever-growing throngs of people using their smartphones to manage more and more of their day-to-day activities, you'd be wise to address customers through this dynamic channel.

But this isn't just a summary of an innovative web site. We need to address how you and your hotel can effectively use this tool—or leverage this tool I might say—to drive new business. As a companion to this, I'd highly suggest you open up an Internet browser and play around with the site just to get the hang of things; this being the case any new web site of this nature.

For starters, Hipmunk is a search engine, not a booking site. It relies on a mash-up of online partners filtered through what I imagine are some very complex algorithms. Hotels are judged on three categories: price, reviews and distance. Distances and location data are gathered via Google Maps, reviews are compiled from Yelp, and price is obtained mostly from Hotels.com, but also from Bookings. com, Getaroom.com, Hrs.com, Otel.com and Skoorsh.com. As well, Hipmunk collects information about your hotel's amenities from these third-party booking sites. The site's fourth scale is dubbed 'Ecstasy' and is based on a combination of price, reviews and amenities. You can further delineate hotel queries by any of these categories or by individual amenities.

When you first complete a search, you're taken to a pleasant Google Maps display for all hotels in the requested city, with the listings sorted in a column on the left-hand side. Your goal is to be at the top of that column. The default landing category for searches is ecstasy, and because this is a compilation, let's focus on its parts.

First up is distance. The pinpoint center of a city is predetermined by Google, and your property is where it is, so there isn't much you can do about this one. No doubt this inherent rigidity is part of the reason why distance is not tabulated for the ecstasy score.

Next up are your Yelp reviews, which seem to play a dominant role towards the ecstasy factor. True, these critiques are written by past guests and you have little control over what they decide to write. But, guests are more prone to laud your property if they are treated well and the services are the best they can be. For this, Hipmunk uses your average score as well as the total number of reviews. It's a quantity of quality game. So, be sure to converse with guests while they are on property and politely ask them to praise your name online. Yelp is relatively unbiased, so if your guest services aren't up to snuff, then don't expect improvements here.

Third up is price, which is where it gets tricky. This category is sorted in ascending order, which means the cheapest rooms get priority at the top. However, the site lets you query results based on three demarcations: cheap, average and pricey. These can also be overlaid for ecstasy, reviews and distance searches. The numerical cutoff points for these delimiters are calculated based on the median price of all listed properties in the city. Thus, if you want to play around with price, your goal is not to become the cheapest place around, but merely the least expensive in your snack bracket.

For example, if your base room rate is listed on Hotels.com as $150 per night and this puts you in the 'normal' third of properties with the threshold for 'cheap' at $115, then you might aim to get as close to $115 as possible. But you wouldn't want to dip below $115 because then you'd show up as a 'cheap' hotel and appear at the bottom of the results column. One other caveat here is that if your entire competitive set starts to lower their pricing to optimize their results in sites like Hipmunk, then the median price point will shift accordingly and you'll all be playing another game of attrition. Moreover, lowering your price will cut into the bottom line and set expectations for future sales periods. Simply put, play with fire at your own risk.

My final suggestion is to look at your own property on Hipmunk and see where it currently stands. Then, work with your team to settle on a feasible six-month goal for improving your position. Are all your amenities listed and properly described on the corresponding third-party sites? Have you read your latest Yelp reviews to see what people are saying? Is your price aggressive or totally unreasonable when juxtaposed to your competitive set? These are all things to consider, and Hipmunk does an excellent job of streamlining such questions.

How Hotels Can Use Room 77

With a straightforward layout, Room 77 is a directory for a hotel's accommodations using room lists and floor plans to display specific rooms in all their detail and grandeur. The big visual draw is this site's use of Google Earth simulated views from each room's windows—easily its most exclusive quality. Moreover, it informs potential guests about such minute details like the proximity to the elevator, noise levels, WiFi strength, bed sizes, smoking or non-smoking, and even if there are interconnecting doors.

What's most enticing is how consumers can refine their search based on room compatibilities that match their preferences. For example, some guests prefer to be in a penthouse with floor-to-ceiling windows, while others prefer to stay grounded. And, of course, as an obligatory for online hotel web sites, you can post reviews after your stay; organized by individual rooms and not merely an amalgamation of all critiques for the entire property.

From the perspective of a hotelier, this may seem like a logistical nightmare. Room 77 takes the tried-and-true methodology of dividing rooms into categories and throws it straight out the window. Instead of managing a 300-room property with 7 different room types, you're now running the same property with 300 different room types.

But there are benefits. Room 77 is free for properties to list on and the only cost is the time needed to set up an account and supply the required specs. Additionally, they send highly targeted traffic (users who look up rooms at length) directly to hotel web sites instead of those dreaded third-party booking engines. They only give suggestions, even recommending the best times to call the hotel and ask about room preferences.

As with all major players in the online realm, involving yourself is not about whether you like a particular channel, it's about where your potential guests are. Of course, this tool may be deemed negligible for those surfing the one or two star cohorts. But, if you're charging a premium, you're likely catering to a discerning and often whimsical customer. So, what can a hotelier do to turn searches on this web site into future sales?

Listing is half the battle, and you can do it quite easily just by signing up. After all, listing gives you access to what users are saying about your hotel, right down to each particular room. That's a pretty good deal if you ask me!

Some customers will really appreciate that you made the effort to get onboard with this new age web platform. It'll give your property a 'tech savvy' image that is sure to attract extra viewers. Plus, there's a section where hotel management can communicate directly with users, advising them on anything from in-room features to general hotel amenities. And as you should already know, any point of contact between you and a consumer may well lead to a sale.

I eagerly await the day when hoteliers start to use this Room 77's cumulative metrics to redefine their pricing structure, but for now, the most important action to take is to get involved; get your hotel's name out to as many online locations as possible.

Is Pinterest a Winner or a Sinner for Hotels?

In late 2011, one of the newest, most interesting and fastest growing social media sites, Pinterest appeared. Pinterest now holds the record for crossing the coveted 10-million-unique-visitors-per-month statistic, completed within months, the fastest stand-alone web site to do so in the history of the Internet. In fact, Mashable.com cited Pinterest as the third most popular social network in the United States in the beginning of 2012, right behind the family names of Facebook and Twitter with 104 million users.

With all this fervor, Pinterest is next to impossible for hotels to ignore. But, as always with social media, will an investment of time and money into this new web site actually bear fruit? Or, will it be yet another cantankerous divergence of much needed human resources?

Set to a clean, minimalist design, Pinterest is a type of online scrapbook where members can 'Pin' visual media to their profiles, organized under a series of 'Pinboards'. From there, it works much like Facebook and Twitter whereby you can follow other users and their Pins will appear in your newsfeed, leaving room for you to like, comment or 'Repin'. Easy to grasp, Pinterest works almost as a system of anonymous recommendations, helping you find and share ideas based on common preferences. As well, members can utilize the 'Tastemakers' page when browsing for more relevant Pins or Pinboards.

As of the summer of 2012, Pinterest has largely been dominated by the wedding crowd within the United States; that is, women within the key demographic of 25-44 years old. This is bound to change as the site expands around the world. It's an excellent tool for any person seeking inspiration to further their own personal interests, and as such, creative communities are driving the early adoption period. Pinterest also integrates with Facebook and Twitter via a seamless notification system.

So, how can hotels use Pinterest? Due to its photo-centric design, this social network can act as a valuable tool to increase inbound traffic to your web site or Facebook page. All pictures shared on Pinterest contain a click-through link back to the source—all the more reason to upkeep your web site with high quality photography. Guest sourcing is also a possibility, allowing you to Repin material from other sources to your Pinboards. Think of it as 'curb appeal' for your property. You give users of the site a sneak peak of what's in store for when they visit your web site, and hopefully, for when they arrive onsite.

For starters, the web site is not a place to advertise your brand, but rather to express a certain lifestyle by posting interesting photos, offering suggestions to other members and, as always, engaging your audience through comments, likes and Repins. The modus operandi of Pinterest is that content drives conversation. You need to have good and current visual content to get people to notice you and drive traffic to an external web site of your choosing.

The difficulty is that this has to occur on a continual basis in order to achieve a desirable efficacy. Suppose you've chosen to use Pinterest to highlight three unique aspects of your hotel (that is, via three different Pinboards) including Cuisine, Décor and Weddings. Not only does this mean more work for your PR department (or for whoever manages your social media), but also for the other departments who generate the content. It takes time and consistency to add real value to your profile. This will require your chef, weddings specialists and other managers to work in tandem with your web gurus to produce the necessary photography or videos for Pinterest as well as write their external host pages, rich keyword descriptions and links between your main site and other networks.

The time adds up, especially when compounded by all the other social media that may be deemed as requirements for business these days. Due to Pinterest's visual nature, it necessitates a full effort, both in terms of strategizing how you will distinguish your brand through various Pinboards and in upkeep. In addition to all this, the lack of direct analytics makes it difficult to measure results over a brief period. There hasn't been any significant evidence to date that suggests the heightened brand awareness from Pinterest has any immediate correlation with increased activity on booking engines.

These negatives aside, Pinterest can be a winner for you if your property has a distinctive character already in place and the photography to boot. So, take a minute and think in terms of furnishings, crafts, architecture, weddings, spas, food, golf, gardening and other popular hobby topics. If you can add to the conversation in any one of these areas on a continual basis, then perhaps Pinterest is worth your time. But it nonetheless requires a significant investment and if you treat it as a blanket marketing solution, then your efforts will be in vain.

Should You Have Your Own Social Media Manager?

I suspect that every hotel manager knows about social media. While they might not personally be fans of Twitter, Facebook and the like, I am sure that everyone has at least once or twice viewed a YouTube video, or read comments on a Facebook post.

Tomes worth have been written on the advent of social media and its ability to generate a positive buzz for your property. The integration of social media into your web site has become paramount for enhancing organic SEO. But beyond this, and being really 'hard-nosed' about it, it is often difficult for social media activities to be directly quantified into a specific return on investment. And without a measurable return, how do you rationalize the direct labor cost in hiring an in-house social media manager?

We've faced this question in our practice at least a dozen times over the past year. The answer is not something that can be expressed by a precise written formula. However, we have developed the following guidelines for you to consider for this decision. These apply to individual properties, whether part of a chain or independent or not. And please keep in mind there are always exceptions to the rule. The goal of this calculator is to define a 35-40 hour work-week for the prospective social media manager.

Social Media Task Calculator

1. Basic social media management such as posting 5-8 items per week about general activities at the property and surrounding area; keeping up with activities; management reporting; organizing an activity calendar pro-actively: **5-10 hours/week**

2. Add a meaningful blog with 1-2 well-researched entries per week, in addition to social media posts, bringing the total posts to 3-4 items per week: **4-6 hours/week**

3. If you have a spa and want to address spa trends and activities: **2-3 hours/week**

4. If you have a golf course and want to integrate activities on the golf course with specific references, course guides and course activities: **2-3 hours/week**

5. For multiple F&B outlets; for instance, suppose your chef has a separate following, you'll want to disseminate recipes and have socially-oriented food events such as a wine tastings or food demonstrations: **5-8 hours/week**

6. If you have any other seasonal activities worth talking about, including skiing, water sports or hiking: **2-3 hours/week**

7. If you want to champion local charitable or cultural activities to make your property a hub for your region: **4-5 hours/week**

8. If you want to generate social media buzz for weddings with a separate bridal photo collection (using Flickr, Instagram, Pinterest, Picassa, etc.): **4-5 hours/week**

Add it all up. I might be generous in my hour allocations, but the fact remains that unless your property is a fully stocked resort with a range of facilities, there really is no need for an onsite social media manager. The issue becomes what to do next. Should you have a part-time position or allocate the work to a third party?

The answer here is more complex. Any staff member or intern, part—or full-time requires supervision. An independent takes more supervisory time than assigning your social media responsibilities to your marketing agency. The latter can be much more tactical.

So, who makes a good social media manager? If you make the decision to hire a part—or full-time social media manager in-house, the next thought is to the type of individual you bring aboard? And, what should be their required skill sets? Our experience is that a young fresh-out-of-college graduate will fit the job description nicely. Look for solid writing skills, an out-going personality with an independent work mentality, basic Photoshop skills (and preferably their own digital camera), and great teambuilding skills.

Give that individual free reign to learn all about your property and embrace it. Monitor the results and encourage your entire team to embrace social media as a core component of your marketing communications plan.

Interview with Felicia Yukich, Manager of Social Media Marketing for Four Seasons Hotels and Resorts

I was fortunate enough to sit down with Felicia Yukich of Four Seasons Hotels and Resorts (FSHR) Corporate Head Office to discuss her role as the Manager of Social Media Marketing. Here's what she has to say about how FSHR has become a leader in the online realm and some of the finer points of this current trend.

1. **Tell us about yourself. How did you become the Social Media Manager for FSHR?**

    My recent transition from Manager Interactive Marketing to Manager Social Media Marketing recognizes our commitment to leadership and innovation in the space. This role is an all-new global role for the company. As a previous member of the Four Seasons Corporate Public Relations team, I managed the PR and social media launch for new hotel openings and worked with our global agencies to coordinate strategic plans, including media events in the US and Brazil as well as launching and overseeing corporate PR efforts in Latin America. Prior to joining Four Seasons, I worked at GCI Group Canada—a leading WPP firm in Toronto—in the Consumer Lifestyle PR Practice. I specialized in digital media initiatives and media relations for international brands including Mattel, Dell and AIR MILES. My previous hotel experience includes hands-on hospitality PR experience at Fairmont Royal York Hotel in Toronto.

2. **How has FSHR differentiated itself in social media versus other luxury hotel chains?**

    The ownership of the brand is now shared because the relationship is now two-way; no longer just marketer to the consumer. The winners in this new age will be the brands that let their fans define it and syndicate it. We've always been a consumer centric culture so the shift to adopting the way guests and clients lead communications for Four Seasons has been rapid. Digital media is now 50% of our brand's marketing efforts with a strong social media presence that facilitates engagement and encourages loyalty.

Four Seasons has quickly and strategically grown its base of Twitter followers and Facebook fans, receiving accolades within the industry. As FSHR continues to incorporate social media into its day-to-day business, the company sees real-time interactions as a natural extension of its service model. Working closely with our properties to embrace this evolution, our unique approach has allowed a center-led global strategy to be localized in meaningful and relevant ways at the hotel level around the world.

On L2 Think Tank's recent 'Digital IQ Index', which measured 89 global airline, hotel and cruise brands, FSHR scored a digital IQ of 138, which is the top end of the 'gifted' classification. We have made digital our priority; it now represents half of our consumer marketing investment. And since content is king, we've combined PR with social media. From virtual wine tastings on Twitter to a vibrant Facebook presence awash with visitor images and timely conversations, to active participation in location-based apps such as Foursquare and Gowalla, to highly curated content on YouTube, which is fast becoming the world's second most important search engine, FSHR has its finger solidly on the pulse of the modern traveler.

3. How are guests responding to your social media presence? What are the metrics?

The FSHR guest is an avid user of social media and expects to have relationships with his or her favorite brands in social media channels too. FSHR has quickly and strategically grown its base of Twitter followers and Facebook fans, receiving accolades within the luxury hotel industry. We invest time in 'listening' to our social media audiences at the global and local level, ensuring that we are connecting the dots between online insights and offline experiences. We strive to serve up content that is interesting and relevant, and our increasing 'return on engagement' is a true testament to that. Our social media metrics are anchored in e-commerce, guest satisfaction and PR effectiveness.

We found that guests use social media, notably Twitter, to comment on their satisfaction during a stay. Because of this, we have incorporated Twitter into our service delivery so we are able to address issues, anticipate needs and generally surprise and delight the guest, using information they have shared publicly as well.

4. **Have you found that your customer base has shifted in recent years as a part of this effort? In other words, has the social media effort lowered the average age of the guest?**

In markets like China, the affluent age is far younger. We are currently developing a social media strategy for that market leveraging native Chinese social media platforms to meet prospective guests where they are. Further, results from our current Facebook campaign shows that we are receiving the strongest response from males and females 25-34.

5. **Can you provide some examples of how social media management has resulted in a change to the product, either physically or from a guest service standpoint?**

Through new technology and social media, consumers can share more information with their favorite brands, so they in turn can respond in a more relevant and customized way. Improvements in technology have enabled marketers to know their customers better and to have an ongoing dialogue with them. We see real-time interactions as a natural extension of our service model. See sample story here:

A) When a guest at Four Seasons Resort The Biltmore went on Twitter to make a light-hearted complaint about the hotel's turndown music, she wasn't expecting anything to come from it. When she returned to her guestroom the next day, she found a bottle of wine and a note from the General Manager apologizing for the 'Muzak' tunes, along with a listing of local radio stations. The FSHR interactive marketing team behind @FourSeasons saw the tweet and took the time to notify the California resort about the problem. The guest is not identified by name on her Twitter account, meaning that FSHR had to do a bit of sleuthing to figure out who she was en route to rectifying what was at most a minor nuisance.

B) A similar situation occurred at Four Seasons Hotel Bangkok. A guest lamented via Twitter that there were no good movies on TV that night. The comment got relayed to the hotel's management, which then informed the guest about the hotel's in-house DVD library.

6. **In addition to corporate social media initiatives, FSHR has separate Facebook and Twitter accounts for each property. How does each hotel manage the labor requirements to keep their social media active? Who performs the work? Was there a training program or standard developed to manage this?**

Our corporate social media team has invested heavily in offline and online hotel training and development. As a result, each hotel is accountable and responsible for their social media activities and meeting our global standards. Like our hotels, each case is unique but the responsibilities lie primarily within the Marketing and PR function, with outside support from Front Office, Sales and even our Concierge in some cases so that the team is truly cross-functional.

7. **How is the effort coordinated between properties? What liberties does each individual hotel have? How does the reporting structure get managed?**

Our corporate social media team is committed to regular two-way communication with all of our properties. Our global strategy is localized with content generation taking place the hotel level; global reporting is then conducted by the corporate team to ensure hotels are meeting our global social media standards and that adequate training and development is provided on an ongoing basis.

8. **A significant problem I've encountered is getting line managers to contribute who might not be that social media savvy. How do you handle this challenge?**

This goes back to our commitment to training and development. We work with our PR and Marketing Directors around the world to build their expertise so that they can in turn help elevate the social media capabilities of their colleagues in operations, ensuring an adequate cross-functional support system is in place.

9. **Where do you think social media is headed?**

The affluent population is unprecedentedly active on social media, having increased their usage across all segments since last year. Regular usage has doubled among the wealthy with target segments including the aspirational at $75k-$199k, the affluent at $200k-$499k and the wealthy at $500k+. We believe this will continue to grow in years to come, with mobile phone and tablets playing an increasing role in social media behavior and content consumption. Trust will continue to be the real currency combined with sound products and services. Much can be gained by engaging in meaningful dialogues and relationships with your customers. Finally, the term 'social media' could become obsolete very quickly since these channels are truly redefining 'communication' as well as how people interact with the world.

Conclusions

So, did you notice any trends? What do all the aforementioned forms of social media have in common? Think of how a network's demographics might align with your target audience. Also of how the titular ostrich and llama paradigms apply to social media.

What I find fascinating is that the term 'social media' might soon become obsolete. It's so pervasive that it, in turn, has become inseparable from other forms of communications, and can thus, not be categorized. And when I think of communications, I'm thinking in terms of how they can affect and improve guest services. If you lens social media through the eyes of the guest and how they perceive an experience with your hotel, then you're bound to succeed.

Oftentimes clients ask me about a new social media site and how to utilize it to heighten business prospects. Managers across the board are skeptical about the real impact of social networks on their ROI. My answer is a 'yes, commit to social media', but only if you act in a very specific manner and commit 100% of your energy to a particular channel. Don't treat it as a blanket task across every site imaginable. You have to get your entire team contributing, making it a fundamental part of your corporate culture.

For example, after Pinterest became the fastest social network to reach ten million unique visitors per month, there was an automatic fervor amongst hoteliers. Everyone somehow needed to get involved and, of course, right away. Instead, when confronting news like this, take a deep breath and ask some questions. Is this social network right for our hotel, the services we provide and the brand we promise? Do we have the web savvy and manpower to fully commit to the upkeep and frequency of interactions necessary to generate a following large enough to tip brand awareness in our favor?

Be forward thinking when developing your plan of attack for assessing new social media and how to use the established industry giants. Do you get a social media person in-house, or do you shop it out? Where do you think the web world will be five or eight years from now? Since no one really knows this answer, it's your job to accept the fact that technology will change and be adaptable.

Branding

*COMO Shambhala Estate in Uma Ubud, Bali is an
oasis of calm. Yoga is the core of a daily regimen amidst
the serenity of a private villa or suite.*

Introduction to Branding

We're living an era of saturation for hoteliers. In every city, in every state, in every country, there's ample supply to meet current demands. We're saturated with hotels in every category—value (commonly known as 'cheap'), business, upscale, luxury, super-luxury or resort.

And this satiety is cause for instability, because with a plethora of options at their disposal, consumers only have more reasons not to stay loyal. This is compounded by online travel agencies which are working to reduce your marketing platform into a series of price figures (more on this later). In the previous sections, I've discussed how guest services and, as an extension of guest services, social media can both be harnessed to increase customer retention. What I'm really talking about is a function of branding.

Guest services and social media should be viewed as an organic part of your branding strategy. The brand, in all its various components, is what customers remember after leaving a property, for better or worse. Your brand is the reputation that you have built for your company and your property over years upon years of guest interactions, advertising campaigns and public relations ventures. Your brand is the promise of what you will deliver for future guests based on this pre-established reputation.

Your goal should be to instill positive memories associated with your brand through superb guest services, unique features, helpful social media channels and exceptional hotel operations. My hope for this section is to not only promote the mentality behind long-term critical thinking at the core of developing a good brand strategy, but also the ability to identify factors that will make your brand identifiable and distinguish your hotel from the glut of competitors. Your saving grace against this saturation and instability will be your uniqueness.

Hotels are from Mars, Resorts are from Venus

John Gray's 1993 bestselling book 'Men are from Mars, Women are from Venus' got me wondering. Are hotels and resorts different? Just think about it. They really are. Yet, for some strange reason we tend to lump them together as simply 'The Hotel Industry.'

Hotels represent the 'male' of the accommodation genus. Typically, hotels are usually comprised of a single multi-story (one might say even phallic!) structure. Guest stays are short, efficient, and with a sense of purpose, such as a business meeting.

Resorts clearly denote their 'female' counterpart, with the building structures softer, often curvier, encompassing a larger footprint and with more illustrious decorations. Resorts are more complex in terms of their amenities, typically including elaborate spas, golf courses, even marinas or beaches. Guest stays are more leisurely with a much higher average night's stay. I could go on with more metaphors, but you get the physical parallels.

From John Gray's depiction, males and females are acclimated to their own planet's society and customs, but not those of the other. One of the ways Gray believes that the genders can be understood in terms of purported differences in how they behave under stress. How true of our industry!

Gray explains that men are known to withdraw until they find a solution to the problem, referring to it as the 'retreating into their caves'. In some cases, this may be more than a metaphorical retreat as, for example, men wander into the garage. The point of this is to take time to reach a decision; behavior consistent with most hotel marketing strategies. When a problem is faced with hotel occupancy, a retreat typically comprises of a rate reduction, as if this is the only tool available to solve the immediate challenge.

Gray then purports that when women are stressed, their natural reaction is to talk about issues, even if talking does not immediately solve the problem. The parallel holds true for resorts, where occupancy issues are rarely addressed through simple rate strategies, but rather through a more complex program that is driven by multi-faceted product offerings. The ultimate solution is not immediate and usually involves discussions amongst the many departments, with all providing input into a collective solution.

In broad terms, ask yourself who is booking at your property. My experience shows that the bulk of hotel reservations are made by men, with the opposite holding true for resorts. This may be a function of the type of stay involved, and your reservations and online live chat staff should clearly recognize this. Perhaps Mr. Gray's book should be dusted off for a re-read, knowing full well how it impacts hotels and resorts.

A Survey of How Early Career Business Travelers Select Their Hotels

A survey completed in the summer of 2011 of hotel purchase behavior indicates some potentially troubling news for hoteliers. In particular, this research reveals a significant weakness in hotel brand recognition.

About the Survey

When I started my business career, travel arrangements were regimented. All requests went through the office travel department—our own in-house travel agency. There were few choices given to the employee. But it didn't matter, I loved to travel. I looked forward to the ad agency visit to New York City, the tradeshow in Orlando, or the plant tour in Michigan. My boss had some pull, and we enjoyed staying in such grand properties as the Waldorf Astoria, the Hay Adams and the Drake. Loyalty programs, the Internet, and, of course, OTAs did not exist.

The world has changed in the past thirty years. Many companies have disbanded their in-house travel arrangements; recognizing the efficiencies of the Internet coupled with a desire to keep costs to a minimum. Given security, travel itself has become more of a chore. As well, the myriad of hotel brands offered to the traveler is sizably greater. The influence of loyalty programs for hotels, airlines, and online booking systems now form critical factors in how travel is both arranged and consumed.

To my knowledge, not much research has been done, or perhaps published, on the young business traveler—those just starting in their business careers. Just as my early experiences in travel (and love of great hotels) were formed by my business trips working with Procter & Gamble and PepsiCo, I was wondering what the travel experience was like for such modern day 'newbies.' Importantly, as habits are formed in our early years, I wanted to see how these travelers were planning their accommodation purchases.

One hundred (useable) one-on-one interviews were conducting in the summer of 2011, split almost equally between male and female respondents and between the ages of 24 and 34. Moreover, respondents were screened for those who had traveled for their business by air at least twice within the past twelve months. Those surveyed lived in Boston, Chicago, Los Angeles, New York City and Toronto, all having worked in a company with at least 25 employees.

Note to reader: With a survey size of only 100, these results require verification through larger scale research programs, and as such, should be considered directional, rather than statistically significant. Nevertheless, the results require careful examination.

Survey Questions and Results

How would you best describe your business travel experiences (pick one of these that best describes your feelings):

> I love to travel and enjoy new surroundings and experiences: 77%
> Business travel creates even more work for me, and is an inconvenience: 4%
> Travel is a necessity of my job/career, I have no choice: 12%
> No response: 7%

Does your employer have written policies that govern travel by air and hotel usage?

> Yes: 60%
> No: 12%
> Not sure: 28%

When traveling on business overnight by air, is this travel primarily:

> Domestic: 88%
> International*: 12%
> (Cross border Canada-US considered as International travel)

For these trips, who makes the majority of your business travel arrangements?

> Reservations done by self: 73%
> Travel agent, office travel coordinator, other: 27%

For those who make travel arrangements themselves, what is the primary method?

> Internet, using an online travel agency such as Expedia, Travelocity, Orbitz, etc.: 68%
> Internet, booking direct with hotels and airlines on their respective web sites: 26%
> Via telephone direct to hotels or airlines: 6%

When you travel by air, how often has this travel required an overnight hotel stay?

> 1 to 3 times in the past 12 months: 74%
> 4 or more times in the past 12 months: 26%

For those who can choose, when traveling on business, what are the criteria you use for selecting your hotel accommodation? (Rated on a scale of zero to ten, where zero is not at all important, ten is most critical.)

> Location relative to destination: 8.1
> Cost of room per night: 7.6
> Free WiFi or fee high-speed Internet: 7.0
> Free breakfast: 4.0
> Room type (suite, bed type): 3.5
> Airline loyalty program points: 3.2
> Hotel brand: 2.5
> Coffee maker in room: 1.5
> Hotel loyalty program: 0.2

Name three major hotel brands (unaided). Top 5 results were:

> Hilton (or Hilton brand variations): 83%
> Marriott (or Marriott brand variations): 76%

Sheraton or Sheraton Four Points: 65%
Expedia: 54%
Holiday Inn: 53%

Have you ever heard of (aided, yes responses)?

Relais & Chateaux: 11%
Preferred Hotels and Resorts Worldwide: 4%
Leading Hotels of the World: 4%
Historic Hotels of America: 0%
Summit Hotels: 0%
Small Luxury Hotels: 0%

How many employees does your company have (your best guess)?

25-100: 24%
101-1,000: 39%
More than 1,000: 37%

Do you belong to at least one airline frequent flyer/loyalty program?

Yes: 64%
No: 36%

Do you belong to at least one hotel frequent guest/loyalty program?

Yes: 5%
No: 95%

Conclusions

While this is only a small-scale snapshot, and is by no means statistically significant, the hotel industry appears to have some work to do.

Despite the economy, there is still some very strong enthusiasm for travel. As expected travel arrangements focus on efficiency and cost, with most of those surveyed going to the OTAs to make their arrangements.

Hotel brands were not really part of their accommodation selection criteria, rating scarily close to the bottom. Perhaps what is most revealing was a response to a question on major hotel brand names, where Expedia beat out Holiday Inn. Since when is Expedia a hotel brand name? Not surprisingly, the survey also indicated a lack of awareness in the hotel affiliation programs such as Preferred or Leading. Hotel loyalty programs are bordering on non-existent.

Indicated Actions

This survey demonstrates a further impact of the OTAs: the decline of brand differentiation amongst the youthful business traveler. Corporate hotel marketers should conduct their own research to validate these findings, and propose ways to penetrate the mindshare of this segment, wholly independent of the OTAs and potentially utilizing their hotel loyalty programs as a (yet untouched) tool. Remember: these customers are the future of our industry.

Jumping On and Off the Brand Bandwagon

It seems like the distant past, but every time I read an article in the press about hotel brands or branding, it reminds me of my old days in Procter & Gamble's brand department. Yes, it was called the 'Brand' Department, not advertising or marketing. Why? As brand (not product!) managers, our responsibility was to manage the critical equity of the company—namely, its brands.

Here's an example from Crest Toothpaste, a brand I managed for several years. When P&G wants to market a new oral care product, it doesn't create a new brand name. Rather, it uses the 'umbrella' brand—Crest 3D Whitestrips, Crest ProHealth, Crest Rinses and so on. All have a common purpose: better oral care. This makes sense to consumers, as they recognize the brand and make purchases of related products based upon their core knowledge. This is the essence of branding: being instantly known for some attribute without further suggestion. This is why brands have value in the marketplace.

Now, let's talk branding in the hotel marketplace. You would think the Marriotts, Hiltons, Hyatts and Starwoods of this world would pound the success of their respective brands into the psyches of travelers. This, after all, would leverage those countless years of recognition amongst the traveling public. Alas, this is not the case, as each of these corporations seems hell-bent on cluttering the hotel landscape with even more brand variations, each requiring its own logo, positioning and, ultimately, marketing support.

This very issue became a discussion topic at a recent ITB-Berlin. Many of the supposed 'hotel gurus' were expressing their concern at the proliferation of brands facing the traveler today. And their dismay is not surprising. We have too many hotel 'brands' chasing travelers who lack the knowledge necessary to differentiate between them, since marketing support of these products is seriously insufficient. Brands need to be rationalized so appropriate marketing efforts for those remaining can be effective.

It cannot come soon enough. Scary as it may seem, I conducted a survey amongst young business travellers who named Expedia as their third choice as a hotel chain! That's what happens when the distribution channel outshines the underlying product. This is a very serious issue for chain hoteliers. Brands need to be nurtured and maintained, or like flowers, they die.

Commoditization: A Wake Up Call for Chain Hotel Management

Just for quick clarification, a commodity is a good that is universal, typically an unprocessed grain, fruit or precious metal. For example, copper is bought and sold on a worldwide exchange with limited relevance to its mine or country of origin. By commodity, we refer to the fact that the buyer does not have to qualify the product, only quantify it.

But how does a service become a commodity? Traditionally, services cannot be commoditized, as there are numerous variables that account for differences between the type and level of service offered by each provider.

The commoditization of hotels started many years ago with the first rating systems. Companies like the American Automobile Association (AAA) and Mobil (now Forbes) ranked hotels into groups rated 1-5 diamonds and 1-5 stars respectively. Each of these categories defined a standard of quality and set of amenities. With these ratings in hand, the consumer could now make a selection based upon the criteria they were interested in. So, without knowing anything about the brand or hotel name, a consumer seeking 4-star, or 4-diamond, quality could shop this group on the basis of price for any given location, knowing that the service offerings would be at least in keeping with the standard.

Then came the upheaval of the OTAs. The arrival of online travel agencies such as Expedia, Travelocity and Orbitz was at first heralded as a new dawn for hotels via rapidly expanded consumer distribution. All a hotel had to do was allocate inventory to the OTAs, then sit back and watch their occupancy soar. True, the REVPAR was affected by the aggressive OTA room rate, but it was all for the good of the hotel chain, wasn't it?

Think about it. All of that hotel investment to build a broad-reaching location base and brand mindshare, only to allocate a significant portion of your distribution channel to a third party, and moreover, pay this third party 25-30% commission for the privilege. The logic in doing this, frankly, escapes me. As a good general manager friend of mine reflected upon this practice, "It's a disease . . . Help!"

The OTAs, like any industry, have recognized the critical importance of advertising to create awareness amongst the general traveling public. They have spent millions of dollars in TV and print advertising to build their brand mindshare. And build they did! For example, how many readers can now quickly place the Travelocity Gnome? Travelers are shifting their purchasing behavior. Now, in many cases, they are much more likely to visit an OTA than book through any hotel chain web site directly.

A recent OTA television ad, I believe for hotels.com, claimed 'four-star properties for a two-star price'. If you are a hotel chain executive and you saw that advertisement, I wonder what thoughts crossed your mind. Not only does this sort of rhetoric lessen your property to a mere category, but it also works to undermine all of the strategic product segmentation that you spent years developing. In effect, the OTAs have positioned themselves as a service with hotels as their commodity. It's an eye-opening realization and a battle cry for change.

Still another OTA allows you to blindly choose a hotel based solely on their 'star' rating. In effect, this ad suggests that the consumer does not care what brand of hotel they purchase/stay at, just so long as the quality is at a prescribed level. In effect, the hotel is "white labeled" and can be any brand, with no reference to any of the so-called elements that make that hotel unique or differentiated from another property. Put another way, its like throwing a Hilton, Marriott, Westin, Hyatt, Sheraton and perhaps an independent or two into a hat and saying pick one, based solely on meeting a price point.

So, what's a hotel chain to do? Change at the strategic level does not happen quickly. Hotels need to differentiate themselves. And this comes primarily from delivering unique benefits to the consumer. These can be in the form of amenities, guest service, room décor, technology applications, value-added extras as well as tried-and-true advertising or market positioning. To me, it's only the combination of all these features that gives the overall, and exceptional, picture of what your hotel is all about.

Next, hotel chains, starting at the 4-star-plus level, have to wean themselves off of distribution channels outside of their own purview. In French, the term is called *maitre chez nous*, roughly meaning 'masters of our own house'. You can ill-afford to have anyone sell your property except your reservations staff, your own web sites (both chain-wide and property-specific), traditional travel agents, and perhaps controlled or very time-limited flash sales.

The simple motto to follow is that you should manage your inventory through your own revenue team. There are risks, particularly during periods of low seasonality. The focus here, however, is a distribution strategy that promises brand success for the long-term, regardless of a few short-term hiccups.

Once you are back on your own turf controlling your own inventory allocation, hotel chains need to beef up their awareness programs. This means mainstream advertising; and not just a 4x or 6x per year media program in *Travel & Leisure* or *Condé Nast Traveler* (both excellent and useful), but a true multi-media program that includes television, print and radio. Set realistic budgets based on market research and specific quantifiable awareness goals. Be bold and inspiring. It will pay off.

Lastly, once you have a firm premium product marketing campaign in place, consider extending your inventory control tactics chain-wide through your 3-star and budget brands. You have the power to prevent commoditization, but you have to start soon before it's too late!

The Independence of Loyalty

Independent hotels boast that they offer a one-in-a-kind experience. The linchpin counter for the big chain hotels has always been their tried-and-true loyalty programs, leveraging their scalability to keep customers faithful—an area where independents could not compete. Well, this is now an area with many shades of gray and it's making for a very interesting landscape in the hotel industry.

Since their inception, chain loyalty programs have become behemoths in their own right. True, guests can cash in their points for hotel rooms and often flights, car rentals, cruises, gift certificates, golf, and other palpable experiences. But, the redemption process is oftentimes limited and confusing. In the end, travelers either use their points inefficiently, or just let them accumulate; residuals acting as rolling 'free finance', or future liability, for the hotels.

Loyalty programs encourage customers to adhere to one chain or one reward program. To give you some visuals, rent the movie *Up in the Air*. There's a great little scene in the middle where George Clooney lists off all his various memberships in astounding detail—hotels, rental cars, airlines etc. And somewhere in there he emphatically suggests that switching programs is a definite faux pas. It's just too much hassle to keep track of more than one.

At first glance, you'd think that most independent hotels are shut out of this potentially lucrative marketing opportunity. For starters, Small Luxury Hotels of the World (SLH) and Leading Hotels of the World (LHW) have been incumbents for a while now, and both have fought to enhance the allure of their members. But, such associations haven't traditionally provided sufficient incentives for guests to stay at other affiliates; after all, they're associations, not conglomerates. It's a tough life for an independent hotel.

This is about to change. LHW has revamped their loyalty program, now called the Leaders Club. Guests pay a $100 yearly fee to gain perks including a free night after five separate stays, a complimentary breakfast, a room upgrade and free Internet access. Or, they can opt for the $1200 annual membership for the 'Unlimited' version with added benefits like access to airport lounges and direct concierge services.

Lo and behold, these are the types of bookings that management wants because they all must come through the LHW portal at full (rack not discounted) price. Assuming the average stay at an LHW location is two nights, guests get approximately 10% of their value back. Not too shabby if you ask me. It's also interesting to note that the other old guard, SLH, has yet to follow suit with a corresponding plan. And Preferred Hotels and Resorts Worldwide has yet to develop a similar program to both LHW and SLH.

But, the real buzz is the three new entrants to the field. It's important to recognize here that, regardless of names or loyalty brands, more independent hotels are aligning themselves in one way or another. With more new entrants come more allegiances, more mutual benefits, more differentiation and more competition. Loyalty programs are a brand tool not only for the big chains, but also for independents around the world. Let's see what the new organizations offer (keeping in mind that the number of incorporated properties and policy specifics may change by the time of this printing).

Stash Hotel Rewards, fairly young, has already partnered with (as of writing) 150 luxury properties in the United States. They offer a clear-cut point system where guests earn five points for every dollar spent on room rate. Member hotels are then free to set their own cost for redemption. The average point-to-price ratio works out to roughly 9:1, meaning guests get about 6 cents back off every dollar spent, usable towards a future stay.

Voila Hotel Rewards was launched by industry giant Hospitality Marketing Concepts within the past decade. Since then, they've found a niche with (as of writing) 235 properties in Europe, Asia and the Middle East. Their only North American locations are the two St. Giles properties in New York City. Like Stash, their system is points-based. Guests earn ten points for every dollar spent on room rate, with a fixed point-to-price ratio of 10:1. A guest gets 10 cents back off every dollar spent, usable towards a future stay, and frequent travelers earn 25-50% in additional bonuses. As well, their points are transferable to several airline partners.

Global Hotel Alliance (GHA) introduced a novel reward concept for their collection of 12 brands encompassing 300 properties. A caveat: GHA isn't a program for independent hotels, only for their brands, but nonetheless worth mentioning for their innovative approach. Rather than a traditional points-based system, they offer 'local experiences' at their member hotels. The quality and quantity of these experiences are respectively determined by how often consumers travel and how many different brands those consumers visit. Currently offered examples range from a tour of the Samuel Adams Brewery in Boston to a private yacht tour of Dubai.

So, will customers switch hotel selection based on these programs? From as unbiased a platform as possible, I believe the majority of customers will not switch to these new loyalty programs at least yet, and here's why.

Whether they are business or leisure travelers, everyone wants points. That's a no brainer. However, loyalty programs are geared towards frequent visits, something that doesn't directly coincide with leisure travel (how often do you vacation each year?). So, if these systems are contingent on appeal within the business sectors, then how is financial success possible?

Business travelers have already succumbed to the allure of a loyalty program with this chain or that. But why? Simple: scalability. Big chains like Hilton and Marriot both have around 3,500 properties under their belts. That's between eight to ten times what these independent loyalty programs currently offer.

The psychology of the business traveler is this: amass points from company trips, spend them on vacations. With thousands of properties to choose from, there's no worry over location. Marriot and Hilton, for example, are in almost every major city in the world, and both have many sites in prime vacation abodes. Stash, Viola and LHW just don't have the critical mass to grant such flexibility. Moreover, these independent reward systems lend themselves more to the upscale market. It's up for debate whether or not the average luxury leisure traveler would pick their next destination based on the allure of a 10% value-back incentive. One will have to see.

The dark horse in this race is GHA, for which I currently fail to see any immediate incentives for repeat stays. Their experience-based policy definitely emphasizes to the leisure element, but the average sightseer wouldn't venture out often enough to reach the upper tiers of the program where the real, cushy rewards are doled out.

Every business on the planet loves selling gift cards because they get an immediate stimulus of cash plus interest, and they may or may not have to provide redemption later. Traditional loyalty programs work the same way. A portion of room revenue is paid into a fund that accrues interest, all while the points may go unredeemed for years if not expire all together. Adoption is a definite consideration.

But, does the revenue from these ventures outweigh the costs of joining? First, let's go through some of the cost estimates, using Voila as our example, with Stash operating in a similar manner. A guest shows up at your hotel as a member of their loyalty program. This means that Voila will get 7.5% of the room rate charged. Now suppose another guest comes to your property wishing to cash in his or her points. Using the 10:1 points-to-price redemption ratio, your hotel will get 75% back off the dollar value of the room.

Confusing, but the gist of it is that Voila skims off the top of BAR for both types of point of purchase. Worse yet, the loyalty card companies manage the cash flow and collect the interest.

But, is the number of new customers acquired from participation enough to warrant the trouble? Statistics on this vary too much from hotel to hotel for a solid inference. Ask yourself if becoming an affiliate of a loyalty program will disenfranchise your existing customer base. The last thing you'd want is to convert your faithful clientele into Stash or Voila clientele. Moreover, will new business from loyalty card guests interfere with other revenue streams; ones that aren't hindered by a loyalty commission off the top.

The other two aforementioned systems are not problem-free either. With the LHW program, at worst, when a customer pays full price, the hotel only buys one-fifth of a free night at another location. It's a good foot-in-the-door policy, but not exactly cheap given the LHW annual fees. In the GHA system, the value of a given 'experience' is often equal in monetary value to the perfunctory welcome gifts at other hotels and only awarded on the first visit to each of the association's 12 brands.

Where do we go from here? Let's consider our options from a manager's perspective.

LHW's Leaders Club appeases both parties. The customer gets free nights, and the hotelier only gets a fee when full price is paid. By placating both ends, however, LHW has created a system where customers might not be fully incentivized to pay the $100 annual fee, leaving the association devoid of the mass market appeal that Stash and

Voila offer. Of course, you have to be a LHW member to participate, which isn't cheap.

As a US-centric program, Stash Hotel Rewards has widespread clout in the region. Thus, it can draw a significant customer base to a prospective location that is close, but not too close to its other members. The problems of loyalty fees and conversation are still ever apparent.

In many ways, Voila Hotel Rewards is the mirror image of Stash. Joining one or the other seems to depend more on a geographical analysis rather than a comparison of benefits. For instance, due to Voila's lack of members in key North American markets (as of writing), a new hotel could leverage this to attain a particular set of European consumers. But then again, how often do Europeans visit the States and vice versa? Is this enough to drive sales by itself?

Although not for independents, the fresh take to GHA's program could elicit some valuable insights. Visit their web site and look at what they offer in terms of reward components and packages. If you currently have an in-house loyalty program, their approach may provide ideas for attracting new guests and retaining your existing clientele.

Personally, I am not yet ready to recommend any independent property's participation. Despite all of their advantages, these systems just don't have the strength in numbers to justify my endorsement. It's a trend to watch closely though, as the loyalty programs continue to grow both in member hotels and general consumers. A geographical assessment should tell you if one organization is a good fit for your hotel or not.

As well, I remain skeptical about how these programs might erode customer loyalty. Sorry for being selfish, but I want guests faithful to my property, not some third-party organization. If you are struggling for occupancy, then perhaps joining could help boost temporary sales. But, if you are already getting by, aim to polish your own brand rather than dilute it under the banner of an external loyalty program.

Hyatt's Hotel Andaz: A Unique Branding Opportunity?

I'm a big fan of Hyatt. If a Four Seasons (my top choice) is not available, I'll opt for a Hyatt product. Park Hyatt, Grand Hyatt and Hyatt Regency properties are comfortable, with friendly staff, excellent service levels and high-quality furnishings. Please don't ask me to tell you the differences among these three brands. I have some difficulty. But that's fodder for another story. What intrigues me now is Hyatt's Andaz brand. This follows an announcement by Hyatt management of plans to double the number of outlets for this relatively new 'chain' through re-flagging and re-branding as well as possible new build-outs.

From an outsider's perspective, it appears Hyatt management has decided to test the concept of a 'non-brand brand'. In effect, Andaz properties are supposed to be chain properties that act as independent hotels with a similar uniqueness and cool factor as the successful Starwood W chain.

But Hyatt already has a terrific brand and all of its current products revolve around the Hyatt name. Does it make sense to have a dozen or so properties floating around with support limited to a web site, the Hyatt reservation system, loyalty program and supplier network? To me, Hyatt had it right before Andaz, which I see as another orphan brand for the company to support. I would hate to burden a successful brand with an offshoot like Andaz. But, perhaps I am too 'old school'. Hyatt, I love what you do, but this one escapes me.

Branding is complex. Hyatt has a great brand name, which has been nurtured through years of excellence in service and product. So, I offer this solution. By slightly changing the name to 'Andaz by Hyatt' the product would be better positioned. This would allow consumers the reassurance of the Hyatt quality standard while recognizing that there is something new and cool about the property. Just food for thought when considering this as a part of the grander scheme at work whereby hotel brands are slowly dissolving in the consumer's mind via too much differentiation.

Clean The World: 300,000 Rooms Down, 15,700,000 To Go

It would be a rare GM or owner that would shun their responsibilities to our environment. Guests are known to appreciate the work done by a property to achieve LEED or Energy Star certification. These programs offer operational savings, but more often than not, the capital costs rarely pay off in the short-term.

However, sustainability should be looked at not only within the property, but also in a broader sense; the world community. Forward-thinking operators are always looking for ways to contribute, especially when the benefits are measurable and the costs of execution are negligible.

Clean The World is an Orlando, Florida-based not-for-profit organization. Yet, in the three years since it commenced operations, properties representing a total of roughly 300,000 guest rooms have come onboard. Their program is simple: take the used bars of soap left by guests in their rooms and refurbish them for distribution to the less fortunate.

I had an opportunity to talk to Shawn Seipler, Co-Founder and CEO, about his successes with Clean The World. Here is an interesting overview of this operation. And if you are not participating, after reading this, you might want to consider.

What is behind the genesis of Clean The World?

Every day, 9,000 children around the world die from diseases such as acute respiratory illness and diarrheal diseases, which can be prevented by proper washing with bar soap. Clean The World has a mission to put soap in the hands of people who need it most to improve hygiene and sanitation conditions, as well as to lessen the impact of disease and promote living environments worldwide.

The idea is very straightforward. Take the estimated 1.5 million soap bars discarded each day by the North American hospitality industry and recycle them to help stop the spread of preventable diseases worldwide.

What is the Genesis of the Organization?

Clean The World was founded in February 2009 by two former e-commerce executives, Shawn Seipler and Paul Till, who happened to ask the question, "What happens to our soaps and shampoos after we leave the hotel rooms?" After calling 30 hotels to find out, they discovered that all of the used amenities were simply thrown away. They decided to change that by forming an organization to collect and recycle those amenities, and then use them to help stop the spread of preventable diseases through proper hand washing.

How does it work?

On average, hotels pay $0.65 per room monthly to participate in our hospitality partnership program. It's a nominal fee that covers the operational costs involved with the collection, shipping, and distribution of soaps and bottled amenities from hotel properties throughout North America to children and families around the globe.

Clean The World provides free shipping of the amenities for participating hotel partners and helps to promote each property's participation in our program through targeted marketing and PR initiatives. Clean The World partners benefit from media coverage, broader awareness via social media and the ability promote their properties as sustainable alternatives making a difference in the lives of others through the hygienic items they provide for their hotel guests.

The involvement of the hotels beyond the daily collection of amenities is minimal. Clean The World provides the turnkey solution for the hospitality industry to recycle soaps and help save lives. Based upon current support levels, the program annually diverts 1.4 million pounds of surfactant waste from polluting local waterways/landfills.

What properties are participating? Is this a property-level program, or do you have chain-wide endorsement?

We covet corporate partnerships and are proud to acknowledge the ones we have. These currently include Walt Disney World Resorts, Starwood Hotels & Resorts, Carlson Rezidor Hotel Group, Caesars

Entertainment, Mandarin Oriental, Best Western International, Joie de Vivre Hotels.

These corporate partners give support to all of their brands and encourage individual properties to join Clean The World. As you may imagine, many of our 1,400 hospitality partners came to us one at a time. These are welcome and we sign new partners every day. But if we can get corporate buy-ins from some of the major hotel chains that understand the benefits of sustainability and wish to promote them to their guests via the Clean The World program, it would make our efforts much easier and more effective.

What are the costs to the property? How does a property implement the program? What do you supply?

We supply the Clean The World-branded bins needed to collect and ship the hygiene items. We provide shipping labels and free shipping of the materials for hotel partners. Participating B&Bs pay for their own shipping without bins, given the lower volume accumulated.

We have a corporate partnership in place with UPS which provides 'carbon neutral' shipping benefits to our hospitality partners, helping improve the sustainability profile and allow for the purchase of carbon credits to lessen the costs involved.

Where is the recycled product distributed?

Our global distribution partners include World Vision, Children International, Harvest Time International, Stop Hunger Now, Food for the Poor, Samaritan's Purse, Operation Christmas Child and others. They have field offices in many countries around the world and we provide the soaps and bottled amenities that are often distributed as part of hygiene kits given to children and families in communities everywhere.

Have you had challenges with unionized workers and complaints from operators based upon increased housekeeping labor costs at the property level?

Not at all! In fact, the Clean The World program doesn't add any work for the housekeeping staff. They simply do what they do ordinarily when cleaning the rooms, but instead of throwing items away, they simply sort soaps and bottles into separate bags before placing them in our collection bins. No extra effort, and to date we have not experienced any negative feedback from unions.

What is the feedback from properties on implementation? Can you give me some personal stories?

Our implementations are quick and thorough. The process is easily understood with regard to how collections of amenities are to be made at each property and how the hotels can promote Clean The World to keep housekeepers motivated. Inspiration comes from the people themselves. The housekeeping staff members at many hotels are often from third-world countries. They understand the value of soap and what it can mean in terms of improved health for an entire community.

Many of our hotel partners report high levels of participation and excitement for our program because their staff members are from Haiti, Mexico, Jamaica, and a host of other Latin American and Caribbean countries that are the receiving end of our distribution.

One story in particular stands out. Cecilia, a housekeeper at The Peabody Orlando, told us that she cried tears of joy when she heard of how many soap bars were being distributed in her native Haiti. Cecilia says, "I am originally from Port-au-Prince. I still have family there and many were affected by the January 2010 earthquake. I don't make much money, but I know that I can give back in a special way each time I clean a room and collect soaps for Clean The World. I collect the soaps that make it back to my family and friends in Haiti. I'm doing something to help and that keeps me motivated to always do more."

You are only in North America at this time, do you plan expansion?

We are planning for expansion. We often receive inquiries from hotel properties in Europe, Asia, Australia, New Zealand and other locations. The program makes sense wherever it is implemented, but we need investment in order to make it a reality.

Once we can find the capital to expand and open additional soap recycling facilities in other continents, we will grow exponentially in efficiency and effectiveness. We will truly be cleaning the world.

What about shampoo, conditioner, and other small bottle amenities: Do you recycle this product as well?

Yes, but the methodology is slightly different. All of these amenities are brought back to our processing plant. Here the exterior of the bottles are washed. If the bottles are judged to be at least three-quarters full, they are recycled for domestic distribution into homeless shelters. Bottles with a lower fill levels are sent for recycling by a company called Newtech, which turns the substrate into plastic decking.

Can you think of any reason why a property would not participate?

The only objection some properties have is the price. As our growth indicates, most hotel companies realize the benefits of our program, but some still get hung up on the idea of paying to recycle products.

We look at it simply. You can throw the items away, gain no PR or marketing benefits, contribute nothing to sustainability and social responsibility, and face disappointing the guests—your customers—who prefer to stay at eco-friendly hotels. Or, you could join with Clean The World, participate in our lifesaving amenities recycling program, and receive all of the benefits of PR, marketing, free shipping of materials, and the knowledge that you are lessening the build-up trash in local landfills.

It's important to note that we're not just collecting soaps and storing them in warehouses. To date, we've shipped 10 million recycled bars of soap, distributing them to over 45 countries.

Hotel companies make their own decisions, but from our perspective, this is a no-brainer in favor of saving lives with soap. With some 16 million hotel rooms in the world, we've got a long way to go. You might wonder why I put this article in the branding section of this book. Simple: your brand must be associated with being a member of the community, assisting others who are more needy then yourselves. Clean The World is an excellent and cost-effective way of starting this process.

Conclusions

Early in my career, one of my bosses at Procter & Gamble said, "If we lose our plants, we'll be back to number one in about a year. Lose our brands and we'll create new brands in about two to three years. But lose our people and we might as well close shop."

The same holds true for the hotel business. The priorities are the same: first people, then brands, and lastly the physical logistics. My sense is that hoteliers can recognize the importance of staff and the maintenance of their properties. What we have forgotten is the central element of the equation—the brand.

Now that I am a member of what is considered the 'older generation', forgive me if I have difficulty understanding the difference between the multitudes of brands that the major chains have launched in recent years. But maybe it's not my fault!

Without educating the consumer through advertising and other streams, how is any potential guest to know the difference between one brand and another? Of all the troubles facing our industry, this one represents a grave area of concern. True, there are exceptions. Four Seasons Hotels and Resorts does a terrific job of branding themselves, admittedly with very little advertising. But again, this is an exception, rather than the rule.

Nearly 20 years ago, an advertising campaign for Westin Hotels used the selling line, "Who is he/she sleeping with?" The campaign was racy and highly memorable. You knew it was Westin. Westin had the buzz and it became the place to go. Sadly, this is one of the last 'memorable' campaigns in all of hotel advertising. Since then, the only hotel ads we see on television are for online travel agencies, and this definitely does not represent branding for any specific hotel chain.

As food for thought, how are you going to invigorate your brand? How are you going to augment your mind share amongst consumers? A llama doesn't grow its fleecy coat overnight and neither will your brand. When it comes to branding, always think long-term.

Operations and Human Resources

The Hilton Garden Inn Carlsbad Beach is a magnet for families, earning kudos from all who stay there. The property underscores a key principle of hospitality: you don't need to be a 5-star hotel to offer superior service.

Introduction to Operations and Human Resources

This section deals with management and personnel issues as they relate to hotel operations. As a going trend, Internet-based technologies are becoming increasingly pervasive throughout every part of a hotel's operations. So, will you be open to new suggestions like a llama, or are you set in your ways like an ostrich?

What I hope you will gain from this section is that despite the efficiency that can be gained from installing new automation software, your operations will nonetheless be reliant on aspects controlled by people. That is, those key personnel who make the important decisions, or the new projects you can undertake in tandem with strategic marketing to stimulate revenues.

A large part of this section is intended for general managers. But even if you aren't a GM, perhaps this will provide some words of wisdom for the future. In fact, every manager should think like a GM and treat the hotel's operations as a personal responsibility.

This is distinguished from the section on traditional marketing which deals more so with strategy, whereas these chapters relate to specific topics that hoteliers can implement to add or improve various property functions.

The Ten Essential Traits of a Great General Manager

Of all the positions in hospitality, none is more revered or desired than that of general manager. When you reach this level, you are at the pinnacle of our profession—in effect, the proverbial 'captain' of the ship!

The road to GM-ship can be long and arduous. There are many different career paths that will lead to the position. Thus, there is no single guaranteed road to success. In my numerous communications with GMs throughout my career, however, I've come to appreciate some of the essential traits that epitomize excellence. Here is my own personal list:

1. **Care.** Care for their property. Care for their guests. Care for their employees. Watch a GM stoop down to pick up a soiled tissue on the floor of an elevator. Why? Their hotel is their home!

2. **Time**. GMs seem to have endless time for their guests, employees, meetings and, yes, their owners, too. If you're thinking the job is nine-to-five, forget it. Try a 12-hour day, six or more days per week.

3. **Acquired knowledge and a great memory.** How is it that a GM knows so much? From F&B to housekeeping, from capital cost analyses to OSHA specifications, not to mention remembering the names of hundreds of past guests, true GMs have an innate curiosity and insatiable desire for understanding.

4. **A love of people**. This is a people job. Every GM I know relishes the opportunity to be with people. The perfect host, the best GMs make everyone feel comfortable around them. And a great GM has a keen ability to build an incredibly successful team and get the most out of them.

5. **Patience.** No plan survives contact with the enemy intact. Great GMs seem to understand this, being able to pivot on a dime and recast their objectives based on the shifting sands of the job.

6. **A keen sense of humor**. Let's face it. Not everything works the way one expects. Being able to joke when all seems lost is an incredible life skill.

7. **The ability to never give up**. Imagine having to grow ADR, RevPAR and occupancy every year. Impossible. Yet somehow, GMs stay motivated and climb the mountain again and again.

8. **A sense of fair play**. I have never seen a great GM disparage a competitor, let alone do anything illegal or immoral. GMs are tough competitors but follow an exceptionally strong moral code. They also respect their suppliers—tough bargainers, but fair.

9. **Energy.** How do you motivate your early shift staff at 6:30AM, run a planning committee meeting all morning, dine with key clients, join an afternoon FAM, attend a marketing presentation, smile through the cocktail hour manager's reception, then drop in on an evening wedding rehearsal? I'm exhausted just thinking about it.

10. **Love of the job**. GMs love their jobs. There is nothing on earth they would rather do. This feeling permeates their work. You can feel it. After all, if you love what you do, then it doesn't feel like work.

When Should You Change Your Director of Marketing

Sometimes business is up. Sometimes it's down. Who's to praise? Who's to punish? The relationship between a general manager and director of marketing is, at best, a strained one. For better or for worse, no single individual in your planning committee has as much potential to change your business as your director of marketing (DofM). So often is the case, however, that I see this role squandered by misplaced tasks that erode its true purpose.

A different role such as the DofM requires specialized talents. You would never promote your rooms division manager to the position of controller, nor would you ever move your executive housekeeper to F&B director. Yet, we've seen countless examples where the director of marketing is promoted from a role in operations. This shift is plainly illogical, underscoring a lack of understanding in marketing complexity and the very unique skill set that an exceptional marketer brings to the role.

By their very nature, marketers are more visionary than pragmatic. Your DofM should have a vision for the future of the property and should be thinking as much about tonight's occupancy as they should for the next six month's opportunities. In fact, the longer the time horizon, the better! Therein lies the conundrum.

Hotel operations tend to focus on the today: VIPs, groups in house, rooms out of order, or service issues identified in the latest OTA guest rating. Hotel marketing, while remaining fully aware of all of this daily information, should nonetheless be focused on scenarios involving package development, positioning, competitive trends and seasonal opportunities. There's very little a DofM can do to magically increase tonight or tomorrow night's occupancy, yet with a good strategy, significant improvements can be made when long-term plans are put into action.

This leads to potential frustration on the part of the GM. The more you ask your DofM to get involved in today's operations, the less time he or she has for planning the future. Sorry, but I side with the DofM on this one. You need your marketer as your scout, your advance planner, your strategic planner, and quite frankly, your risk taker. A good DofM manages the relationship between revenue management, the sales team, and senior operations. A great DofM builds fundamental bridges between these often-desperate groups and leads them according to the vision. If their time is taken up with too many smaller tasks, they won't be able to visualize the bigger picture.

But where do you find these evangelic and charismatic DofMs? Surprisingly, my recommendation is not in our hotel industry. Simply put, there are typically insufficient opportunities for gaining the prerequisite marketing experience on property. Packaged goods firms offer one potential resource; in particular, those with backgrounds in perishable goods such as soft drinks or snack foods. I note that my own background of marketing with Procter & Gamble and Frito Lay served me well in quickly adapting to hospitality. Another potential reserve is financial marketing, especially those in retail banking where customer acquisition strategies are meticulously honed.

In 30 years of working with hotels, I have had the pleasure of learning from more than forty different DofMs. The bulk of these individuals came up through the sales stream, typically moving from the director of sales position. I suspect, more often than not, adding the marketing title to their directorship was a cost savings measure as opposed to hiring two separate positions. That is not to say that this was a bad HR decision, or that the individuals who held this position were inferior. Rather, the marketing approach was by and large an extension of sales efforts: conservative and traditional. And for most market situations, this works more than satisfactory.

But these are not traditional times. If you are a DofM reading this article, take charge. Hotel marketers need to rattle their GMs' cages. And vice versa, GMs need to support their DofMs through this process. Set the tone for the future. Cast off the shackles of trying to measure every bit of minutia to the nth degree.

Remember you were hired as a marketer, not as an accountant. Identify new opportunities and take some calculated risks. Then test ideas with new ad creative, new web initiatives and ventures into new market segments. Take command by helping mold the future of your property. Remember, without risk, there is no reward.

A key trait of a marketer is adaptability. This goes without saying, but it is oh so important to reiterate. DofMs must accept the present conditions with all their idiosyncrasies then find some way to be unique amongst a slew of competitors. The Internet can really serve to your advantage here as it offers another direct channel to connect with your consumers.

Building on this notion, loyalty programs are a superb example. Now a mainstay of hotel chains, you should reflect on the broad acceptance of these initiatives, so you can take them to the next level.

Kudos to the marketers at Kimpton who delivered pet goldfish to befriend single travelers. And let's not forget the success of the Holiday Inn and Howard Johnson's 'This Summer Kids Eat and Stay for Free' campaign. Brilliant. What thumbprints has your property's marketing team delivered lately to adjust to an industry of tighter margins and heightened expectations?

Ask yourself: is your hotel adapting to meet the rigors of a modern world? A comparative look at revenue forecasts should give you some indication. So, when is it time to look for a new director of marketing? As a GM, here are the questions you should ask yourself before even considering this difficult action:

- Are your DofM's bonus goals based on short term (this fiscal/ calendar year) or geared at least in some portion to long-term success?
- Do you allow your DofM to test new initiatives, and does your marketing budget reflect this belief with a specifically identified allocation for these activities?
- Have you encouraged your DofM to bring new ideas to your team garnered from companies outside of the hotel industry?
- Have you rejected your DofM's business building proposals when they are either unproven or cannot be specifically quantified?
- Do you regularly allocate funds for guest research to provide inferences for testing initiatives?
- How involved is your DofM with day-to-day operations? Have you bridged the topic with them to find out if they need more time for proper long-term planning?

Great marketing requires a special type of leader—both visionary and malleable. As a GM, you not only need to seek that individual, but nurture them with an environment that allows for their success. The results can be beyond your wildest imagination.

Looking for Mr. Goodbar: Searching for the Ideal Director of Marketing

Over thirty years of being the 'outside-agency-consultant-guy' to literally hundreds of GMs and DofMs, I've seen everything from gifted marketers to the much less so. Our team has served almost every form of relationship, from being the acting marketing head to, quite literally, a supplier of paper or electronic services. Looking at the forest rather than individual trees, I am able to draw some interesting and useful conclusions on how you as a GM should manage and work with the most critical position on the planning committee: your lead marketer. Here then is my short primer on the subject:

1. **Marketing is the lifeblood of your property.** Your DofM has to truly understand the fundamentals of marketing: how to separate strategy from tactic and how to balance the entire wheel of marketing, from PR to advertising and from web to in-house activities. What is his or her background, and how much of that 'wheel' does he or she comprehend?

2. **Marketing is not sales.** These two must be considered distinctly different activities. The sales department has its own strategic requirements. I have seen very few individuals who can juggle both portfolios successfully. Make sure you do not confuse these two disciplines.

3. **Marketing is not operations.** I've seen marketing people dragged so deeply into day-to-day operations that they lack the time necessary to serve their function as a marketer. Think of marketing as your guest services ambassadors outside of the property. Let your operations team take over once the guest crosses your threshold.

4. **Good marketers listen, great marketers act.** If you want a 'yes man', keep them off your marketing team. To move your property ahead, you need a marketer who is thinking about occupancies and rates three to six months in advance. Ask the right questions

and see how far ahead your marketing leaders are thinking and planning.

5. **"C'mon baby, light my fire."** That's what your DofM should be doing for you and your team! If your DofM is not making you a little bit edgy or uncomfortable with recommendations to test initiatives, you have the wrong person at the marketing helm. Of course, this requires you, as GM, to be receptive to new ideas and initiatives. You are, aren't you?

6. **It's not about measuring minutia.** Rather, it's about growing the business and maximizing long-term asset values. The latest fad in marketing is measuring every single 'spit' to see how it performed; short-term thinking from bean counters. This isn't marketing. See if your marketing leader understands the differences between long-term branding and short-term business building.

7. **What are your marketing folks getting from their external agency?** No DofM has sufficient in-house staff to do everything. As a GM, you need to understand the role the agency is playing and its importance in contributing to the property's success. When was the last time you, as GM, met one-on-one with your ad agency?

8. **What is your succession plan for your marketing head?** Chances are, you have none, and unfortunately, you are not alone. If you have a great DofM, protect his or her position now!

Revenue Manager: The Property's 'Master of the Universe'

When I started in the hotel marketing business, the role of revenue manager did not yet exist. We were all neophytes to the concepts of channel strategy and yield management. Ask a senior marketing director about pricing, and they would refer you to seasonal or weekend promotions. I can even remember the time when the Inn on the Park in London had one price for each room type, independent of the day of the week or month. The only exceptions were for groups and high-volume customers. The evolution of the revenue manager position has solved many of these earlier pricing inefficiencies, but has left a dearth of areas that still need improvement.

Times have certainly changed. The sheer range of prices offered to a property's channel partners is daunting enough for anyone short of a post-secondary education in finance. At the same time, PMS tools now allow us to adjust pricing by the minute in much the same way as a modern day stock market. It's micromanagement as much as technological advancements will abide. How can a GM properly regulate this mercurial job and at the same time ensure quality guest service?

Enter the revenue manager; the computer wizard of numbers and Houdini of profitability. A good RM manipulates the prices within the channels, room types and days of month to maximize return. A great RM, however, carries this to the next level; reading competitive rates and previous years' data to squeeze the most out of system reservations.

Revenue management is a combination of numerical skills, a thorough comprehension of the property's operating systems, and strong empirical capabilities. It is a tireless, often thankless job. Hotels that have solid RMs should protect them through appropriate financial incentives. Are they worth their weight in gold? Well, at $1,500 an ounce, that could be $3 million. And, in fact, that might be what they can contribute to a thousand-room property annually.

The role of revenue manager is focused on data and hard to merge in with other numbers-focused jobs. The types of individuals who do well in this position are mathematically oriented, likening them to avid stock or derivatives traders. But, what about considering a promotion for them? After a few years of success, does it not make sense to give them a director's role? Would this not be an effective way to reward them for what they bring to the table? From my experience, the answer is a resounding no.

The role of director of marketing may be thought of as the logical next step. Here is an individual who is well versed in all aspects of the property and knows where the revenue opportunities are. The promotion, therefore, reflects a natural progression.

But, let's examine the DofM role a bit closer. Your DofM clearly recognizes the importance of revenue, but has a much broader role; casting the vision for the future. And here lies the conundrum. Do you want to have a DofM that looks to the future, or manages strictly for today and maybe tomorrow?

The answer is teamwork. An ideal approach is to have a strong director of marketing, reinforced by a knowledgeable revenue manager. Working together, the DofM creates the programs that grow the business while the RM guides the execution of these programs to ensure that the maximum revenue is obtained. Each position has an important role to build your property, but they never truly converge on the same areas of expertise. The risk of promoting the RM is that they will naturally tend to focus on their area of strength: the numbers.

What we have seen during the past recession is a dubious, almost desperate, reliance on the revenue manager. Why worry about the future when there is so much uncertainty in the present? As a result, when budgets tightened, the RM position was never the place to make a cut, while the DofM was left far more open for a game of musical chairs.

But now that the industry has regained its foothold, the prospects to bolster marketing are omnipresent. Rewarding the RM with a promotion makes sense. It is the obvious move to want to progress individuals within the organizational hierarchy. Ultimately, it is a choice that a GM should be very hesitant to sanction. The fear is that without a promotion, your RM will search for a higher status position elsewhere. Instead, keep your RM happy with two basic strategies: appropriate bonuses and a solid marketing partner.

Directors of marketing and revenue managers are critical but separate roles. Both have important skills to offer your property. Merging the positions is seldom the answer for property growth. But rather, you should seek out individuals suited to one role or the other and who work well together.

Do You Have a Crisis Communications Plan?

Do you remember the pictures from the Japanese tsunami of 2011? Utterly devastating. Destruction on an epic scale and the deaths of thousands of innocent people are hard to fully comprehend. My thoughts go out to the families of loved ones who perished.

With this in mind, I ask the naïve question: could it happen here in North America? Or, how about in Europe? The short answer is a definite yes. Nowadays, the landscape of New Orleans still reels from the damage caused by Hurricane Katrina and California shares in the earthquake-prone 'Pacific Ring of Fire' alongside Japan.

It could happen, often in the most unpredictable and tragic ways imaginable. Some ten years ago, I was working in Manhattan on property during the 9/11 terrorist attacks. Witnessing firsthand the crisis management undertaken, the memories of this incredible situation and the approach taken by hotel staff are permanent reminders of the crucial nature of this task.

Nothing can fully prepare an oceanfront property for a full-scale tsunami. The loss of property is unimaginable. But at the same time, it is a fundamental responsibility of every hotel and resort operator to ensure the safety of his or her guests. Your property does not have to be located on the ocean to be subject to risk, either through natural disaster (earthquakes, for example), or manmade tragedy (such as a fire on property).

Planning is mandatory. In the wake of the catastrophe in Japan, I quickly polled a dozen luxury properties to better understand their preparatory status. Thankfully, all claimed to have a procedure for crisis management of some sort. However, only one had a clearly defined crisis communications plan—one that had not been reviewed in several years.

In this era of social media and otherwise rapid communication, I find this totally unacceptable. This is a project that should be assigned as a top priority to your director of marketing in conjunction with your risk management team. It should be undertaken now, not later. Your failure as a GM to act could cost you, both in terms of revenue management as well as long-term protection of asset value.

At a minimum, your crisis communications plan should include the following precautionary factors:

- A complete contact list for all senior staff, including home telephone and cell numbers, as well as personal (not property) email accounts
- A contact list for senior advertising and public relations staff
- Permission lists for your web site, blog, Facebook account, Twitter account and any other company social media
- A series of protocols that identify who will be the spokesperson for your property and how communications are to be handled by staff during a crisis
- An incidence reporting structure to document issues and responses
- Training tips on dealing with the media
- Sample scripts for news releases and your social media outlets

We recommend a separate in-depth team meeting to address crisis situations. Apart from reviewing the plan, role-play can form an important part of bringing the plan to life. As an example, split into teams and assign each team hypothetical scenarios for which they have to manage. Have them follow your crisis communications plan, craft responses and note any suggestions that must be made to properly handle each specific event.

Your team will appreciate the challenges and be better equipped to supervise a difficult state of affairs. Most importantly, be sure to revisit your plan every year. An ideal reminder might be to coincide this with your annual budget planning.

Crises that affect your business may not occur on property. A regional crisis can be just as detrimental to your business. Some examples worthy of consideration: a flood or earthquake in your major feeder market, the closure of your local airport, or a breakdown of utilities such as electrical power or fresh water.

All of us will probably be faced with a crisis at one time or another. No matter what the ordeal, the situations are always stressful. How we as GMs deal with these situations are the true tests of our ability as hoteliers and communicators. Having a crisis communications plan reduces the risks that stem from such miscues. You owe it to yourself, your staff and your guests to be as prepared as possible.

Interns: Anything But Free

Free! It's the golden word that stops shoppers in their tracks. It's the word that interrupts the casual reading of a newspaper. But how does free apply to the world of employment and, most notably, internships?

For the record, until recently, I was dead against accepting free interns in our business. My rationale was simple. Anyone who was not paid would treat the position with less enthusiasm and less commitment and, as a result, would produce lower-quality work. It appeared that I was the last holdout to the tidal wave of 'free' interns in the business. Our most recent intern experience proved me wrong.

Internships are an opportunity for an individual in college to gain some initial experience in our business. Be it sales, marketing, F&B, operations, front desk or any other aspect of hotel-keeping, there are young and enthusiastic individuals who want to gain a firsthand experience that can only be found on the job. To offer an internship is truly a positive opportunity for these individuals. The offer of income is secondary and, for the most part, not part of the acceptance decision.

But while payroll might not be significantly affected by adding an intern or two to your staff, you should not treat any intern as free or cheap labor. Remember, interns are there to learn and to embrace the profession. Their assignment should not be treated lightly. It would be totally inappropriate to hire an intern to clean up a storeroom or merely to assist in an office move. That would be considered an abuse of the learning contract that you have with this individual. I have developed the following principles that you should consider before you add an intern to any of your departments:

- Each intern needs a mentor or trainer. GMs rarely have time, so this mentor must be committed to the value of interns and their training, and must complete the appropriate evaluation forms.
- While you might not be paying a salary to the intern, you still need to abide by OSHA and other standards of employment. Your HR department should establish appropriate guidelines.
- Internships should be linked to a specific college or university program. This ensures some degree of performance guarantee.

When an internship is a mandatory part of a certificate in hospitality management, or another program, you can be assured candidates are committed to their success.

- Your interns should be treated as every other employee, with the same respect and fringe benefits. I am not referring to health and pension, but rather, cafeteria, dry cleaning, guest room use for family, office events, etc.
- Regardless of what department the intern is hired to work in, you should ensure that he or she gets a broader exposure to your whole operation, including attending at least one senior staff meeting.
- Volunteer to pay an intern's basic transportation costs to and from your property.
- At the successful completion of an internship, you should reward interns with a financial incentive, subject to your available funds.

The future of hospitality depends upon ensuring that today's youth are given a positive 'sampling' of this industry. It's a mutually beneficial opportunity. Embrace it.

Would You Spend $189 for a 15% Productivity Increase?

Okay, I'm a little bit of a technology geek. I have a pretty fast laptop, tablet and smartphone. And while I can't fully keep pace with all of the twenty-somethings in my office, I'm reasonably good at most programs and Internet-related activities. Yet, even a codger like me can learn a trick or two.

Our production studio is a terrific team, all using shiny, new computers coupled with great software. But what had differentiated this group from our account staff was that each operating station had a second computer monitor. At first, the 'Doubting Thomas' in me said that this was merely for them to stay connected to their friends, with one monitor showing their Facebook and the other showing the task at hand. I was soon proven wrong.

We conducted productivity tests on the modification of several databases as well as clerical functions involving reservations-style activities such as viewing an Internet page and copying data into a form. The results showed a significant timesaving of anywhere from 15% to 40%, depending upon the task.

Again, not trusting the data, I took an LED TV in my office and moved it over to my desktop, plugging it into the external monitor spot on my laptop. Instantly, I too had joined the dual monitor crowd. While the ergonomics of the layout are probably not perfect, I use my main monitor for work such as emails, documents and spreadsheets, with the second monitor showing a related web site or simply a summary of file listings for easy access. You can configure the monitors in any way you want, so spend some time getting the setup best for you.

Like any step forward in technology, once you move to a two-monitor set up, you'll be hooked. I went on Best Buy's web site and found many monitors for less than US$200. Costco has a great selection as well. My suggestion is to look for a monitor that is wider rather than square. Do you need your IT folks to do this for you? Unless you are all thumbs, this is a plug-and-play affair, so the answer is no. Do you need to get this approved as a capital expense and review it as part of your ongoing capital program? Well, for you, I doubt it.

However, if you really want to see some improvement in productivity, plan one for every workstation in your organization. Start with your sales department, where you can easily rationalize the cost. On second thought, go cold turkey and convert the entire team. You'll be glad you did.

And They Call It Puppy Love

People travelling with their pets can mean big business if you do it right. By now it should be common knowledge for hotel marketers that this is a prominent, and still growing, segment of travelers. If you need statistical proof of this, a Google search will suffice.

My purpose isn't to restate the numbers behind this trend, but to address the next steps for hoteliers wanting to target this niche group of consumers. And for others who might be reluctant to shift into the pet friendly business, hopefully I can convince you otherwise.

To start, let me dispel some cons. True, pets require special attention and a particular set of skills, both equating to further costs. However, vacationing owners fully expect to pay a little extra for accommodating an animal, effectively neutralizing any additive expenditure. Plus, we're dealing with methods to attract new customers and drive up occupancy.

Secondly, the presence of pets may repel others from coming. To this, I've noted that most traveling pets are accustomed to such journeys and are very well behaved. Otherwise they wouldn't have made the cut! Beyond this, you'd have to survey your existing customer base to discern if pets are merely a tolerable inconvenience or an outright deal breaker. And to approach this from a positive angle, not owning pets doesn't stop people from liking them. A friendly animal encounter may add to the experiences of other guests, heightening the flavor and overall appeal of your property.

Dogs are by far the most frequent traveling animal companion and thus I'll focus my attention on how to best appeal specifically to dog owners. However, cats represent the next most common pet type, and most of my dog friendly suggestions are easily transferrable. Here are some more pet owner behavioral patterns worth noting:

- Most owners travel with their pets on average once a year (think repeat business)
- They will likely choose their hotel based on whether it has a pet friendly policy or not
- Pet safety is the top priority above price

- Taking a pet on an airplane is still a nuisance, and as such, most pet owners will arrive by car, truck or RV
- Also due to the hassles of flying with pets, most of these travelers will not be international, but they won't necessarily be local either

Based on these characteristics, you'll likely to be able to formulate your own plan of attack to address incoming pet owners. Here are the steps I would recommend:

- **Decision:** You have to decide upfront whether the benefits of attracting pet owners will outweigh the costs of executing this shift, promoting this new positioning and possibly deterring existing customers. Look at your competitive set to see if any other hotels in your region are already pet friendly or whether you can get first mover advantage.
- **Planning:** Take this time to outline your pet friendly policy in its entirety. Are there any places in the hotel that will be off limits? How many pets per room? Are there any size restrictions? How will you deal with unruly animal guests? Moreover, what will you offer pets and their owners on top of general admission? What pet services will you offer? How will you make the experience both exceptional and fun?
- **Room Segregation:** Reallocate a section of your rooms for people traveling with pets. This will give those under the 'tolerable inconvenience' category an easy way to enjoy their stay while avoiding any potential barking or allergic reactions. As well, it'll make your housekeeping efforts more efficient.
- **Local Relationships:** Make a list of vets, groomers, dog walkers and pet stores in your area, then connect with them to establish a rapport and a build a support community. As well, they might have some great insider suggestions for getting off on the right foot.
- **Pet Guide:** Develop a thorough guide for what owners can do with their pets around the hotel. This starts with the list you've made in the previous step, and should also highlight parks, outdoor attractions and pet friendly restaurants. Ideally, have this available in print and web formats.

- **Training:** Front desk and housekeeping must be amicable to pets and comfortable dealing with pet emergencies. Your staff should be fully versed on your pet friendly policy, your pet guide to the area, and any other necessary procedures.
- **Web Site:** Design a section of your site to outline what pet-specific features your hotel has as well as any price considerations. Steer people here by putting a note on your home page and social media sites. Update your SEO keywords and tags to reflect this.
- **Advertise:** In tandem with getting all the elements in place, you have to get the word out that your hotel is now pet friendly. Target pet magazines and use your PR team to galvanize local newspapers, news web sites and bloggers. Submit your information to web sites that list pet friendly hotels and their policies. Use social media to directly reach out to vacationers seeking a pet friendly hotel. Host an event to launch this new positioning, making sure to invite the press and talk about it online.

Most of these steps are fairly straightforward, except for the planning phase, which opens the doors to a lot of creativity. To help inspire you, here are three excellent examples of hotels that have their pet friendly aspects down pat:

- **New York's Hotel Pennsylvania:** This property is the host hotel for the Westminster Kennel Club Dog Show held across the street at Madison Square Garden, and is often called the #1 Dog Hotel in the World because of this. For a week in February every year, the hotel hosts over a thousand dogs as well as their owners, groomers and handlers. For the event, they set up an onsite dog spa, fill and replenish half a floor with hay for use as washrooms, and even have a Doggie Concierge to cater to individual needs.
- **Ojai Valley Inn & Spa:** This five-star resort just north of Los Angeles has made a tremendous effort to extend its luxury pampering to pets. Specialized rooms are fitted with dog beds and adjoining lawn enclosures so animals can do their business

without leaving the room proper. They also have a gourmet dog menu so pets don't get left out of the fine dining experience.

- **Four Seasons Hotels and Resorts:** This chain has distinguished itself as the luxury pet friendly provider with services like pet vet care, dog walkers and in-room spa treatments, in addition to special cots and pet menus. Not every hotel in the chain accommodates pets though, so check beforehand.

Minibar, Maxi Profits

One aspect of a hotel room that definitely merits more discussion from a profitability and customer satisfaction standpoint is the minibar. Truth be told, I seldom use the minibar when I travel. I like to eat out and experience the city I'm in. Plus, there's the stigma of paying exorbitant fees for staple goods.

With this in mind, the minibar is one aspect primed for reimagining, and to help kick start the call to action, I sat down with Sandeep Sharma, the Vice President of Account Management at Minibar Systems, a pre-eminent supplier in this segment, to address the issue.

PKF's 2011 annual Trends® in the Hotel Industry report examined minibar utilization. With 727 hotels (out of 6,500) reporting minibar revenue in 2009 and 2010, the results indicated:

- In 2009, minibar revenue averaged $143 per available room, 61 cents per occupied room, or 0.23% of total hotel revenue.
- In 2010, minibar revenue averaged $152 per available room, 60 cents per occupied room, or 0.24% of total hotel revenue.

Therefore, it appears that minibar revenue grew 6.3% as a source of revenue for the sample of hotels, but much was attributable to the increase in occupied rooms. For reference purposes, room service at these hotels averaged $775 per room in 2010, or 1.2% of total hotel revenue.

Sandeep, I noticed from the latest PKF data that minibars represent only a minor revenue source for hotels. Yet, I can't remember a hotel that doesn't have a minibar. What is your take on this data?

It is true that the average hotel guest at a full-service, reputable hotel expects his/her guestroom to have a minibar. From the hotel's perspective, besides offering the convenience of a minibar to make the guest's stay more pleasurable, there's also an opportunity to generate incremental revenue. That's why minibars are found in most reputable hotels and hotel chains.

While it's also true that minibar revenue is a minor source of revenue (when compared to rooms, restaurants or banquets), those hotels that have our equipment averaged a Sales Per Occupied Room (SPOR) of $2.01 in 2009 and $2.41 in 2010. This was largely a result of higher ADR and occupancy trends in the industry. In our opinion, a hotel that is doing $0.60 SPOR really shouldn't have minibars because at that revenue level, it's impossible to make a profit given the fixed and controllable expenses of a minibar department.

You mentioned that automatic bars were becoming an increasingly important business. Can you explain the impact of this phenomena and where it is most prevalent.

One of the biggest expenses that a hotel has is labor. With honor bars, labor expense (in high labor cost cities) can run as high as 80% of revenues. Automation drastically reduces a hotel's labor expense. A minibar attendant can service 130 occupied rooms in a hotel that has honor bars. That productivity goes up to 350 occupied rooms in a hotel that might use our SmartCube automated bar system.

I noticed a move towards minibars with automated accounting; remove a bottle and the guest gets charged by a computer. What is the feedback from hotels? Have you seen a lot of complaints from guests?

A hotel that has a well-run minibar department will ensure that the daily routine includes the process of refunding all such charges to a guest's account where the attendant identifies that the guest has not consumed the item. Educating the guest about the new amenity is also critical in keeping guest complaints down. This is done by the Front Desk on guest check-in as well as by having signage and collateral in guest rooms which provide information about the automated nature of the bars.

There are some growing pains when a hotel that has had honor bars switches to automated bars. However, if properly managed, automation actually has the ability to cut down on minibar-related guest complaints for the following reasons:

- You are not disturbing those guests who have not moved anything in the minibar. Compare this to honor bars where you have to knock on every occupied room.
- Billing takes place in real time, so the chances of a guest being billed in error are minimized.
- Because all activity in the bar is stamped with a date and time and saved on our SmartCube S3 Software, it acts as a deterrent against employee theft from the minibars.

With a trend towards healthier products, how have you guided your hotels in planning their product selection?

Our studies indicate that the trend towards healthy options in the general marketplace does not transfer over to minibars. With the exception of Spring Water and Orange Juice, 'healthy' items perform poorly in minibars. While we advise that hotels have one healthy item (such as a granola bar) offered in the minibar, for a hotel where profit is the main objective, our advise is against loading the minibar with 'healthy' items. The 10 top selling and most profitable items sold in minibars have mostly remained unchanged over the years.

Despite the reasons given above, we always engineer menus based on the hotel type and guest demographic. For instance, if a hotel is a spa resort, we will engineer a menu that focuses on that particular theme.

What can a hotel do to maximize return on their mini-bar capital investment?

This is a very interesting question and one that hotels often struggle with. A majority of the hotels don't treat their minibar department as a profit center and never provide the focus and attention it needs. As a result, they have unprofitable minibar departments. The key to success consists of three simple steps:

- Procure equipment from a well established and reputable company such as Minibar Systems.
- Ensure that the company doesn't just install the minibars and disappear. It's critical that the company provides technical and

operational support for the minibars as well as the point of sale system that it installs.

- If the hotel doesn't want to dedicate the time and resources needed to manage the operation, then partner with a company, such as Minibar Systems, which has an established track record of providing minibar consulting and management services to the hotel industry.

What is the funniest or most unusual minibar story that you can tell us?

This story comes from Garrett Warren, our Senior Account Manager and minibar expert-at-large. A guest was checking out of her hotel room and had been automatically charged for all of the minibar items in the external snack basket. When the guest realized she had already been billed, she said she had all of the items in her suitcase and opened it up to retrieve the items. As she pulled out all of the snacks, she also pulled out guest towels, hair dryer and hotel room iron. When the Front Desk Agent asked if she wanted to return these items as well, the guest replied, "No, why should I return them if I haven't been billed for them?" The Front Desk Agent fell over laughing.

What is the future of minibar systems? Do you see expansion within the accommodation marketplace? What are the latest trends in minibar management and marketing?

While the viability of the minibar concept is often debated, the fact remains that guests of upscale hotels expect minibars in their rooms. They enjoy having some of their favorite beverages and snacks available at an arm's reach in their guest room and that they can get what they want immediately without having to call or talk to someone.

With the advent of new technology, the way minibars work will continue to change. For instance, Minibar Systems now offers a communication platform called PowerPlus that enables our SmartCube Minibars to work over the hotel's electrical infrastructure. Hotels no longer have to spend on costly wiring and cabling infrastructure to have an automated minibar in their guest rooms.

The latest trend is for hotels to outsource the operation of individual departments to companies that have the expertise, and this is happening with minibars as well. F&B Directors have too many tasks going on and don't really have the time to focus on an operation that contributes limited revenue to his division.

This is where Minibar Systems steps in and takes over the operation to ensure that the right focuses and direction are provided. The overall goal is, of course, to make the minibar department profitable. We give our customers different options that they can choose from depending on how much they want to be involved.

Some properties retain us for consulting services. For this, we assign one of our experienced Regional Account Managers who makes periodic onsite visits to audit the operation and make specific recommendations targeted to improve revenues and reduce expenses. Some hotels enter into revenue sharing agreements with us wherein they have no capital costs. We provide the hotel with the equipment as well as technical and operational support. Then we recover our costs by sharing the revenues generated by the minibar department. Other hotels do a full 'outsource' of their minibar department to us, wherein we provide the equipment, the product that is sold in the minibars and an onsite manager to operate the hotel's minibar department. There's plenty of options to maximize profits.

Congee: Breakfast of Champions

It's a given that there can be vast cultural differences between East and West, North and South, or between any other national divide. These range from the grand-scale like architectural patterns to the miniscule nuances of daily interactions. When people travel to a foreign location, they are indeed yearning for that localized, authentic experience, but it's nonetheless comforting to have some semblance of normality while regrouping at the home base, and that home base should be your hotel!

Hoteliers now have to look well beyond their own backyards for customers, and there's no better place to start than the world's most populous country—China. According to the Pacific Asia Travel Association, China's outbound travel increased by 54% between 2005 and 2009 from 31 million to 47 million trips. As per the US Department of Commerce, in 2010, the United States received $5 billion from Chinese visitors alone. No doubt this is an outcome of China's economic proliferation during the past two decades, and if current forecasts hold, there'll be more Chinese travelers coming to a tourist destination near you.

Knowing that this is a burgeoning demographic, how can a property best present itself to attract new business? A total overhaul is out of scope both from the perspective of time and money, but there are many subtle changes you can make that will amount to a world of difference. And it all starts with a good breakfast.

Congee is a traditional rice porridge dish popular not only in China, but throughout Asia from East India to Japan, with a host of styles, varieties and infusions. I emphasize Congee because it's relatively simple (which restaurant doesn't use rice in some form or another?) and because it fits the 'home base' mentality. Before a traveler embarks on the day's adventure, he or she needs to reboot in a stable, calm environment. For me, this is a cup of coffee, some granola and a silent read-through of the daily newspaper. For others, it might be a bowl of congee with tea. Regardless of the cultural specifics, breakfast sets the tone for the rest of the day and ultimately, it will play a significant role in determining how guests perceive your hotel.

Alas, this isn't necessarily a novel concept. Marriott, Starwood and Hilton have all announced plans to revamp their dining menus to better appeal to Chinese travelers. Starwood has taken this a step further by planning to offer specific services for Chinese travelers such as in-room tea kettles, slippers, translation services and at least one team member who speaks a Chinese dialect at many of its properties. Hilton is training Mandarin-speaking concierges and installing Chinese television stations at select locales.

All three hotel brands are leveraging their scale and preexisting penetration of the Chinese market, but this doesn't mean that these are actions exclusive to big chains. Bringing in Mandarin-speaking front desk staff may be far-fetched for an independent hotel, but can you say the same for adding a few new rice-based dishes to the breakfast buffet? How about hiring a translation service to add Mandarin to your dining menus and feature cards? Does your web site have a default version for Chinese visitors?

A big component here boils down to how you train your staff to adjust to foreign value systems. In China, persistence equals interest. As the host, you might be expected to offer something multiple times, even though a guest may initially decline. Unlike in the West where good eye contact demonstrates strength of character, a customer from China may view it as a gesture of attitude or defiance. Also, it is not in their custom to tip a full 15% to 20%, so ensure your restaurant staff members are not offended if this occurs. And if you plan to surprise guests with flowers in their rooms, avoid white as plants of this color denote mourning and funerals.

You could write a whole book on these sorts of differences (and indeed someone already has!) but there are also many key similarities between east and west, especially when it comes to respect and formality. Never forget to treat all your guests as you would expect yourself, and don't let this air of geniality break down due to language barriers. That is, the fundamentals of guest services ring true universally.

Imagine yourself as a Chinese tourist visiting an American city where the only real spoken languages are English and Spanish. Outside of the foremost tourist attractions, how do you get around and communicate with other people? What happens if you get lost? It's a scary thought. Now imagine waking up in the morning with all this whirling through your mind, and there's something familiar on the breakfast menu—Congee. You breathe a sigh of relief. The property's respect for your culture isn't a grand gesture, but just enough to nudge you towards feeling good about the day and make the hotel memorable.

The point of all this is to leave a good impression. Word of mouth is still one of the most powerful ways to market your business. If you succeed with one guest from China, then expect more to follow. And to do this, all it could take is a few behavioral changes, a touch of empathy for their conventions and a hearty Congee breakfast.

Everyone Loves Pizza

Your in-house restaurant acts as a beacon for guests looking to unwind with a fresh meal close to home base, thus improving the overall quality of their stay. Common knowledge. What I've found is a trend towards the standardization of onsite eateries. Every hotel restaurant I visit seems to offer the same general assortment: salads, pasta, burgers, pizza and a few meat entrees. It's rare that I find anything new, bold, or that catches the eye.

Frankly, most hotel restaurant menus are becoming rather boring, and in an industry where excitement is a key facet of success, this needs to change. You should have a minimum of one or two select dishes that can really wow your guests; dishes that will delight the senses as well as offer a distinctive experience. The conventional strategy here, on top of repeat business, is to generate word of mouth by giving your visitors something worth talking about.

Fortunately, there's a quick solution that might be worth a try. Just about everyone loves pizza. They're fun, they're filling, they're sharable, and they're loaded with flavor. If your kitchen can craft one right, it's all the more reason for a positive appraisal at the end of a guest's stay or a visitor's repast.

True, any part of your menu can be modified. You may even want to revamp the entire restaurant with a chic new look and a grand reopening. But this is expensive. I offer up pizza innovation as, more or less, a band-aid solution to get the ball rolling and gauge consumer response prior to any other more substantial upgrades.

The beauty of pizza, apart from the aforementioned advantages, is that it isn't too hard to get the basic recipe down pat and the ingredients aren't too pricey either. There are many people who will only ever want the perfectly crafted, and quite conventional, margherita or pepperoni slice. Beyond these two staples, however, pizza is prime turf for experimentation and adventurous combinations. People want bountiful toppings as well as tasty, creative infusions of sauce, cheese, meats, veggies, and, in some cases, even fruit.

Take the 'Meat Lover's' for example (bear with me vegetarians!). What comes first when you imagine this combo? For me, it's a minimum of three meats likely consisting of salami, ham, bacon or ground beef, all piled high over cheese and dough. Good on the tongue, but not so much for the arteries. Now picture my chagrin when a meat lover's pizza is served and it resembles a pepperoni with a few added slices of cured meat. A friend at the table asks how it tastes and my answer is a brusque, "It's good."

Not exactly the response of someone who's going to remember what they ate 48 hours later, let alone go out of their way to extol such a meal. In this day and age, 'good' isn't good enough, even when it comes to something as simple as tomato sauce lathered over bread. Too many restaurants have gussied up their pizza varieties to the extreme, especially when it comes to the unbridled excess of the 'Meat Lover's' combo. Our expectations are high. In order to positively impact your guests, you have to go beyond, with pie and everything else on your menu for that matter.

Again, a large part of your success is to get creative. Any restaurant can offer a do-it-yourself pizza bar to outsource this ingenuity, but many will always be inclined to try a menu's pre-packaged flavors—the 'expert's opinion'. And if you can offer an array of truly savory topping combinations, then it will only act in your favor.

Think truffle oil, oyster mushrooms, sundried tomatoes, broccoli, fried eggplant and zucchini flowers. Instead of a 'Four Cheese' with mozzarella, cheddar, parmesan and bocconcini, think goat cheese, asiago, stilton, halloumi, feta or camembert. Give some combinations the piquant touch with banana peppers, cayenne, chillis and a spicy tomato sauce. Add herbs like thyme, tarragon, parsley, sage or rosemary.

Also consider the presentation. How vibrant does your pizza look? How are the toppings layered? Do you use full spinach leaves or chop them up? In 1889, the first pizza margherita was crafted for Queen Margherita of Italy with the toppings of tomato sauce, fresh basil and mozzarella to resemble the colors of the Italian flag. Remember that people eat with their eyes as much as they do with their mouths.

Pizzas are also a great way to expand into some more vegan-friendly territory. Think wholewheat crust, pesto sauce, fresh veggies and a layer of steamed kale; healthy as ever. Be inclusive, and keep in mind that vegetarians are just as bold as carnivores when it comes to their pies. So throw in your caramelized onions, baked ziti, artichokes and butternut squash. If available, focus on locally grown ingredients and describe accordingly. Experiment with different varieties of your base toppings like tomatoes, peppers, leafy greens and sauces, then find a mix that is unique to your restaurant.

As well, pizzas tend to be at the core of the late night ordering-in crowd. If you are known for good pie, then perhaps your room service will beat out Dominos, Pizza Hut and any other fast food delivery pizza conglomerate that caters to this demographic. Be known for making great pizza. At worst, it beats not being known for great pizza! Just remember that pizza quality is inversely related to the length of time between taking it out of the oven and first bite. Coordination of room service delivery is essential.

Your CFO will be pleased with your initiative. Pizza costs, even with premium ingredients will rarely exceed 20% of selling price (white truffle variants aside), making this a very solid decision financially. I'm not suggesting you specialize in pie, but given that it's a staple of many modern diets, being proficient in this area will surely be a plus. Start by eating at another restaurant around town that actually focuses on pizzas and see what they do and how they do it. Learn from the best, then innovate as you see fit.

Hotel Reputational Harm Insurance

Most of the time, hotel and resort reviews on popular travel web sites are honest and reasonably objective. Most of the time, these critiques are written by real, unaffiliated guests with the purpose of informing other potential customers of a product's true worth. But occasionally, the system is abused and the property may suffer lost business as a result.

A guest may denigrate a hotel to well below what is fair, based solely on what would otherwise be perceived as a minor grievance, or even a misperception. Online anonymity makes it easy for someone with a personal grudge to take on the appearance of a paying, and very angry, guest. A false, and perhaps highly scathing, rumor may go viral and reach tens of thousands of individuals before countermeasures can be enacted. These are just three out of many possible scenarios that may ultimately lead to a financial loss.

How do hoteliers deal with these headaches? First and foremost will always be guest services. If you eliminate the points of contention and keep your guests happy, then it's hard for people to complain. But, even with all your affairs in order, there is still the possibility that something beyond your control will occur and subsequently damage your reputation.

For one example, look to Lloyd's of London with their new type of protection—Hotel Reputational Harm Insurance. These policies are designed specifically to reimburse properties that have suffered from an adverse media event; that is, publication of a statement that has caused direct loss of RevPAR. Properties that qualify are compensated for their RevPAR deficits during the period of indemnity and for crisis management costs incurred while trying to avoid such RevPAR losses. Of course there are numerous eligibility details and exclusions, but those can all be discussed with your loss prevention/insurance provider.

Hotel Reputational Harm Insurance is not a blanket solution, however. It's still your job as the hotelier to first mitigate any damages through reasonable actions proportional to the level of risk. This includes following the recommendations of approved crisis management professionals such as legal advisors specializing in media strategy, crisis consultants and public relations experts.

Touching on a few of the caveats, this policy does not cover perils that affect a larger portion of the market, such as political lobbying efforts, published surveys or product reclassifications, unless your property is specifically mentioned. Your property must be up to code with the latest regulations for sanitation, cleanliness and water systems. Lastly, adverse media events arising from labor strikes or acts of violence are not covered. Despite all this, Hotel Reputational Harm Insurance is a serious step in the right direction when it comes to developing a strategic safeguard against damage incurred as a result of Internet activity.

Hail to the Chief! Steward, That Is.

Most discussions relating to food & beverage talk about some new chef, food costs or techniques. Rarely, however, do they mention the unsung back-of-the-house heroes—the Stewarding Department.

The position of Chief Steward is often overlooked and misunderstood. A good chief steward makes everyone in F&B shine; a great one is a rare find. I am fortunate in Toronto to have such an individual at one of our landmark properties.

Mike Braykovich proudly holds this title at the Fairmont Royal York, managing a team of 75 for this 1,472 room property. For those unfamiliar, the 'Royal York' as it's known locally has been a centerpiece of the Toronto skyline since its completion in 1929; is directly opposite the city's main train terminal and financial district; and is the primary lodging for the British royal family and other heads of state whenever they visit the city. The hotel's F&B department is a bedlam of daily activity and responsibilities.

As Mike explains it, stewarding is the 'palette' upon which the chefs can create their vision. Mike sees stewarding as the roots of a tree, the branches of the tree being the culinary, banquets, and restaurant outlets. In effect, stewarding is the program through which all the F&B programs operate. A chief stewards responsibilities include:

- Maintaining operating procedures for the department
- Developing appropriate successor plans
- Instigating and supporting employee empowerment
- Ensuring internal customer satisfaction (internal customers for the stewarding department are the members of the food and beverage team)
- Integrating stewarding activities with other departments for cost savings
- Monitoring and implementing technological advances
- Championing recycling and energy savings efforts
- Managing equipment maintenance
- Ensuring the health and safety of the F&B staff

No doubt, the function of stewarding in the hotel is significant. Mike cited several excellent examples of the Stewarding Department acting as the main facilitator of new innovations; many directly impacting the bottom line.

First, through his 'green stewarding' initiatives, the property has increased recycling to a waste diversion rate of 67%, with sizeable reductions in water, gas and electricity utilization. Although these forms of energy conservation affect the bottom line indirectly, they are nonetheless technological advances (and capital expenditures) that a good chief steward is responsible to report to the general manager for due consideration.

Mike also heightened the hotel's anti-breakage program, selecting china, glassware and flatware based not only on design, but also on durability to cut replacement costs. It's his department's responsibility to track the trends, locations and factors that contribute to costly onsite breakages, and then reduce accordingly. A good chief steward must also his educate his team about fiscal responsibility and how such breakages might play towards the property's bottom line.

Mike stresses the need for stewards to get the sense of providing outstanding customer service; getting in the right frame of mind. For successful stewarding, it's important to build a culture of employee engagement and a sense of internal customer responsibility. To accomplish this task, he undertook an Internal Guest Survey Program as a measuring tool. This survey was completed with banquet servers, bartenders, line cooks and supervisors to fully understand how stewards were directly impacting their jobs. This survey approach opened a dialogue between the departments, changing the conversation amongst stewards from 'the other staff keep bothering us' to 'how can we help them better serve guests'.

Here's another example of how a great chief steward can enhance operations. Being an older property, the back-of-the-house layout of the Fairmont Royal York has numerous nooks and crannies. Responsibility and maintenance for these grey-zones fall outside of stewarding, banquets and housekeeping. Mike wanted to eliminate these 'no man land' areas. To accomplish this, he created an interdepartmental task force that walked through and simply assigned maintenance responsibilities on an ad hoc basis. There was no need for senior management input and no additional costs or consumption of resources. Rather, it was just a matter of understanding boundaries and supporting each other.

Mike sees the Fairmont leadership's focus on innovation as one of the keys to his department's success. The Fairmont Royal York's general manager understands that there's no 'curtain' between the front and back of the house, stressing that guest service success starts in the back of the house. The senior management at the Royal York believe in team empowerment, and have nurtured an engaging corporate culture where Mike and his team can make better decisions. This ultimately leads to a better customer experience and happier employees, helping make the Stewarding Department a true 'heart of the house'.

(Since the publishing of this article, Mike has been promoted to Director of Banquets at the Fairmont Royal York, the largest banquet department in the Fairmont chain.)

The Benefits of Group Interviews from Wave Crest Hotels and Resorts

As the management firm for Hilton Garden Inn Carlsbad Beach and the Hilton Carlsbad Oceanfront Resort and Spa in California, Wave Crest Hotels and Resorts has developed a premier reputation for sustaining exceptional staff, translating into superb guest services, critical praise and customer loyalty.

Renato Alesiani, the CEO, was quick to point out that this virtuous cycle begins well before staff training. He contends that Wave Crest's regimented group interview process ensures they recruit only the most passionate employees in a very time-efficient manner. Reduced staff turnover and six to seven digit cost savings on new hire starting wages are also key benefits. The practice has become integral to the overall quality and community satisfaction of Wave Crest's hotels.

Applicants take the initial step by coming onsite and inquiring about potential job openings. Wave Crest wants them to feel special and appreciated from the start. The front desk staff members know to treat applicants like guests, offering comfortable seating and beverages while they fill out the required paperwork. From there, all potential employees are scheduled into a group interview timeslot, usually biweekly. The idea is to wow the applicants from the beginning and imbue a standard for success.

The HR director spearheads the process, organizing the day and time for all group interviews. Next, the HR director leads the potential employees through a hotel tour, the job, benefits, environment and expectations. After a roundtable introduction from each interviewee, there's the group exercise. Successful applicants get a call back within two business days.

With the GM and three department heads also present alongside the HR director, the group interview process is designed to weed out undesirable applicants. These five acutely observe how the group interacts, individual attitudes and team spirit. Character deficits in these areas may not present themselves in a one-on-one interview, but will be apparent during the group exercise where applicants are divided into small teams and given a five-minute scenario to solve. The senior managers judge how each candidate works in a team environment.

Are they participating or aloof, active or overbearing, indecisive or assertive, inclusive or exclusive? There's typically no right or wrong to the scenarios; it's the thought process that counts.

No one can overrule another's decision to strike an applicant out. The five senior managers have to trust each other's instincts when it comes to who should not be given a chance to reach the next stage. And having no experience is never a reason to disqualify a candidate at this point—no lengthy talks of past accomplishments, only gut feelings based on character. In fact, being a neophyte is often a plus because they are free of bad habits and preconceptions. "A job can be taught, attitude cannot," as Renato puts it.

All applicants who pass the group interview stage are always given a second, one-on-one interview with the pertinent department head and the HR director, regardless of whether there's an opening or not. This phase is far more traditional in design. Interviewees are now expected to wow the interviewer. Due to the groundwork already completed during the group interview, the discussions here go far more in-depth with regard to applicant background and career goals.

It's also a practice of aligning the right applicant with the right department. For instance, someone applies intent on sales, but there are no openings at that time. If this individual has a genuine personality, they might be offered a job at the front desk and given a chance to shine until a sales position becomes available. The GM may even grant such an applicant a sales job from the start to keep the pressure on the other new hires.

By disqualifying the less suitable candidates during the initial round, it ensures that all hires are made from a more capable pool of applicants. Only those who really want the job will make it through. It sets the precedent that there are elevated expectations to meet. New hires will have a higher satisfaction at a starting wage lower than our competitors. They'll see a long and fruitful future as a Wave Crest employee, vastly reducing turnover and saving managers the time of interviewing too many people.

Then there's the 'hip pocket' effect. An applicant may wow the managers throughout, only to find there are no immediate opportunities in his or her desired position. In this case, the HR director will add this person to a 'ready for hire' list. The minute there's an opening, such an applicant is called back, sustaining the high quality of service by minimizing productivity loss and overtime.

When Wave Crest initiated the group interview process, there was a widespread stigma that placing new hires at lower starting wages would deter the best prospects and increase the turnover rate. Neither of which was the case. The key barrier was teaching the HR Director and other senior managers how to properly conduct the group interviews so they could accurately judge each interviewee in a limited timeframe. Managers had to be trained to focus more on assessing character traits and critical thinking than technical knowledge. It took nearly six months to master the process, but now that it's in place, the benefits could never be better.

Conclusions

Up until very recently, every time I visited a hotel client, I was continually amazed by the mounds of paper on the average manager's desk. Daily report after daily report, section after section. I love the way the Internet and other associated software have worked to reduce this stack and helped clear many managers' desk space. But has the pendulum swung too far?

Whether you are for or against, part of the success of your operations nowadays is directly tied to how well you use technology to streamline operations. Although I'd argue that these new electronic solutions are essential, as hoteliers we've become over-reliant on Internet-based systems to fix our problems. Oftentimes a creative solution is a good viable option to grow your business.

Hopefully the previous chapters have given you some inspiration to seek out new answers aside from the perfunctory 'just use the latest software' solutions. Whether it's incorporating a new type of food or making your hotel more appealing to pets, an original idea can go a long way to boost occupancy and invigorate your marketing efforts. And as with your branding and guest services, the success of your operations is dependent on the integrity and work ethic of your staff. Never neglect the human aspects of your business!

Traditional Marketing

The Hazelton Hotel in Toronto, Canada is among the finest boutique properties in the world, with opulent rooms and a million dollar art collection. It's known as the hangout of choice for Hollywood celebs when they visit town.

Introduction to Traditional Marketing

With all of the focus on social media, Internet advertising, SEO, OTAs and the myriad of pseudo-marketing activities that have emerged in this electronic age, one would think that there would be no place left for traditional marketing in the realm of hotels and resorts. Nothing could be further from the truth.

Plain and simple, some may think outright that traditional hotel marketing is boring; others adamantly claim that it works at delivering more guests and increased revenue opportunities. Again, it's a matter of bipartisan consideration (llama) rather than unwavering assertion (ostrich). I acknowledge that it is right to have a solid value system and defend those beliefs, but especially when it comes to the ever-vacillating domain of marketing, you have to keep an open mind.

Many of the items outlined in this section are based on experiences with properties large and small; high-end and moderately priced. The key is to recognize marketing opportunities as they exist and use them to differentiate your property amongst potential guests. Don't associate traditional marketing exclusively with high-priced advertising. Often a great traditional marketing idea can leverage all aspects of your communications program.

Is It Time to Start Traditional Marketing Again?

The hospitality industry suffered a definitive slump following the 2008 market crash—one, probably two years of hard times. Then early 2011 data projected signs of full recovery, yet with a vast discrepancy. Key metrics such as RevPAR, ADR and profitability were lagging behind occupancy increases. So, what was the cause?

Look no further than the OTAs. In their infancy, the OTAs seemed lucrative: you simply transferred your remnant inventory to them, which added instant cash to the bottom line. Sure the rates were not terrific, yet occupancies improved and total revenues increased. But a monster was created, and a gluttonous one at that.

Giving these online sites leftover rooms the odd weekend or off period week was one thing. Thanks to those original occupancy-booster sales, the OTAs garnered their own loyal customer bases that they consolidated in the wake of slim consumer confidence and a depressed marketplace. The OTAs emerged as the primary method for vacationers and businesspeople alike to find cheap rooms, raking in a staggering commission from each sale—25-30% on average compared to the traditional 10% travel agent commission.

And that is the new bottom line. Many consumers bow to the almighty Expedia, Orbitz, or Travelocity. For instance, if you work at a resort in Florida, don't plan on seeing too many of the same friendly faces year after year, unless, of course, you are offering the best deals for the OTAs. Compare this to over a decade ago where guests interacted more directly with the hotels, many becoming steady, and perhaps lifelong customers.

While hotel profitability has floundered, juggernauts like Expedia have grown by several billion dollars; a quintessential example of wealth transference. What started off as a quick fix to generate more hotel revenue through these snappy online agencies has caused a serious paradigm shift within the customers' minds. They are loyal to the OTAs and don't necessarily care about individual hotels. This caused the discrepancy, so now let's look towards a solution.

The answer is marketing, or more correctly, replenishing the dire shortage out there at the moment. The depressed economy of years past forced our hand to analyze costs more scrupulously, and advertising dollars were immediately trimmed across the board. We accepted this hike as a necessary short-term fix, but better economic forecasts calls for a return to normalcy, or however much is possible in this increasingly online world.

Even in this modern day and age, television still represents a highly effective and potent mass advertising medium. But when was the last time you saw a hotel ad on TV, and not just on the free, in-room 'What's Happening' channel? Probably never. Compare this with the advertising undertaken by Expedia, Orbitz and Travelocity. These corporations have invested heavily to boost their franchises' mind share through solid broadcast campaigns.

Television obviously isn't for everyone, as it is quite expensive on a national network basis. However, chains like Hilton, Sheraton, Marriott and even luxury brands like Ritz-Carlton would likely benefit from a heightened voice share on this medium. And with the advent of targeted local cable channels, television advertising is no longer out of reach for individual properties in their key feeder markets.

On the contrary, you might say that hotels are wiser than OTAs by diverting their ad expenditures to more modern media, such as Google, YouTube or Yahoo sponsored links. Well, there certainly has been some hotel presence in this regard. But as a test, check any destination, and you'll see that the OTAs are quite pervasive on this front; often holding the number one, two and three link positions.

Then there's what I consider as a middle ground: magazines. Pick up any of the leading travel magazines and you will find some terrific ads for many hotels, both for chains as well as individual properties. By and large, the ads are well written and art directed. However, their potential to reach the target audience is a mere drop in the bucket compared to what is needed to maintain, let alone grow a franchise.

Get back to the basics. How long has it been since you commissioned a real marketing plan, with specific objectives, goals, and a budget to make it effective? I'm not talking about the twenty pages of 'gobbly-gook' that's churned out every season. Rather, I'm talking about a marketing plan that has some teeth; marketing plans that have concepts and programs with both risks and the potential for sizeable returns.

Real marketing campaigns are not measured as a single-digit percentage of operating budget or by carrying forward last year's paltry allotment. Real marketing, and its respective budget, is based on analysis, target audiences and consumer research. More importantly, however, real marketing involves the development of concepts that will serve to differentiate your property or chain in a unique way from other hospitality options.

And that's the true challenge. Rather than throwing money at electronic room hawkers, use those funds to create new meaningful advantages for your product. Embrace new technology by creating mobile platforms for learning and booking your property. Expand your social media presence with online concierge activities. Create value by becoming masters of your local scene through a genuine understanding of what's happening. Secure community involvement in the arts, sports or other programs of regional interest. Be proactive.

Look to Westin Hotels & Resorts and their $30 million ad campaign titled 'For a Better You' distributed across popular news and lifestyle web sites as well as newspapers and magazines like *The New York Times, The Wall Street Journal, Condé Nast Traveler* and *Travel + Leisure*. The objective was to make people feel better throughout their stay, leaving guests restored and revitalized upon checkout. Westin employed an independent New York City-based firm for this task, creating six intricate sets of imagery for their various locations.

They strived to convey the message in a sophisticated yet lighthearted manner without relying on computer graphics. Not using any standard property or room shots, the campaign instead focuses on the various amenities and features at their locales—the 'Elements of Well Being' as they are called. Take their 'Heavenly Bed' advertisement for instance, which offered the insight that a good night sleep is vital for your health and memory retention.

All things considered, this is a great brand strategy—making the experience a centerpiece and not relying solely on each property's physical attributes. Considering that this was the first Westin ad campaign in the last five years, I think that the results were remarkably positive.

Using this example as a wakeup call, it's time to bring back hotel marketing. It's time to give revenue managers a true marketing partner in their efforts to maximize revenue, not just by building occupancy, but also by restoring ADR through significant value with each and every reservation. This is a job that the director of marketing has to champion, with less of a stranglehold from the budgetary committee.

Furthermore, this can only be accomplished once guests are involved directly with the property and not through an independent, electronic intermediary. If you can work to restore the connection with your consumers and supersede the middleman, then your brand presence, and profitability, will continue to grow, no matter which OTA gets in the way.

Save Paper, Time and Money by Burning Your Marketing Plan: Then Build a New One

As an industry consultant, the marketing planning process for hospitality never ceases to amaze me. For our hotel and resort properties, the discourse generally starts around late July. With great gusto, the GM calls a meeting with the direction of marketing, the ad/PR/Internet agencies and other planning committee luminaries in tow to talk about the great initiatives for the upcoming year; most likely entailing a determination to increase average rate and a desire for continued growth in occupancy.

The next step involves the DofM spending every working hour for the next two to three months writing a thesis-length document. During this period, any semblance of real business growth is thwarted as all efforts are always fixated on the next fiscal year. Sound familiar?

If you gave an affirmative, then ponder these questions. After the marketing plan presentation is completed, how many times is it subsequently referred to by your managers? Where does this tome ultimately reside: on the desk of the DofM and the GM for immediate reference, or on a bookshelf, neatly displayed with the previous year's incarnations, like some sort of collector series?

The last time I've seen a marketing plan seriously referenced is the budget meeting. That's a lot of forest turned to pulp for nothing, let alone the hundreds of hours consumed in its development by the DofM. But it doesn't have to be this way. Just as the electronic revolution has overthrown virtually every other aspect of hotel management, it's now time to revamp the marketing planning process.

So, what's the most important aspect of a marketing plan? For one, a clear and actionable strategy for long-term success. Though it's easy to say, it's hard to actually implement. Most GMs and DofMs are compelled, whether by the owners or through their own virtue, to produce on a quarter-by-quarter basis, but if this is the only purpose, then inevitably, you'll reach a crisis of sorts. Planning long-term is imperative for every budgetary meeting, and balancing both the long and the short will require all your mettle. You have to think in terms of developing a specific brand identity and projecting that image to maintain a solid base of loyal customers.

Now let's talk about a new type of marketing plan. When I was starting my marketing career, my first employer was Procter & Gamble. This marquee firm had precise rules for their marketing plans that should serve as prime examples for the hospitality industry. Fundamental to their doctrine is brevity: if you can't say it within a few pages, it is probably not worth saying.

While with P&G, I wrote half a dozen of these plans. For many of them, the revenue and expenditures would easily exceed that of a 10,000-room hotel chain. And yet, the marketing plan was never more than four or five pages in length. Cut to the chase, as they would say.

Writing such a concise document is painstaking, but has great merit. The final plan might actually be useful to all stakeholders. It's hard to find time to read a 100-page document, so a five-page summary ensures that all managers have read it and can offer feedback. Moreover, since the plan is now stripped to only its most essential components, it'll adhere to what's needed to deliver the core objectives.

There is some skill required in writing such a condensed document. Key to success is using a formal structure. Here is what an outline for an independent property might look like. Remember, the focus is on brevity:

- **The Marketplace:** general factors and competitors
- **Your Product:** a true assessment of the property and what it offers guests
- **Research and Reports:** where you stand in terms of ratings and recent research studies
- **Rooms and Revenue Forecast:** including all the usual details, but in topline format
- **Channel Strategy:** OTAs, web, traditional agents, preferred clients, etc.
- **Pricing and Promotions Strategy:** goals, not just plans
- **Sales Strategy:** your sales program, fully integrated with marketing activities and goals
- **Communications Strategy:** what you hope to achieve through both traditional and electronic means
- **Tactical Execution:** specific details of your advertising, local community activities, social media programs, promotions,

SEO/paid search/links, direct response, web site and collateral replacement plans

The focus is to provide a solid road map, with a concentration on the strategies, rather than specific and minute details. Why? As every good GM or DofM knows, tactics change often, but strategies last for a while. So, save your resources by keeping the marketing plan short and sweet. And while you're at it, you'll be helping the environment by saving forests too.

The Seven Deadly Sins of Hotel Marketing

Despite all the literature out there on the topic, I still believe that marketing is an area for vast budgetary improvements. Here is my version of the 'Seven Deadly Sins' as a quick message for what to do and what to avoid during this often-turbulent process.

- **Pride:** Don't ask the DofM to produce a multi-tabbed, 100-page marketing manuscript. Rather, call for a document that is a useful working tool for the business. Define appropriate strategies for each segment of the marketplace, and once these are set, adhere to them for the entire year, modifying tactics as necessary and readdressing only if dire circumstances intervene.
- **Sloth:** Make sure your team does their homework and reviews what worked and what did not work the previous year. Ask the question: how can we learn from my mistakes and not repeat them ever again? Strategically plan your advertising purchases. Don't aim to just buy remnants, or "one-off" media on deep discount. Rather, work hard and strive to build a direct relationship with the audience based on generating frequency with a selected publication.
- **Wrath:** Don't overanalyze everything that's done in the marketing department. Look at campaigns instead of individual ads or events. Listen and reflect rather than acting impulsively from a reactionary standpoint.
- **Greed:** Don't increase rates without justification. Your guests will know when greed has set in, and they won't be impressed. On the flipside, don't aggressively increase occupancy targets without prudent rationale. And above all, don't illogically increase both rate and occupancy while at the same time reducing marketing funds.
- **Envy**: Don't just pay lip service to social marketing, but embrace the concept by responding to customers and enhancing your B2C relationships. There are so many ways to stand out and make an exceptional impact via these online channels. Be original in your thinking and not just a copycat of other similar properties.

- **Lust:** Once a budget is set, don't create a 'stretch budget' without rewarding the team, which delivered the base plan. Unless there are extenuating circumstances, stick to the document you have and don't overzealously fine-tune it while stalling execution. Focus on diligently marketing your property, directing your lust not at the budget itself, but at your property's exceptional aspects and its quality of guest service.
- **Gluttony:** Wean yourself off OTA activities and avoid the lure of flash sales. Refocus on your own web site, your supporters and the strengths of your own brand.

Credibility in the Age of the Incredulous

A casual browse of advertising agencies and PR firms on Twitter sparked me to rethink how the marketing world is evolving in this age of instant communication and endless noise we are presently facing. Reading through account descriptions, several common phrases kept reappearing. The two that stuck in my head were 'search engine expert' and 'social media guru'. An avid fan of game theory, I wanted to test how this economic principle applied to everyday encounters like this. I thought to myself, "If everyone says they're an expert or a guru, then who's telling the truth?"

My initial thought was one of doubt. I brooded over similar questions like, "How does one actually become a bona fide whiz in social media?" and, "What does it even mean to be an SEO expert?" For the latter, is it simply a matter of researching the nuances of Google Analytics, reading industry blogs, knowing how meta tags work and being under 35 years old? Or, is there an earned and laborious process to this involving formal education and experience towards mastery? How does one distinguish between the true masters and those selling snake oil?

Our culture has seen a tremendous evolution over the past decade and the maturation of the Internet and related technologies are primary influencers. But it's not all good. Emails are continuously spammed by fraudsters. Photoshop lets us alter images or beautify people, objects and places beyond their true selves. Banner ads assault our browsers, all advocating unsurpassed products, services or destinations. This technology satiety has made us exceedingly disbelieving of the message, so much so that electronic skepticism is an unconscious defense mechanism.

This isn't anything ground-breaking, but perhaps it can be mined for some new insights for the hospitality industry. Examine how the phrase 'the best hotel' is used in the online realms, and also through more traditional advertising mediums. Hotels and hoteliers are constantly boasting that they're the best at something; be it best in the region, best dining or best amenities. Why wouldn't they? Managers are proud of their property and they're trying to make a buck. And heaven forbid an advertiser not promote them as the best. They'd lose the contract!

However, much like my game theory dilemma with the use of the words expert and guru, apply this to your competitive set. If every property claims to be the best, than who is the consumer supposed to believe? When everyone's a winner, no one is. And there's the problem: comparative modifiers are far too subjective. By purporting that you're the best without a specific and legitimate third-party credential—like a top placement in an annual magazine ranking—you're imbuing a sense of distrust right from the start of the customer interaction.

From there, everything the customer sees or hears about you is lensed through a grain of salt. People will scrutinize every adjective used to sell rooms. What exactly do 'finest quality' or 'superior amenities' mean anyway? Ditto for airbrushed photography. No doubt the imagery on your web site is stunning, but nowadays everyone knows it's an exaggeration of what's actually there. Moreover, a colorful, easy-to-navigate homepage is the standard for hotels across the globe. Unless your programming team installs some palpably different features, you're only meeting customer expectations with your web site, not wowing them.

Your efforts are becoming counterproductive. By claiming your superiority, you've instilled the need for customers to fact check via Google. Any reasonably savvy surfer will open another browser window and consult TripAdvisor or other such travel review web sites for the real answer. Congratulations, the OTAs have become the authority on your property, not you.

In the old days, hotels were given diamonds and stars by trained and qualified members of AAA and Forbes respectively based on set criteria for each level. AAA and Forbes still exist, but they aren't foremost on the average consumer's mind. The OTAs have that job now. Favorable as it may be to have ordinary people lending their opinions, there's no regulation to how hotels are judged. Someone's vacation might be exquisite except for one tiny error that lowered the review to three stars instead of five. Offering complementary bottles of water might score higher in one guest's mind than access to a million-dollar spa that's lavish by anyone's standards. Add to this the ability for vengeful guests to maliciously assault or paid employees to fantastically augment a hotel's rank, the aura of online disbelief is only destined to increase.

I firmly believe you can still greatly reinforce your hotel's brand reputation by utilizing traditional media like newspaper and magazine editorials, but fortunate or unfortunate as it might be, the Internet is swiftly usurping these long-established channels. Accept and adapt. Even within this electronic landscape of lies, it is possible to gain credibility amongst customers and branch out to new ones.

Step one is to ensure your online scorecard is tiptop. Essential to this is guest services. Regardless of the décor quality or amenities, everyone appreciates a friendly conversation and helpful staff. People will not expect the world when staying at a midlevel property, but they will always expect attentiveness to their needs. Nowadays, the margin for error is zero. To this end, I consider every employee a member of the guest services department. From custodians to executives, all must know and be enthusiastic about mingling with guests.

Train your staff in all matters related to guest services. Each employee-guest interaction is a chance to lockdown a stellar review. When a guest makes a request, your team has to know how to rapidly coordinate an effective response. They must know how to go above the call to rectify any errors. The customer is always right, and if you keep this on the back of your mind, then your online reputation amongst the OTAs—that is, the much sought third-party credibility—will prosper. The few fraudulent diatribes that seep through will be drowned out by the other 500 genuine and likely positive critiques. Strength in numbers asserts real quality.

Next, ask yourself how you would distinguish yourself when all your competitors have passing grades on the OTAs? Research has shown that prior to making a reservation, guests will undoubtedly check your homepage for a closer look, whether they book through you or the OTA. Thus, upgrade your hotel's web site to set you apart.

My solution: differentiation through specification. It's unreasonable to call yourself the best hotel or boast that you have the best restaurant. Instead, think of a select few details that you can earnestly proscribe the royal treatment. For instance, promote your lobby bar by talking about how many different martinis your bartenders can create. Perhaps you just implemented a tablet menu system at your flagship restaurant that remembers past meals and recommends similar dishes or wine pairings. Advertise the superiority of your rooms by highlighting the materials used to make the linens soft and the mattresses comfortable. Gain credibility and sell through descriptive qualifiers rather than ambiguous comparatives. The devil is in the details.

Just as the OTAs are commoditizing the hospitality industry by reducing properties to a rating and a price, you can fight back by treating your guests to features that are undeniably unique. People will always remember the experience over a price, provided that the experience is a good one. It's not just about being situated downtown; it's about being a two minute walk to the train station and the express corporate package streamlining all the minutia for a weary business traveler. It's not just about the spa facilities; it's about offering a few brilliant treatments you won't find anywhere else. Locally sourced, organic products are a great start as well.

Be prudent and focus your efforts—target everything and you achieve nothing. Those few aspects which are truly extraordinary will be the ones people talk about and the ones that drive repeat business. The way I see it: specificity is credibility.

Next, tie this all together through your social media channels. Sites like Facebook and Twitter are great places to solidify your fan base by showing off your character in earnest. Much like how I encourage staff training for guest services, all top tiers managers have to be active on their hotel's Facebook and Twitter accounts. Lead by example then the rest of your team and your fans will follow. Once you have that core momentum, post quick facts, fun events, resourceful feedback and plenty of candid photography. Whereas your web site will set the tone, your social media will give your story its narrative spine. Your past guests will friend or follow you online, and maybe talk about it with a few of their friends, but how you breach untested waters? How do you find new customers with completely different social circles?

What you need are specific features to incentivize new prospective consumers to seek you out because you are just that irresistible. For this, your social media marketing campaign has to be empowered from the executive level. Your social media manager needs the fiscal leeway to offer an eye-popping promotion to your Facebook fans as well as a slice of the web budget to support fancy customizations and proper Twitter management software.

The tricky part is to incentivize without diluting your core. That's why it's best to think of these types of promotions as bonuses towards an already outstanding product. For instance, how about a $50-$100 one-time F&B coupon available once a customer likes your Facebook page? How about four complimentary spa treatments when you book two nights or more using a reservation code only found on Twitter?

People everywhere are talking about embracing social media, but again, apply your game theory mindset. Top down social media marketing necessitates drastic action for you to stand apart from all the white noise. This can only happen if the executives endorse a more radical way of thinking. A reasonably well-off (and somewhat radical for its time) company once used the words 'Think Different' for their slogan, and you should too.

Is It Time to Get Bullish on Meetings?

The concept of pent-up demand is one I have heard of many times and it can be employed to merit some optimistic results for the meetings business. It works this way: you have a car and you typically replace it every five years. Right now business may be a little soft, then year five comes around and you elect to hold off for a while. That 'overdue' sale is considered pent-up demand. The older a vehicle gets, the higher the propensity for a purchase.

Does the same concept apply to the meetings marketplace? In other words, do you believe that a company withholding or cutting back its conventions budget will create a pent-up demand for future meetings? To shed some light on this, I contacted three colleagues, all senior sales executives in Fortune 50 firms. While they aren't directly involved in the arrangements or authorization of specific meeting plans, each has a good pulse on his or her company's activities.

Firstly, they acknowledged a significant reduction in budgeted meeting expenses over the 2008-2011 recession blip. When asked if they felt the trend would start to reverse in 2012 and beyond, they were somewhat guarded, but expressed some positive thoughts. As it was explained to me, the 'new normal' embraces more technology and less face time. Nevertheless, they all acknowledged a need to get more team involvement.

You should always strive to maintain a high frequency of meetings at your hotel or resort, but the period immediately following a recession is perhaps the best chance to ramp up your efforts, both for the actual deals and for hiring some top-flight sales managers. In spite of all the recent technological advances, face time is near irreplaceable. Companies will always be looking for a great spot to rendezvous for a midweek or weekend, teambuilding jaunt.

Rack Brochure: Rest in Peace

I remember my first ad agency assignment in hospitality, nearly thirty years ago. I had to design and produce a 'rack brochure' for the Inn on the Park Hotel in Toronto. At the time, the project was considered the quintessential component of their marketing plan, requiring both significant design effort and budget given the substantial print runs. The advent of the Internet has all but arrested the rack brochure status and marketing funds, but does down necessarily mean out?

The history of the rack brochure dates back to the post-Korean War 1950s, when the travel agency business was booming, and often storefront oriented. Prospective travel customers would visit an in-store display unit housing equally-sized printed literature for destinations, hotels, cruise lines and attractions. The size of the slots within these display units were standardized and cantilevered, thus creating the eponymous rack. Brochures produced by all travel participants were sized to fit these display units. You can still see this style of racks in some chain properties displaying other chain members, regional tourism welcome offices and, of course, in the (remaining) traditional travel agencies.

At our advertising agency, I've seen the typical print runs of rack brochures drop significantly within the past three years. As of this writing, our current production quantities rarely exceed 2-4,000 units, compared to runs of 25,000+ units less than a decade ago. You need only look at newspaper and magazine companies worldwide to corroborate this decline.

As Mark Twain said, "The reports of my death are greatly exaggerated." So too, I suspect, can be said of the rack brochure. I did a quick survey of about fifty hotels and resorts, both independents as well as chain properties, and not one general manager was prepared to totally abandon rack brochure production availability for their property.

Today's modern printing techniques have brought us new opportunities for this venerable marketing element. To begin with, the costs of printing have plummeted. Modern digital printing technology allows for shorter runs without the need for creating films and plates. Customization, such as personalization to the recipient, is both feasible and highly cost-effective. The size of the brochure is also no longer a constant. Whereas every rack brochure used to be designed in a 'portrait' format, brochures now are just as likely to be in a 'landscape' format, consistent with the high-definition feel of modern web sites. And that's just the orientation change. Rack brochures have increased in size, with the only restriction appearing to be the cost of mailing.

This may be reason to postpone a quick collapse of the brochure business into a more gradual decline. But there's another subliminal force at work whether we hoteliers can put it into words or not. You can always buffer your web site with a PDF brochure and ten times the amount of enticing benefits and graphic photography, but the rack brochure is a physical entity. Customers can feel it in their hands.

Psychologically speaking, touch relays to some powerful emotional centers in the brain. This same reasoning underlies many other common sales practices. Houses are rarely sold without the buyer first touring the property, brushing the balustrades, sitting on the living room sofa and literally feeling its design. Ditto for cars. Even with online shopping, clothing stores persist as most people inherently like to touch and try the goods before making a purchase. Why else are products on display at an electronics store if not for you to see them with your own eyes and feel them in your hands? As humans, we trust that which is tactile.

Sales are emotional. By having potential guests grasp and leave with a rack brochure, marketers are cleverly channeling the age-old practice of making customers feel positive about the sale. Our genetic makeup hasn't changed nearly enough in the past twenty years to completely disregard the function of the rack brochure.

Thus, I believe this paper product will continue to exist for a long time, albeit even in smaller quantities, even as we rapidly shift into a paperless world. Before you plan to create your next brochure, ask yourself the following questions:

1. Define your strategic goals for the piece. What do you hope to accomplish and who is the brochure targeted at?
2. How will the brochure be distributed and what is the annual forecast quantity to each distribution channel, including mail, travel agencies, in-house, trade shows, phone requests, front desk and any others you can think of?

3. How long do you anticipate the brochure to be in use? Nowadays, think in terms of months, not years!

4. Do you need separate brochures or variations for groups, weddings, or catering? Plan your quantity requirements for each variation.

5. If personalizing, how large is your database? What portion of the print run would be kept generic and not personalized?

6. What percentage will be mailed? If this number is considerable, then mailing costs will be a more important factor.

Once you have all of the data assembled, your communications agency should be able to provide you with a strategic production plan, which you should review before committing to any creative design elements. Think of a printed brochure as more of a support element to important one-on-one communications. The rack brochure, if used correctly, is nonetheless a great sales tool.

Fixing the Dead Spot: Quick Ideas for the Thanksgiving to Xmas Blues

For many hoteliers the period between Thanksgiving and Christmas is filled with angst. The Thanksgiving and Christmas holiday breaks offer great occupancy and revenue with often predetermined agendas and strategies. But the period in between is wrought with uncertainty.

I recall working for an all-season resort in New England, where the period from early November through to the Holidays was called the 'Serene Season'; autumn foliage almost all on the ground and too early to ski on neighboring mountain tops but too cold for anything more than a brisk walk. The solution was to reduce staff and close a portion of the property for some well-deserved renovations.

But for most properties, the idea of shuttering a wide swath of product is out of the question—definitely not a sturdy tactic for an urban hotel! With this in mind, here are some tactical approaches and programs that have proven successful.

Plan Ahead: Your directors of sales and marketing, in conjunction with your revenue Manager, should have your plan for the serene season locked up well before Columbus Day (early October). The plan should include all of the necessary promotional programs and marketing support allocations. Define your goals for the period, weighted less towards ADR or occupancy and more on RevPOR as ancillary income from F&B.

Look to Groups: Your plan for this period should be based upon a solid book of group business. This group business will typically have a short lead-time and be comprised of smaller local or regional meetings that reflect both year-end and new year strategy sessions. It's not uncommon for sales teams of Fortune 500 firms to meet on a unit or group basis locally across the country, recognizing that managers have a need to stay closer to home prior to the holiday season. Be sure to map out your targeting of local businesses accordingly.

Encourage Corporate Social Events: Catering has the edge in this season. For this period, more than any time during the year, your catering team will help drive your room sales. Develop programs that support year-end events on property and encourage the sale of guest rooms to support the prevention of drinking and driving. Prepare to offer aggressive room rates to your catering sales team and create incentives for the sale of room blocks with each event they close.

Shop Until You Drop: Christmas shopping will definitely be on your guests' minds. For those who have urban properties, create shopper special packages with guest room price points that make sense for your market. Features here can include discounts at local stores, coupons from affiliated retailers, gift wrapping centers in the lobby, assistance with gift pick up from local stores and even packing for FedEx/UPS delivery. Be sure to promote these packages to your guest lists through electronic channels and social media.

Think Like a Retailer: You know the routine. It seems as if the turkey leftovers have barely been consumed, and stores are decorated as if Christmas is immediately upon us. Your property should look festive on the same schedule. A strong holiday spirit encourages guest spending and positive attitudes amongst your staff. Plan your schedule of activities early and post it to your web site well in advance. Use electronic communications to share this schedule with your customer base.

Don't Forget Gift Cards: Even if you don't have a retail shop of your own, promote the sale of gift cards for future nights' stays. Create promotions around the sale, including gift-wrapping, special cards and overnight delivery services. If you don't have an established gift card program, consider creating a seasonal package certificate that offers the recipient a blend of accommodations with F&B, selling this through all of your usual marketing channels.

The Spirit of Giving: Don't forget that there are others less fortunate than us. Ensure your holiday plans include a charitable component. This should not be an add-on or token effort, but rather an intrinsic part of your message as a good corporate citizen. As always, share your efforts through your social media channels.

Measurement is Future Learning: While I am not a fan of programs that measure the minutia of every marketing detail, it is important to gain learning experience with your approach. Therefore, each of the programs you undertake should be well defined with records taken that correlate to their response and efficacy. And remember, you'll be back at this twelve months from now!

Ten Quick Ideas to Market Your Property Better Now

Many GMs think that marketing planning is done once a year, typically in the fall and in advance of the coming fiscal year. Here are a series of quick points you can spring on your director of marketing to see to help keep your marketing program on track.

- **Repeat Customers Are Easier To Cultivate Than New Guests.** Therefore, make sure you don't forget to capture as much information as you can from each guest. Expand your database to know why they visited and what they did. Then, maintain a relationship with your past guests, encouraging them to revisit by appealing to their interests.
- **To Everything There Is A Season.** Mark your calendar in advance. Plan holidays with military precision. Unlike every other promotional program you create, these no-brainer events deserve your full attention. You have the knowledge and the power to be wholly booked out. Just do it, no excuses.
- **Everybody Eats.** Of course, you might also have a spa and a golf course. But at best a quarter of people regularly visit spas and lower numbers for golf. However, with almost perfect certainty, I can guarantee that your guests eat. Make it your business to ensure they eat with you. Create menus and venues that give your guests what they want. Incentivize them with room and food packages if need be.
- **Remember There Are Five Weekdays And Two Days In The Weekend.** Depending upon your property's location, this simple ratio typically dictates that business groups take precedence to leisure travel. Now examine your sales and marketing plan spending. Is this reality accurately reflected?
- **Marketing Needs To Start The Minute Your Guest Interacts With You.** Initial experiences are vastly underrated. A welcome packet on check-in beats a myriad of tent cards.
- **You Don't Control Price; The Market Does**. Only your owners are interested in comparisons to pre-2008 ADRs. Be realistic in your expectations. It's a different world out there. If

your competitive set is at $250 per night, don't even think that the old days of $400 per night are in the cards. Remember that without occupancy, rate is irrelevant.

- **The Minute You Wean Yourself Off The OTAs, The Better.** Sure they provide a quick fill. But they drive your rate down and do nothing to generate loyalty in your product. For example, the latest OTA deal offers a 4-star property at a 2-star price. Think about it for a moment. They are commoditizing all the work it took you to get to four stars, relegating you to an equal with others at that level.

- **Invest In Your Local Neighborhood.** Hire and train. Promote and motivate. Donate and participate. Give back and tell everyone about it. It pays to be a friend and a community leader. Treat everyone as family and they will return in kind.

- **Socially Savvy Makes Sense.** Don't just start a corporate account on Facebook, Twitter and YouTube. Invest in appropriate programs to harness the energy of these programs and fully integrate them into your marketing programs and brand strategy.

- **Your Website Is Your Window To The World.** Make it sing and make sure that it works effectively. Don't expect to be first in a Google search if you are an independent in a busy/large market. Use creative programs to drive links. Think big and enticing photography.

Did You Share the Love on Valentine's Day?

Valentine's Day is one of those commercial holidays you don't find on any government-issued calendar. Yet, do I even need to state its inherent value for hotels? A 'blip' on the winter cash flow radar, every precocious marketer has no doubt initiated plans months ahead of time to guarantee room and restaurant sellouts. But, do you have the necessary measurements in place so you can learn and enhance next year's experience? This article serves to identify some important steps to take to maximize next year's fiscal return.

- **Learn. Learn. Learn.** What activities did you undertake this year? What was successful? What can you quantify? What did your competitive set promote and how did their performance for the week compare? Examine F&B results: what were the top sellers? What was the typical bottle price range for wine sales? What type of wine was most popular? What anecdotal information can you glean from serving staff, concierge, front desk and any other managers who interacted with guests?

- **Database.** Capture and create a list of your Valentine's Day customers from this year and previous years. Strategically consider this list for a special exclusive offer next year. The same applies for restaurant-only guests. Add to this database every bride and groom that has celebrated wedding day with you. The key is to pinpoint specific groups within this collection of data and then market according to what they already might want in a Valentine's Day promotion.

- **Plan Based Upon the Day of the Week.** Is a property more successful if Valentine's Day falls on the Saturday night? From my experience, it doesn't matter! The customer will choose to celebrate on the day that is most convenient to their schedule. What is important to your property is to ensure that you don't put up roadblocks that prevent your customers from celebrating on the day they want. In other words, plan your Valentine's Day for the weekend, week or even the entire month. The most successful Valentine's Day I've experienced was when the day fell on a Wednesday—two weekends along with midweek jaunts were all supported on an equal basis.

- **Be Real.** Establish realistic goals and build the Valentine's Day program around your property's unique advantages. Review previous years then set an appropriate growth target for occupancy and rate. To maximize success, look at what your property has to offer based upon location, amenities, and F&B. Build packages that include lavish spa treatments along with F&B. If it can be arranged, a babysitting option is also worthwhile.

- **Themed Months.** While it may sound corny, this is one time where romance and romantic themes prevail. Just make sure that whatever you're promoting, it's consistent with your branding and target audience.

- **Promotional Period.** Define a temporal spending program based on specific revenue benchmarks. This is a straightforward financial exercise arising from your fiscal goals, margins and returns. Define the expenditures and give your agency ample time to prepare a marketing campaign. Building blocks for the media program should include: public relations, local print media, Google Adwords, web site promotions, in-room flyers, restaurant check stuffers. Consider a tie-in with a local radio station or news web sites to add reach and exposure.

- **Loyalty Bonus.** Whatever the promotional offer, provide a little extra for return guests. Send an electronic note to past guests 2-3 weeks in advance of the promotional announcement. Create value-added extras, rather than focus on price reduction. Then, when your loyal members come onsite, surprise them again with chocolates, wine, flowers or a delicious appetizer for two.

- **Don't Forget Your Staff.** Create an environment of romance that transcends the front-end displays. Roses in the accounting office; chocolates in the staff lunch room. Be equal in your presentation to everyone, from housekeeping to your sales staff and managers. Any gratitude you give your team will spill over into the exuberance with which they interact with the guests.

Remember, Valentine's Day comes every year, so keep track of everything this coming year, so you'll be more than ready to do even better twelve months from now.

Let's Make Love: How Hotels Can Target the Niche Market of Honeymooners

Does your hotel accommodate weddings? If yes, I'll bet management keeps a record of how many they've held in the past year, and I'll double down that they have a calculated goal for how many they expect in the upcoming years. Weddings are big business for all involved, and they've always received their just dues in the corporate limelight.

But as the shorter sibling to this gigantic revenue maker, honeymoons are often overlooked as a niche market for hotels to target. Do you keep track of how many honeymoons were held on property in the past twelve months? More importantly, do you have a specific strategy in place to attract honeymooners? Collaborating with Kristin Stark, the owner of Honeymoon Wishes, I'd like to explore this issue and draw upon some useful pointers for hotels looking to expand their weddings and honeymoon travel business.

By gross estimate, the worldwide valuation of weddings is somewhere in the ballpark of $50 billion, but honeymoons are not far off with a market cap of $12 billion. Honeymoons also follow weddings in terms of seasonality with peaks from June to September and nadirs in January and February (ostensibly reversed for those living south of the equator). By Kristin's accounts (and listed alphabetically), the most popular destinations for US lovebirds are the Bahamas, Fiji, Florida, Hawaii, Italy, Jamaica, Mexico, St. Lucia and Tahiti, while for those from the UK, the top choices are Cypress, India, the Maldives, South Africa, Thailand, Turkey and the United States. Using these two nations as examples, hopefully you can fathom the notion that honeymoons are enormous ventures and that they're everywhere.

So why do we not stock a dedicated Honeymoons Department much like we do for weddings? For starters, many hotels don't know if guests are honeymooners until after they arrive, whereas weddings are prepared in tandem with hotel staff for months if not years prior. Secondly, weddings require a much more substantial alignment of resources as they often entail providing hundreds of guests with F&B and accommodations for a very limited time, necessitating such scrupulous preparations. Many hotels still don't track honeymooners, even when such couples identify themselves on arrival. It seems as though a lot of us are missing out on a great opportunity. Prior to launching into marketing strategies, let's consider the average mindset of the honeymooner demographic.

Honeymooners typically book four to six months in advance for an average stay of seven nights. Not surprisingly, over 80% of these people now use the Internet for research and planning. In terms of selection patterns, the far majority of couples choose their destinations prior to individual hotels or resorts.

The rationale for picking one specific place or another varies, but there's nonetheless one overarching constant. Honeymooners want a no stress, romantic spot in the sun. And as a close second linked to this desire, the more accessible the locale and the more carefree the experience offered, the more likely a hotel is to attract honeymooners. This is why all-inclusive resorts, couples-only properties and cruises are so popular. A honeymoon can often be the newlyweds' first extended vacation together, so any convenience factor that reduces decision-making and heightens romance is a definite plus.

Quite ironically, off-site adventures like hiking and scuba diving do not rank as high on honeymooning to-do lists after arrival, even though such attractions play a major role when picking this region or that. Couples want to have options, but more often than not, they'll spend their vacation time poolside or on the beach, drink in hand. This serves to emphasize the importance of good onsite attractions such as themed restaurants, in-house activities, specialty spa services and live music.

In terms of actually attracting honeymooners, let's start with what's most accessible—that is, after they drop their bags and let your staff in on their secret. Everyone remembers their honeymoon, and what separates this vacation apart is that it's a topic of discussion for many years to come. Anything you can do to make a couple's experience all the more exceptional will contribute to the positive word of mouth thereafter.

Knowing that the most common welcome gifts are a bottle of champagne and couples massages, an easy way to set yourself apart is to go above and beyond with your initial greetings and everything past that. Instead of welcoming newlyweds with liquor and a coupon, how about adding chocolate, flowers or a honeymooners' special for when they visit the restaurant? What types of entertainment do you have onsite, and can they be enhanced to offer a more unique flavor? Do managers come out to personally congratulate newlyweds? Do you offer a car service to pick guests up directly from the airport? There are scores of little touches you can add without running in the red or being too intrusive.

The real marketing, however, has to happen before guests arrive, and it has to start from your web site. Create a dedicated page to elaborate on your property's benefits and packages written from a couples-only perspective. Use your site to connect your property to the region's most exciting and romantic attractions.

If you're planning to launch a honeymoon-specific package, focus your advertising on unique offerings for couples as well as anything inclusive you will provide to make the experience as carefree as possible. Hone your advertising efforts through media channels that cater to honeymoons and weddings, but also reach out to travel agents, gift registry programs, wedding planners and other established networks.

Honeymoon Wishes, for instance, offers partnership opportunities to jumpstart your presence in this niche market. Following the template of a bridal registry, a couple preselects an affiliated hotel or cruise and then creates a 'wish list' for their honeymoon. Friends and family can then bestow gifts through contributions to airfare, nights at the hotel, romantic dinners, sightseeing excursions, spa treatments or any other amenities your hotel provides.

Each property gets its own profile page, fully customizable to qualify your brand. Honeymoon Wishes will do its part to endorse your hotel through banner placements that catch the searching eyes of honeymooners and viral marketing via their thousands of affiliates. Considering their average registry accrues an average of $2,500, honeymooners preselecting your hotel will certainly look good for cash flow.

Honeymoons are generally not some spur of the moment summer escape, meaning that your planning today will see benefits for the next fiscal year, but only if you start now. We've heard of weddings scaled back due to financial pressures, but this is far less applicable to newlywed jaunts, largely because the couples only have to provide for themselves. Dare I say, it's as if they're recession proof! Make it easy, make it romantic, and above all, make it an experience of a lifetime. Then, find a suitable way to reach honeymooners, and you'll undoubtedly be in good shape.

Romantically Seasoned: A New Floor for Hotels

Four Seasons Hotels and Resorts (FSHR) is universally recognized as an industry leader—its product quality and service levels continually setting luxury standards. Programs pioneered by this chain have become de rigueur for properties in all price ranges. Thus, innovative marketing programs being undertaken by FSHR are worthy of reflection.

The Four Seasons Singapore is one their magnificent properties located just off the incredible Orchard Road shopping district. Knowing that it was our thirtieth anniversary when I visited, the hotel put us on their special couples' floor, which they call '11 for 2'.

Dubbed their Ultimate Couples Getaway, the idea was to create a quieter floor with lower corridor traffic and a softer, more romantic ambiance through a number of subtle soft goods changes. With added amenities, enhanced concierge services and some solid marketing packages to sell this product, Four Seasons Singapore has created something very distinctive within the marketplace. Here are some of the specifics that make this package work:

- Check out time has been extended to 1PM. Housekeeping services have been delayed to start in the afternoon, leaving the whole morning to indulge in breakfast in bed, with no corridor noise or interruptions.
- The couples experience starts at the eleventh floor elevator lobby, where complimentary fruits and chocolates are refreshed three times daily. The corridors have been redecorated and the lighting has been themed, changing throughout the day and night to set the mood.
- Each room's king-size bed, which dominates the room, is festooned with a number of wild, decorative throw pillows. The side table has a collection of snack jars loaded with commercial candies. A book of Love Poems was also provided as well as a set of romantic DVDs for musical selection. Most intriguing was a Love Box—an upholstered jewelry box containing about one hundred business-sized cards designed to inspire, with such single lines on them as 'Eat Dinner by Candlelight', or 'Play a Sport Together'.

- The concierge has been repositioned as the Experiential Assistant (EA) with the role of enhancing guests' stay with many pre-arrival services. Noteworthy, the EA delivers breakfast and assists with planning your stay, creating a butler-like experience.

Promotions for this experience comprise of a series of what they call 'indulgent morning experiences'. In effect, they are add-ons to the room rate, thereby simplifying the yield. Different selections were offered, ranging from breakfast in bed, tennis, yoga, spa treatments or in-room couples massages.

Through several informal talks with guests we met on the floor, the experience was highly positive. Comments included 'cute', 'fun', 'innovative', 'refreshing' and 'kind-of-sexy'. All of these were descriptions that meet the product criteria. Once again, Four Seasons refused to rest on its laurels, setting the standard for others to follow.

Say, 'I Do' To More Wedding Revenue: An Interview with Carley Roney of TheKnot.com

The real quandary over weddings pertains to how your property can cash in. Rather than approach this from the hotelier's perspective, let's take the viewpoint of the bride and groom.

And to get a good insider's perspective, I interviewed Carley Roney of TheKnot.com and WeddingChannel.com. While the bridal market, for the most part, tends to be highly localized, The Knot was one of the pioneers in terms of approaching the business on a national level by creating regional micro-sites with national sponsors and editorials. Together, both sites represent one of the largest online resources for brides-to-be.

In the US, just how big is the wedding market? How many couples were married in 2011 for example? What was the average spending per wedding? What are the trends in costs and cost allocations?

The wedding industry is a $74 billion industry that includes honeymoon, registries, engagement rings and all things related to weddings. Each year we conduct a Real Weddings study and according to TheKnot. com and WeddingChannel.com 2010 Real Weddings Study, the national average wedding spend is $26,984. Here's the overall wedding spend breakdown:

Category	2010 National Average Spend
Overall Wedding (excluding honeymoon)	$26,984
Ceremony Site	$1,393
Reception Venue	$12,124
Reception Band	$3,081
Reception DJ	$900

Category	2010 National Average Spend
Photographer	$2,320
Videographer	$1,463
Wedding Gown	$1,099
Florist/Décor	$1,988
Wedding Cake	$540
Ceremony Musicians	$503
Wedding Day Transportation	$667
Rehearsal Dinner	$1,127
Engagement Ring	$5,392

Everyone says weddings are recession proof. How has the economy influenced wedding and bridal spending?

The bridal industry is recession resistant, as brides will still spend money for their wedding no matter the state of the economy. Less than a third (31%) of brides said the economy affected their wedding budget, a decrease from 34% in 2009. However, when it comes to lowering the wedding budget, one successful cost-cutting tactic used by brides is to trim the number of wedding guests—141 was the average in 2010, compared with 149 in 2009. Despite the decrease in wedding guests, wedding standards weren't affected, as the average wedding spend per guest remained the same as it was in 2009 at $194.

Statistics say the average bride is older. What are the facts and how does this influence spending? Who's paying for these weddings?

The average age of the bride in 2010 was 29, an increase from 2009 when the average age was 28. The average age of the groom in 2010 was 31, an increase from 2009 when the average age was 30. Because couples are older and more established in their careers, they're paying for more of the wedding. The couple paid for 42% of the wedding in

2010, while the bride's parents paid for 45% and the groom's paid for 12%. Everyone's contributing to overall spend, not just bride's parents anymore.

When selecting a reception venue, what are the key factors that a bride looks for? How influential is the groom in the wedding location selection? What about parents?

When choosing a venue, the first thing you want to ensure is that the room is large enough to accommodate the number of people on your guest list. It may look big enough when it's empty, but you won't get a good idea until it's filled with chairs, tables, a dance floor, food and drinks. Ask to see photos of the space when it's set up for another wedding of equal size as yours.

Light can also make or break the mood and the space. If you're marrying during the day, make sure your venue has plenty of windows. If it's an evening affair, make sure the room's not too dim. You also need ample outlets. Take a look around the room to make sure there are lots of outlets, especially if you've chosen a space that doesn't normally host weddings or events.

Finally, good acoustics are a must. If the place has echoes, it could alter the sound of the band, or make it difficult for guests to hear speeches and even each other. A tile or wood floor, will amplify sounds, while a thick carpet tends to muffle them. Again, visit the space during an event so you can hear the room's sound quality yourself.

The groom and parent's influence on the selection of the wedding reception varies with each couple. Some grooms are very involved in the planning process, while others will ask to have more of a say in the food or the honeymoon planning. If parents are paying for the wedding they may have more say in the decisions than if the couple is paying for it themselves.

The factors that influence wedding reception location are: word of mouth, wedding shows, past experience, referrals, wedding shows, magazines, broadcast, and online. Can you comment on the importance of each?

The power of word of mouth, referrals, magazines, broadcast and online promotions are very powerful. Never underestimate PR. When we launched, there was no expert in weddings or an easily recognized voice. So instead of focusing on advertising, we invested in PR. We believe that if you're doing things that are interesting enough, people will talk about it. Essentially, PR was the first social media!

On WeddingChannel.com, we have reviews where brides can easily search and review more than 130,000 of the top wedding vendors. In turn, vendors can interact directly with brides. Vendors should encourage their brides to post reviews on WeddingChannel.com reviews as well as check out other bride's tried and true reviews.

Are destination weddings gaining in popularity, or are the bulk of receptions still local?

Destination weddings rose the past two years, with an increase of 20% since 2008. In fact, approximately one in four couples considered their wedding a destination wedding in 2010.

What new trends in weddings and wedding receptions are you seeing?

A new trend for 2012 is the Ritzy Ranch Wedding. Picture a 200-year-old barn complete with long exposed-wood tables, large chandeliers and ambient lighting. For flowers, think lace-wrapped bouquets of wild roses, lilies of the valley, Queen Anne's lace and gardenias. Food includes delicate wild game like juniper-spiced venison, cider-braised pheasant and pan-roasted quail. Brides will be channeling the Old West with a rustic-elegant spin.

Brides nowadays are inspired to wear wedding gowns that are light and airy, but with a mysterious and sexy vibe. Vera Wang's stunning witchcraft-inspired wedding dresses are already a bride's first stop. For wedding décor, magical and fantasy settings will be big with brides opting for a woodsy vibe. Think soft, decadent bouquets filled with flowers like cabbage roses, peonies and dinner plate dahlias.

Tell us more about appealing to the growing ethnic markets within the USA.

On Weddings.com, we have an entire collection of niche wedding-planning sites devoted to reaching these markets—Asian weddings, Indian weddings, Jewish weddings, Muslim weddings and many others. Each site features a collection of custom content, vendor listings, message boards and real weddings to offer inspiration.

Beyond the US, we've expanded globally. In November 2010, we launched Ijie.com, a web site that provides Western inspiration and local advice for weddings, relationships and pregnancy for the Chinese consumer. We also recently announced a partnership with SINA, one of the most trafficked news and lifestyle portals in China with 170 million daily unique visitors, in which we have a cobranded weddings channel under the SINA E-ladies section. Not to mention, we also have a partnership with Youku, the largest video hosting site in China.

What is your advice for a venue that wants to be totally wedding friendly?

Having an attitude of 'no request can't be met' is essential. The venue should answer emails and phone calls in a timely manner. They should work with brides to reasonably negotiate within their budget and meet their needs. It's also advisable they have a presence wherever brides are (eg. Facebook, Twitter, TheKnot.com, WeddingChannel.com, etc.).

O Canada, True North Strong, But Not Free

I am a proud Canadian. Except for Quebec, Canadians speak the same language as our US counterparts, albeit with a slightly different accent. We shop at the same stores: the GAP, Wal-Mart, Old Navy and soon we'll even have Target! Travel to one of our large cities and you'll see the usual hotel chains too: Hilton, Marriott and most of the Starwood varieties. One could even mistake downtown Toronto for Chicago. Often it is, too, as many Hollywood films supposedly set in Chicago are really filmed on location in Toronto.

Flashback 10 or 20 years to when Canada was a poor cousin of the USA. The Canadian dollar was lucky to hit 80 cents American. At the dollar's nadir, it was worth 62 cents American. Unemployment was stubbornly 2 to 3 percentage points higher than our southern neighbor as well. Our economic picture was somber, and accordingly, we were ignored as an origination market for tours and travel, with an assignment of second or even third tier status.

Well, wake up world, and especially our southern friends—Canada is on fire! Here are some facts that may provide some perspective.

- There's no housing or mortgage crisis here. The average house prices in Canada actually grew every year from 2008 through 2011. In Toronto and Vancouver, low interest rates have propelled the housing markets into what could be considered as 'bubble' territory. For perspective, my own home has almost tripled in value from my purchase price of just nine years ago.
- The Canadian dollar now hovers around par with the greenback and often tracks above it, thereby increasing Canadians' buying power. Canadian travel outside of the country has grown in double digits over the past three years as Canadians exercise their newly discovered economic muscle.
- Canadian unemployment levels are lower than the US and are in a range consistent with those experienced prior to the dismissal 2008 recession year.
- About 56% of Canadians have a passport, compared with just 37% of Americans. A passport is required for Canadians to

travel to the USA, as it is for Americans to travel to Canada and the world.

One look around my adopted hometown of Toronto, with a metropolitan area population of about 5.6 million according to the latest census, exudes a definite 'wow' factor. There are nearly 150 high rises, mostly condominiums, now under construction or consideration in our city. For comparison, the next highest is New York with just over 50. A drive in downtown Toronto will reveal a sea of construction cranes.

So, as an hotelier, how do you take advantage of this vibrant, potentially untapped market? Canada's motto of 'True North Strong and Free' is a good start, but unfortunately, it's not going to be free. Most American ad agencies haven't a foggy clue as to how to approach this market. The questions I am often asked by even the brightest of this group are downright embarrassing. Canadians, on the other hand, are well-familiar with the USA, given strong penetration of US stations on our cable TV networks. Before coming to this vast northern expanse, you should consider the following.

- Define the Canadian market that best suits your geographic needs. This is a big country, so consider regionalized, targeted programs.
- Try testing Canadian-targeted Google Adwords.
- Look to participating with local CVB's or state tourism offices on their next mission to Canada. If a state doesn't host Canadian delegates, invite them.
- Consider some FAM trips for targeted Canadian PR writers.
- Consider participating with key Canadian tour operators.
- Seek assistance from Canadian market experts.

It used to be said that when the USA gets a cold, Canada sneezes. Canada is doing fine, thank you, while the US appears to be looking for some cold and sinus capsules. And don't get me started on health care differences as Canada does quite a few things better there as well!

What I hope you'll learn is that like Canada, there are many other countries held under certain outdated assumptions. Reevaluating certain nations as strong consumers, both for targeted marketing campaigns and possible expansions, may be a prudent strategic move. Come to Toronto and see for yourself!

Customer Loyalty and Toronto's New Luxury Hotels

It seems as though every luxury hotel chain on earth decided that Toronto is the place to be nowadays, and all within a narrow timeframe. Looking at the luxury hotel segment, here are the newcomers, in order of their opening date:

- Thompson Hotel, opened Spring 2010, 102 rooms
- Hotel Le Germain at Maple Leaf Square, opened Fall 2010, 171 rooms
- The Ritz-Carlton, opened early in 2011, 267 rooms
- Trump International Hotel & Tower, opened late 2011, 256 rooms
- Four Seasons Hotel & Residences (replacing the existing Four Seasons), opened late-Summer 2012, 253 rooms
- Shangri-La Hotel & Residences, opened Fall 2012, 220 rooms

Before this upscale onslaught, Toronto's total luxury room count was 1,125, based on the following property set: the Hazelton Hotel; the Windsor Arms, the 'old' Four Seasons Hotel, the current Hotel Le Germain, and two Metropolitan properties. A caveat to this sum is that I did not include niche luxury hotels—those with a double-digit quantity of rooms. Nevertheless, the statistics are still quite remarkable. The city is experiencing an addition of 1,279 new luxury rooms, which represents a staggering increase of 113% over the current base.

To a certain extent, Toronto has lagged behind other metropolises insofar as luxury stock, so this may be partly considered as pure catch-up. Call it pride, but I like to think of this more as a 'coming out' party; a distinction that marks Toronto's ascension into the upper echelons of worldly cities. With this, there are several macro and micro considerations.

First, the Canadian banking system, largely centred on Toronto's Bay Street, has been far more conservative than others within the past decade. As such, the city was not as heavily hit by the recent economic downturn, implying two major stimuli for luxury hotels. Second, stable banks equate to steady cash flow, which means no stalls on construction projects. And third, the top tier Canadian banks flourished in the wake of the recession, leading to more high-end business travellers to and from the city. This is a whole separate topic, but the gist of it is that the city is flourishing, with a prosperous core of banks as the foundation.

As something that only a local can truly observe, Toronto's neighbourhoods have undergone significant change recently. Originally, if you wanted a high-end room, you stayed in Yorkville, which is our ultra chic and quite expensive shopping district. And so it became saturated with hotels. But with a consistent condominium boom over the past decade (again, a whole other topic), many other downtown areas along the lakefront have gentrified with more sightseeing, more shopping and more nightlife. This has paved the way for luxury brands to consider properties in other areas where land is more plentiful than the overdeveloped Yorkville hub. Of those newcomers listed, only the Four Seasons is based in Yorkville, and it is replacing the existing Four Seasons just a few blocks away.

On a more microeconomic level is the Toronto International Film Festival (TIFF). Started in 1976, it was a niche event clustered in Yorkville, then a burgeoning artists' enclave. As of 2010, however, TIFF is a citywide festival, drawing over a quarter of a million people and rivaling Cannes as the foremost symposium of back-end movie deals. And all those actors, directors, producers and studio execs want luxury rooms for these business negotiations, right? Toronto has done an excellent job to bolster such premium events throughout the year, likely heightening demand for luxury rooms.

Last of note, many foremost luxury brands were devoid of a Toronto locale, and to cycle back on the city's rise to worldly prominence, it has now become fitting for those hotel chains to claim their piece of the pie, whether be driven by namesake, loyalty programs or overall brand strategy. No doubt this was a consideration for Trump, Shangri-La and the Ritz-Carlton.

As each new product launches they have to be aggressive in their marketing to nudge their way into a crowded sector. What first comes to mind is the 'what's new factor'. That is, new properties often launch with programs that generate fresh customer trials with rates that are typically less than the ADR level targeted for the long run.

These introductory discounts are hard for consumers to resist, whether we are talking about Toronto or any other commercial center. Here is what can be expected in anticipated priority order:

- Targeting customers on their own corporate loyalty programs, introducing their newest destination
- Aggressive pay-per-click advertising using the new destination as a key word
- Organic SEO programs that include the new destination
- Local public relations that announce the new property
- Open house events for travel agents and meeting planners
- Tradeshow representation for meetings and weddings
- Direct marketing lists of potential guests who have utilized nearby accommodations
- Local advertising targeting leisure weekends

So, how can you cope under these conditions? Recognize that your instincts will tell you to go into defensive mode. You will probably lose business as the supply has significantly increased without any proportionate growth in demand. But, don't just sit there and expect everything to even out in the long run. Do something. Now is the time to really take advantage of your pre-existing customer loyalty, and here's how:

- If you are a chain, review your loyalty point category and program participation
- Target your marketing to past guests and encourage repeat visits with value-added discounts and best rate guarantees
- Recognize past guests through social media to create rewarding, targeted promotions
- Spruce up your electronic communications programs with select offers for past guests
- Spend the time with your sales team to develop pro-active strategies to protect your business base
- Be prepared to spend more in marketing on a per-room-sold basis than you needed to over the past two years

The addition of this many luxury rooms will probably be fully absorbed in the long-run given Toronto's continued growth, which has no stoppage in sight. If you're local region experiences similar conditions, understand the short-term surges will inevitably lead to some losses. All operators should expect to see occupancy erosion due to all the new competitors. A smart operator will recognize this and plan accordingly for the long-term.

As a case study, I find this to be a fascinating little experiment. Will all these hotels, both new and old, survive? As always, only time will tell.

Conclusions

What did you infer from the previous chapters? Did you notice any common themes?

First, are you convinced that weddings and honeymoons are a big source of revenue for hotels? They're both staple industries and aligning your resources to appeal to these markets will surely deliver a solid revenue stream. If you find that you are dwindling in this department, get a think-tank together of senior managers from your weddings department and other related areas of your operations, then decide on a few key measures you can incorporate into next year's marketing plan. And if you are already a known destination for weddings and honeymoons, look towards developing tools to measure your performance and gain honest feedback so you can continue this success well into the future.

I hope that despite labeling this section as 'Traditional Marketing', you've realized that there's nothing traditional about it. I used this title as a way to delineate it from those topics entirely devoted to 'Internet Marketing' and to 'Social Media'. But even then, is there really any type of marketing that can exist without considering the Internet these days?

All modern marketing techniques can be fused with social media, but I advise that this be done with caution. I'm still wary about exactly how much a social media following translates into sales. Managers are so focused on the actual quantity that they forget about the quality. This is something I've touched on and will continue to note during the upcoming section focused on Internet marketing tactics.

Regardless, don't discount 'traditional' methods in favor of the purely electronic-born. The 'space' in cyberspace has created too wide a gap between the consumer and hotel personnel. Keeping this in mind, let's talk about some ways you can you use the Internet to your advantage.

Internet Marketing

The Montage Beverly Hills is everything you'd expect from a world-class establishment in this star-struck city, and a whole lot more! (Photo credit: Scott Frances)

Introduction to Internet Marketing

At the intersection of traditional marketing and social media are a series of tools and components that I've grouped into a section entitled 'Internet Marketing'. Much of this section is devoted to trends that are becoming essential marketing components for hotels, starting with tablets (such as the iPad) and flash sales.

What I hope you will gain from this section is that although these new technologies can probably aid your business, they should first be properly evaluated prior to implementation. You need to evaluate whether they are worth the investment, or merely constitute a novelty. Almost every new venture will be a double-edged sword.

Tablets may present themselves as flashy, palpable sales tools, but they are also costly in terms of physical purchases, software development and maintenance. There are also theft and obsolescence risk issues. Flash sales may be great for boosting occupancy in low periods, but they also undermine your long term ADR strategies. Everything has pros and cons to some degree, and it's your job as a hotelier to see both sides of the argument.

As always, don't rush to immediate conclusions. Consider all aspects then reach your own decision based on long-term strategic plans. I have always supported incorporating new technologies and Internet applications to your advantage, but only if executed properly. Hopefully the following chapters will inspire you to rethink how you judge these new tools.

Either way, hotels will be in a period of transition for quite some time. There's always lag between when a new technology first arises and when it can be feasibly incorporated into hotel operations. Remember, you do not have to be the early adopter, but you should definitely not be a late adapter. Finding the correct timing balance is often the greatest challenge.

How Your Hotel Can Use Tablets

In case you haven't noticed, there's this great piece of technology gaining massive acceptance, generically called the Tablet. Your guests will be arriving with them. Your competitors will be using them. So what are you doing about it?

If you're not convinced that this new technology is important, consider this: Apple, the world's leading tablet computer manufacturer, shipped over 14 million iPads in Q1 2012 alone, nearly quadruple the amount of laptops (MacBooks) they sold in the same period. On an industry scale, sales of tablets are up about 400% year-over-year for 2011-2012, while sales of notebook PCs have basically plateaued. This adoption rate is faster than just about any new technology to hit the marketplace in recent history, including the DVD player, PC, or smartphone.

The first question to ask yourself is whether or not your hotel is tablet friendly. Have you checked your web site on a tablet to see how it looks? Can customers book from a tablet as easily as they can on a computer? Most tablets will only have two plugs—one to connect to a computer or power source and another for headphones. Without an Ethernet port, you better have WiFi available for your tablet guests and, ideally, at no additional cost. Hardwired Internet just doesn't cut it anymore, pun intended.

Once a guest arrives, there are many other points of interaction where tablets can make a strong impression. Rather than having your concierge show someone a paper brochure for an amenity or activity, why not present it to them on a tablet? It'll impress your guests and allow you to show them a variety of material without interruption, introducing and enticing them to use more of your services. I have also seen great use of tablets at the concierge desk displaying the weather in many destination markets, as well as live airport flight departure times.

At your restaurant, try showcasing your wine list with an app for users to browse by type, price and vintage. You'll save big on menu reprints. Many wine list apps today can integrate with your inventory to only show those that are presently available, as well as ideal food pairings. You might even consider using tablets to replace the paper menu all together!

At check-in, consider having a tablet available so your front desk staff can use them to up-sell rooms. It's easy to create simple presentations on features in a quick slideshow of illustrious photography. Helping guests visualize the benefits of a larger room makes it that much easier to get them excited about the upgrade.

What about behind the scenes? Think about how your staff members can keep track of guest requirements. Integrating a tablet app with your property PMS can go a long way to help reduce the waste associated with daily room printouts as well as speed up internal communication. Having a tablet ready is a great way to pass along notes about a certain guest or a guest request to give guest services a boost.

These are just some of the ways that tablets can integrate into your hotel's operation. Mind you, it's not an overnight adjustment because there's the fixed cost of purchasing each unit and there are some security issues (never mind that you might have to install WiFi throughout your hotel). However, with their exponential adoption rate, you'll need to be tablet-compatible and tablet-chic if you want to attract the younger tech-savvy crowd. Best get with the program before it's too late!

The Year of the Tablet

Tablets are all the rage. They fill the new and cool factor and they're a tool to enrich your guests' experience. The real quandary is whether their integration is feasible for this fiscal year? Let me convince you.

Let me first share my experiences with the iPad. It started as a novel device. I hacked around with apps that I'd never really use more than once every six months. As that wore off, I settled into using my tablet primary for email, web surfing and reading. For those three functions, it is near perfect. I don't even buy paper books anymore.

After awhile, I started substituting the far lighter iPad for my laptop on short business and leisure trips. I brought it everywhere. One time, I brought it into a restaurant and the waiter greeted me with another iPad as their menu. Seeing I was already in possession of one, she was more than happy to let me download their menu to keep for future use. It was a fun exchange and the new age sensibility left a positive impression; something worth talking about.

The first place to consider tablets is for your front-end staff. Used a replacement for standardized printouts, such as a menu, spa brochure or sales pamphlet, the tablet becomes an incredibly versatile device; the associated integration costs far outweighing printer bills over the long run. Think of letting the concierge use one to fact check and better direct guests. How about providing a couple for the front desk set to a rolling slideshow of calming photography and exciting activities available on property?

Then there's the aforementioned F&B. It's a fun and interactive way to liven the atmosphere. Tablets afford the restaurant menu to be more malleable towards regular chef alterations. Guests might actually remember the specials for once! You can even install features that give recommendations based on past orders or alluring wine pairings. Or, imagine having several tablets propped up at your lobby bar so customers can flip through your array of elixirs while they sip away on their first beverage. If you are worried about theft, then why not just start with tablets just for waiters to use as a presentation instrument?

Consider tablets as in-room, universal devices controlling such things as the TV, your alarm clock and room service. This is more far-fetched, but with new apps for the iPad and Android-based tablets coming out every day as well as more programmers being fluent in both languages, it's not hard to see this as an option for the very near future. However bold this might be, its installation is bolder.

A tablet in every room is a serious cost, but it might not be as heavy as in previous years given that there are sturdy models hitting the market for well about $400 per unit. The more elusive cost is that of an app to serve your needs. What I recommend is looking into a provider of a standardized app that leaves space for augmentation once you've received feedback.

Any way you put it, this is still a major overhaul, but think back to the time you had to switch from a CRT to a plasma or LCD television—an enormous cost, but necessary nonetheless. Who still groans over the flat screen TV upgrades? The way we perceive tablets will be in the same boat soon enough, so you'd be best to invest now and reap the word-of-mouth results for being an early adopter.

The third prominent area to incorporate tablets is for your housekeeping, maintenance and other back-end team members requiring mobility. Picture it as a checklist clipboard substitute. Housekeepers could use it to jot down which rooms require what and to note minibar consumption, damage and theft.

With Internet access, tablets easily become handy communication devices, able to relay emergencies or other critical guest service needs. This is where engineering steps in. Maintenance workers can be alerted to problems and give quick status updates, ensuring that all operations run as smoothly as possible, all while having a full tablet-sized screen to reference for key information. Of course, such functions would require a healthy dose of training, but the barriers aren't too overbearing for straightforward touch-and-go applications.

While you're at it, think about upgrading the WiFi coverage for your property so that it includes all the rooms, restaurants and back-end areas. This is obvious for situations where you require your staff to use tablets while on the move, but consider your guests as well. Many brands don't even house an Ethernet port, so WiFi accessibility is a must. And if you want your property to be deemed as a true 'tablet friendly' zone, that Internet connection better be free.

A fourth major use is for the planning committee. Instead of relying on stacks of paper for the weekly briefings, a robust file reader with PMS integration can ameliorate the mounds of reports that accumulate over a year's time. This affords managers a quick access point to know what's happening on property whether they are at a remote location or offsite entirely.

With feasible uses for front-end staff, housekeeping, maintenance workers and managers, integrating tablets is a good step towards keeping in line with future technology trends. I have to draw the distinction between 'tablet compatible' and 'tablet chic'. I want you to be the latter. It implies so much more about your progressive strategy towards integrating the device across all levels of your operations as well as your empathy for the new generation of tech savvy travelers. Be a forward thinker and when the planning committee meets next, think of making the tablet in your hotel a reality.

Jumping Jack Flash: The Pros and Cons of Flash Sales

You see them on sites like Jetsetters, Living Social Escapes, Hotel Tonight, Groupon and several others: "Deluxe Vacation in Paradise, Regularly $2,000, Book Now for Only $1,000, Save 50%." The promotional text is crisp; the offers relatively straightforward. The question is, should you as an hotelier participate in these programs?

For those unfamiliar, a flash sale as an Internet-based promotion offered to potential guests for an extremely short period of time (one to seven days). The offer is typically for an inventory-restrictive packaged program available over a specified month or season, and is priced at a discount significantly below BAR. Most flash sales require full payment at time of booking. Once purchased, they are generally non-cancellable and may also be non-transferrable.

As you might expect, consumers love a sale. In the research report from Q2 2011 conducted by *Condé Nast Traveler* entitled 'What Matters Now, Volume XLI,' two out of three respondents agree: "I'm intrigued by travel 'flash' sales." Of that same group, 11% have already booked travel or accommodations through a flash site, with another 44% planning to do so in the near future. Condé Nast concluded with their opinion that flash sales are here to stay, and I'd be inclined to agree.

Flash sales can appeal to hoteliers for several reasons. The ability to unload rooms from a non-productive period is the dominant attractor. It's a clutch tactic to increase occupancy and shore up dry spells. If these rooms can be bundled with value-added extras, the loss in ADR can be made up somewhat through a balanced RevPAR. Flash sales can also be utilized as a tool to push suite upgrades, golf rounds, kids camps and even F&B programs. Hoteliers might also execute a flash sale just to invigorate their leisure sales team.

As a further bonus, you'll know your results within a very short period of time, making it very easy to plan further actions. With programs prepaid, there's limited financial risk and immediate cash flow. Flash sale web sites give your product a higher awareness to a new set of consumers. And, for those who tried your product at this incredible low price, there's the potential for them to be converted to regulars.

On the flip side, liken flash sales to the use of an addictive drug. There's a certain rush from the first time you see hundreds of thousands of revenue dollars come in from a single program in a very short period of time. It's hard to fathom and the idea of repeating a flash sale again and again will quickly come to mind. Each successive use, however, actually delivers less of a thrill and less of a business bump. Like any addiction, it's hard to get out of the cycle.

When used repeatedly over the years, flash sales lower your brand's perceived value, weakening your ADR. Nowadays you're likely dealing with a more web-savvy crowd, one that's fully acclimatized to breakneck marketing tactics. Once these consumers get a habitual taste for flash sales, that's all they'll want in their diet. There's also the risk of displacement. A flash release is received by all subscribers to a given site. If one of your subscribers just so happens to be booked at your hotel for that same period, they may demand compensation.

The costs of managing a flash sale also have to be taken into consideration. Flash sale providers with large, dedicated subscriber bases will not distribute your product to their database for free. In addition to the discount you offer the customer, anticipate a further percentage for the middleman taken straight off of the top of your yield.

My old bosses at Procter & Gamble—a marketing-oriented, packaged-goods firm of pretty good standing—taught me that trial strategies are often necessary in driving new customers to your product. Indeed, thinking of a flash sale as a trial generator might be a logical rationale for the exercise. But the costs incurred through any trial strategy are high, and the lost margins need to be rationalized through a percentage conversion of these trial candidates to regular, loyal customers.

Think of any trial program you undertake as being only the first step of a multi-level program designed to convince these customers to become repeat guests. These strategies should be honed to include effective use of databases and electronic marketing programs, as offered by most reservations systems. Again, the secret here is capturing all the trial data on your system, not on some third-party flash sale supplier.

My personal feeling is that flash sale sites have their time and place, albeit very rare. If you are dead set on using them, do so sparingly and don't include them as part of your core marketing plan. This'll prevent consumer displacement and negate any long-term ADR declines. No more than once or twice during the fiscal year, and only for periods that need real bolstering.

And always remember, the more you offer deep discounts like this, the harder it is to restore your true value proposition. If you have a soft spot, why not reward past guests with excellent pricing or complimentary value-added extras that make your property irresistible? Offering a short-term promotion program to a past customer is called a reward for loyalty. Giving this to a total stranger is called foolhardy.

Ten Questions for a Solid Website Foundation

When my advertising agency reached the one hundred mark, we stopped counting the number of web sites we had already built. Regardless of the size of your property, its star ranking, location or feature set, the development of any successful site is based upon your ability to provide appropriate input to your web design team.

I imagine your house was built on a solid foundation. So too should your web site! By utilizing this as checklist for deciding which direction to take, you'll be able to help yourself get the web site that meets your business needs.

- What is wrong with your current web site? What are you hoping to accomplish with a new website? What do you see as the strengths and weaknesses of your current site?
- What other property websites do you like and why? What other (non-hotel) web sites do you like and why?
- What is your property's primary raison d'etre (that is, leisure, business, wedding, weekends, etc.)?
- Define your competitive set. How do you differentiate your property from your competitors? What do you like and dislike about their web sites?
- Who is your core target market: demographically, geographically and psychographically?
- How do your guests view you? What differences do they perceive when comparing your property to your competitors?
- How do your competitors view you? What would they perceive as your key strengths and points of difference?
- How would you describe the character of your property? What special values do your property and management consider critical?
- What are your key success measurements including ADR, REVPAR, Average Rate, Occupancy or OTA ranking (not necessarily all so select priorities)?

- Everyone wants site visitors to immediately make an online booking from your site. In addition to this, what key selling point would you like users to take away from your site?

Now that you have this comprehensive brief, make good use of it. Share it with you team and confirm their consensus to these responses. Use this to help start your agency discussions.

Top Five Functions Your Website CMS Should Be Doing

A content management system (CMS) is the administrative controls to the back-end of your web site, letting you modify what appears on the front-end without having to know any coding languages. It's generally an extra cost in your web site's development, but what you get in return is the flexibility to manage day-by-day happenings and keep your site in tempo with the rapidity of the Internet. Still not convinced? Here are five specific reasons why you should have a CMS.

1. **Blog.** A web log portion to your web site lets you readily update your guests, both past and future, about recent happenings and neighbourhood hotspots. It's entertainment and a good motive for customers to frequent your web site more often than they are right now. The content is easily shareable via your social media outlets to further heighten content generation and awareness through those channels. As well, writing with keywords in mind will do wonders for your SEO.

2. **Promotion Management.** With total control over this portion of your web site, you can better promote packages and specials in as timely a manner as possible. Not having this control means that every modification becomes an addition both in lost time and money. Plus, last minute changes are a breeze, letting you can stay ahead of the competition.

3. **Calendar of Events.** The goal is to have a quick list of everything happening at your hotel in the near future so guests are well informed and can plan accordingly. Along the same lines as your blog, a CMS lets you take control of upcoming events so no intermediary is required for last minute updates.

4. **Specific Updates.** With a bit more complex tinkering, a CMS can be rigged to manage any other portion of your web site, including accommodations, dining or weddings. As business needs evolve, so may the needs for the types and quantity of information on your

web site. Having the flexibility to complete near instantaneous alterations is a must for proper business strategy.

5. **Getting Staff Involved.** The real beauty of a CMS is that it's easy for any staff member to update the web site. Systems these days are very intuitive and necessitate very little training for tech-savvy individuals. If everyone knows how to use your CMS, it ensures that content is posted in as timely a manner as possible. Your posts will be far more authentic than if everything is relayed through the IT team.

Going Mobile: Website or App?

Bar none, making your web site mobile friendly is essential. I'm frequently asked to review a mobile application (app for short) on behalf of a client property. The main question on their minds is: Is it worth it? Definitely yes—it's where the technology and customers are headed. At this point, however, a more critical question to ask is: Should you strive for a full-scale native mobile app or a mobile-friendly version of your web site?

The construction and marketing of mobile apps represents a rapidly proliferating subsection of the web development business. The number of apps available for the iPhone is in the hundreds of thousands and approaching a million. The other smartphones (chiefly Android and Blackberry) currently trail in numbers to Apple, but there's still an abundance of apps to choose from. In the travel world, airlines, magazines, rental car companies and cruise lines all have apps. Just as it's now almost incomprehensible to not engage customers through social media networks, so too must hotels investigate their options to support mobile devices.

The main differences between a mobile web site and a traditional web site are the size of user interface elements, layouts, viewable areas, and accommodating 'swiping' rather than 'scrolling'. Traditional web sites are built for computer monitors (over 1024 pixel x 768 pixel resolution) and navigation using a mouse or trackpad. The user experience for a traditional web site does not consider the much smaller, compacted screen of a mobile device. After all, the finger is much larger and less precise than a mouse pointer.

A traditional web site is viewable on a smartphone, but this can often involve excessive scrolling and difficulties using some of the site's functions such as dropdown menus, Flash elements and other hoverable actions. Consider that a traditional site may be coded with a width of 960 pixels, but the ideal width of a mobile site is 320 pixels. A mobile web site is designed specifically for the smaller screen and the finger as the primarily navigation tool.

The good news is there are a number of ways to serve a mobile version of the site to users visiting from specific devices. One of the more optimal methods to achieve this at the moment is by following the principles of 'responsive' web design for your main web site. This essentially includes building your web site so its layout elements will respond and flex to the various devices accessing the site. Of course, there are other ways to detect mobile devices, including the actual detection of the specific device using a server-side language, or even by creating a completely separate mobile web site for smaller device screen sizes.

In terms of advantages, there's no question of that certain cool factor associated with having your own app. Mobile apps can be designed for very easy access of information that guests might want. Or, you can cater different apps to different markets, such as a spa-only app or a golf app. Such 'native' apps tend to feel smoother and run faster on smartphones than HTML5 processes which are the norm for mobile web sites.

One of the single greatest barriers for native apps is the cost involved in developing a separate app for each mobile platform. For example, if you want to be compatible with iPhone, Android and Blackberry's operating systems, you'd need to develop three individual apps in completely different programming languages. Apps also require downloading though a facility such as iTunes, which in itself is a minor turnoff. And although you may set your price as free, the app may not be readily found by those not already searching it.

When it comes to updates, your app users will have to download each one, still one more step that doesn't concern mobile sites. Plus, app updates are cumbersome; each revision in essence relates to a new version of the app that must be approved by the app marketplace. On the other hand, content management systems (CMS) allow you to simultaneously push changes to both your regular and mobile sites, making repeated updates a cinch.

Lastly, think of your target audience and their booking frequency. Does it make sense to have your customers go through the effort of downloading an app just for something they'll access on average once or twice a year? Hardly.

Alas, I'm tackling this largely from the perspective of an independent hotel. If you're part of a major chain like Hilton or Marriott, then an app makes good sense. In the same way an airline app provides a user with updated flight information and flexible booking resources, a hotel app aimed at a large demographic might garner enough utilization to make it worthwhile. For this, I stress that it's the ability to get frequent use out of the app that makes it valuable.

As a relatively new technology, mobile app prices are restricted to those vendors capable of producing them. Native apps can become quite expensive primarily because a separate version is required for each mobile device. Also, some web shops exclusively develop iPhone apps, which would require working with several companies to cover multiple platforms.

Depending on creative decisions and site capabilities, a solid mobile site can typically be built for a fraction of the price as a relatively complex web site, depending upon functionality and content management programs. Because this mobile site would be designed to synchronize with your regular site, additional maintenance fees would be nominal, if any. You should also consider that this might well be the faster of the two executions to implement.

Therefore, if you were considering this upgrade for an independent property, I'd advise that you shy away from creating your own hotel app. However, you don't want to miss out on traffic and potential bookings by leaving your web site unformatted for smartphones, so definitely plan a mobile version of your site for this year's marketing plan. Conversely, if you operate one of the major chains, it would be smart to review your options for a mobile app. These dedicated programs will allow you to slate aspects of your property distinctively for smartphones as well as give you that chic 'more than just a website' buzz.

Either way, mobile devices are here to stay. Website or app, you have to pick a solution to ensure that you are well positioned to handle customers reaching you via smartphone. As always, sooner is better.

SEO: Modern Day Snake Oil?

It never ceases to amaze me as to how many unsolicited emails my clients get from companies promising to do wonders for a hotel's web site in terms of search engine optimization. Usually, these missives are well written in an onerous tone that has GMs questioning their web sites, their web agencies, their directors of marketing and often all of the above. What's a GM to do? Just how important is SEO, and can a 'specialist' company really help? Above all, is there any value to the whole exercise in terms of true revenue generation?

Some notes. I'm focusing on Google, which at this current time processes more than two-thirds of all search activity. For those who use Google Adwords, you know the sponsored links on the right hand side or top of the page, which are not influenced by SEO tactics. Positioning your product in these pay-for arenas combined with SEO is called Search Engine Marketing, or SEM, and is a whole other discussion.

Why is SEO important? If a person is looking for a hotel in a foreign city, doing a Google search is the easiest way to find accommodations. Surely every GM knows this is not the only approach that a potential guest would take in their quest to find the perfect room to rest their weary legs. But it's typically the first. Other resources include travel agents, OTAs, Facebook, Twitter, other social media, other travel sites, hotel chain sites and association sites such as Preferred Hotels and Resorts Worldwide, Small Luxury Hotels, or Leading Hotels of the World.

With so many methods to find your hotel, being in first place for a broad Google search is far from being the panacea to your occupancy challenges. In fact, it may be almost insignificant depending upon how relevant new customer searches are to your marketing strategy. Certainly, it can't hurt to be in the top two or three as a matter of search results, but it is not Armageddon if you miss this spot.

The rationale is simple: the more 'optimized' your site is, the more relevant it is within the Google search algorithms, resulting in a higher placement for all posted results. But Google rankings cannot be fooled. Don't think that hiring some third party sales company will take you from an eighth ranked page to a top three position in a matter of days or weeks. It doesn't work that way. Moreover, Google is wary of the tactics these proverbial snake oil salesmen utilize and likely has algorithms that negate such surreptitious tactics.

Start by taking the initiative yourself. A basic optimization strategy is quite easy to do internally. Review your web site as you do your property, both strategically and tactically. Here is a typical checklist of what you should look for before seeking external help.

- A flawless site, with clear text and no internal errors
- Correct and accurate tags (title, keyword, page and headers)
- Optimized images with photo alt tags
- Fully linked and active blog, including social media sharing opportunities
- Fully linked and active social media (primarily Facebook, Twitter and YouTube)
- Your URL registered for at least 24 months before it expires
- Active RSS feed
- At least one data collection form
- Clear navigation structure of indexed pages with sitemap files
- A number of quality in-bound links
- A site that is regularly updated

Many of these items can be costly to execute, both in terms of coding upgrades and time spent uploading new images, articles and quick factoids. But the dynamically driven content offered by your blog and social media is important for SEO. Google correlates these to how often your site is updated and therefore relevant.

The last item is more challenging. In-bound links are ones that come from other sites referring to yours. Within Google, however, not all links are considered equal. Those from high traffic sites, such as CNN, are far more important that those from a 'no name' URL. There are some proven approaches to garnish these quality in-bound links; most reside outside of the realm of Internet marketing and lean more towards the public relations side. Certainly, be wary of the 'come on' offers of 10,000 inbound links for only $99! These may actually do more harm to your SEO that good, as a jump of inbound links of this magnitude is not consistent with slow-build, organic growth.

If it's that straightforward, then why do these SEO specialists exist? If you don't have a web agency, and you built the site yourself, then yes, the SEO work from these specialty teams might be useful. Furthermore, there is a definite skill in developing the appropriate tag sequences. Some ad agencies are just weak in SEO, and thus, an outside firm might be an approach to consider. But, like anything sold in bulk over the Internet, caveat emptor!

In the end, SEO is just one more item on your checklist, but for the most part, it won't be the most critical for success. Ask your web agency for a monthly report on their results, both in terms of SEO and site analytics. Next, make sure you have an active social media platform that is in tune with your brand strategy. And when those snake oil emails arrive in your inbox, remember these words as you hit delete.

Black Friday: Make It Green for Your Hotel

Make no mistake: Black Friday is a pivotal day in marketing. I'm not referring to the stock market crash in 1929, but rather the busiest shopping day of the year occurring over the US Thanksgiving long weekend. The day is hugely important for retailers with billions of dollars in sales, and I see no reason why your hotel can't also capitalize. First, let's review some history and how it ties into present day consumer expectations.

The Thanksgiving weekend is the traditional time for people to start their Christmas gift purchases; something established long before the official naming of this grand sales event. Our current iteration of 'Black Friday' originated in Philadelphia in the 1960s when the combination of fans for the annual Army-Navy football game and shoppers drove the city into a bottleneck. It has since evolved to more generically reference the bedlam at malls nationwide and the point at which retailers go from red to black in the accounting books.

With most people taking time off work and its prime placement before the upcoming holiday season, Black Friday has always been destined for great things. In an effort to lure this blip of consumers and heighten impulse buys, a few select retailers started by offering Black Friday promotions. This in turn caused other vendors to compete with their own Thanksgiving specials and extended shopping hours. Soon, everyone had their own limited-time deals, all vying for customer dollars.

Then came the Internet and this behavior has gone haywire. Loud web sites and gluts of social media messages inform potential buyers of Black Friday promotions well in advance of the day as well as inundate consumers with reminders. Many companies now offer Internet-only specials. The World Wide Web also lets people comparison shop to better locate where the best deals are truly hiding.

It's peer pressure on a massive scale. Retailers and hoteliers who aren't involved may feel as though they're missing out or be coerced by owners into action, while those already in the fray may feel inclined to ramp up deals to stay ahead of the pack. As such, Black Friday specials are the norm. In order to continually draw attention, many retailers have now resorted to exorbitant discounts, often far exceeding anything else during the year. This has also perpetuated a 'wait until Black Friday' mentality that translates to even more focus on this day.

Purchasing hotel rooms, however, is quite different from more traditional retail purchases. The best way to get the ball rolling is to use your web site to promote your deal as well as provide a smooth avenue for transactions via your online booking engine. Alas, it's not that simple. With slashed prices everywhere, a regular deal will only be met with a ho-hum response. You'll have to be aggressive and add a touch of creativity if you really want to stand out and profit.

For starters, map out an offer your guests can't refuse. The easy way is with strong discounts on room rate. This tactic makes sense if you are offering rooms in a forecasted lower occupancy period, but it might also erode ADR to the point of putting you back in the red.

You can avoid this dip by limiting the number of rooms at this deep discount. Or, in lieu of a significant markdown, build a moderate price reduction into a leisure package which could be value-added to include transportation, meals or spa treatments—anything that will make the future experience streamlined and carefree. Lastly, to mitigate loss, consider adding criteria such as full pre-payment and a restrictive refund/cancellation policy.

Next, create your own standalone flash sale site to further differentiate your Black Friday specials from your other promotions. The goal is to market your deal explicitly and drive impulse buys. The design should be straightforward with the specs bolded in a list on the home page, social media icons populated correctly and a direct path to purchase. Emphasize the holiday spirit of gift giving and perhaps consider placing a countdown ticker, keeping in mind that web sales don't have to abide by regular store hours.

But all your web efforts and RevPAR number crunching will be in vain if you don't promote the endeavor. Your home base is your web site. Add a tiny banner or JavaScript announcement to the corner of the screen that links to your dedicated sales page or flash site. Next, leverage your social media connections to build anticipation with a slow drip of the inside scoop. These networks are very pervasive tools to coerce shoppers on the day of the sale and to answer questions about your deal.

The only real way to build this anticipation is through diligent preparation. If you're going to rake in the crowds like some of the current retail juggernauts, you have to form a plan by the end of September at the latest so the marketing engine won't have to resort to last minute tactics. If you give this project your full attention, I see no reason why Black Friday can't be green for your hotel. I warn you though. This tactic is a type of flash sale, and if you already have several of those under your belt during the fiscal year, then definitely consider another approach for the Thanksgiving weekend.

Customized Loyalty: What Hotels Can Learn from Airlines and Amazon

Have you ever browsed or purchased from Amazon? Easy question. If yes, then you're no doubt familiar with how well the web site will remember your individual tastes. The next time you log on, it'll offer you specific recommendations built right into the homepage based on what you looked at last. Their e-blasts and each specific product page both work the same way. Being an Amazon member certainly has its privileges—personal recommendations and special deals foremost on the mind.

Many airlines apply similar principles. For repeat customers, you can get increased mileage accumulation, priority luggage, the ability to reserve seats and reduced fees. Their marketing principles are driving loyalty and this loyalty means steady, incremental revenue increases without the heavy costs of seeking new customers eating away at your profit margins. So, what can you apply to your property?

Just as each hotel is unique, each customer is also unique. I wholeheartedly encourage you and other managers to get out on the lobby floor and engage your guests face-to-face. This is really a 'no brainer.' If you really want to know every habitué, however, you better start collecting data. The more data you have for past customers, the better you will meet and exceed their future desires, so much so that you'll know a person's preferences before he or she arrives.

The idea that sparked me to investigate this principle occurred while I was touring Southeast Asia. One evening, my wife and I dined at the hotel's restaurant, casually mentioning that it was our thirtieth anniversary. After dessert, our waiter presented an engraved menu with both of our meals printed on the inside covers. During the ensuing conversation, this staff member also told me that our meal was recorded on computer, so whenever we visited next they could prepare it to the tee.

Imagine how this application of data collection could be applied to the weddings and engagement dinner business. It is very often and quite romantically the case that couples will revisit the restaurant where one of the two planted a knee and asked the question of all questions. This could happen at your hotel, and it'd be wise to take note of what each of the two had so they could relive that moment upon their return. Better yet, tell them you have their meal on file so they're more inclined to return.

The custom menu was an astonishing extra; a total surprise. There's no reason you can't set up a template for your in-house printers to manage this task. Not only will you demonstrate how much you value guests sharing one of their most intimate moments on your property, but giving them enough impetus to talk ecstatically about how much you actually care. Repeat business aside, it's all about word of mouth generated by excelsior guest services.

And this is not a new concept. When I call to order pizza, I'm first prompted by an automated voice to select whether I want the same order as before. This system has been in place for years. Mind you, I'm ordering off of a regional call center for a national pizza restaurant chain, but the kernel of the idea remains the same. The automated voice offers me selective deals on how I've ordered in the past, and then allows me to streamline my favorite order, helping reduce their labor costs in the process.

My experience in Asia was simply the flawless execution of this model. Imagine if every hotel you stay at remembers all your previous meals at their in-house restaurants? The waiter approaches you with this knowledge, and he or she can already make suggestions more attuned to your individual tastes, whether it be appetizers, mains, desserts or wine pairings. Now picture tablets used in place of menus and the personalized suggestions scrolling along like they appear on Amazon. Then, extend this idea to room service, spa amenities and your reservation system.

The key is to use technology to build rapport so your guests aren't just your consumers, but your friends as well. For consumers you ask questions, but for friends you already know the answer. Staying with the topic of food, suppose that a recurrent guest consistently orders the same appetizer or has expressed admiration for the dish. Why not reward such loyalty and show your gratitude by having that appetizer ready in their room upon arrival? Your friends would remember such minor details about you, so why not a hotel? And this doesn't just apply to frequently purchased menu items, but also whether a person has specific allergies. If you are allergic to nuts, then wouldn't you be relieved to know that you don't have to remind the restaurant staff over and over again?

Since returning from Asia, I've had many insightful conversations about how hotels are already applying customized loyalty principles to make for better consumer experiences. In particular, when it comes to business trips, consistency in specific necessities is paramount, helping bring peace of mind to wearied travelers who wants everything in order upon arrival. Much like how you can reserve a window seat on an airplane because you don't want to be disturbed, you should also be able to reserve a room far from the elevator to reduce hallway noise. And the hotel in question (along with its sister properties if it's part of a franchise) would be wise to remember and automatically execute this preference for the next time you travel. Even better, book the same room for a loyal guest and then offer recommendations on other similar rooms which may be worth trying.

Remembering the little details that complete your guests' experiences will not only make them more loyal, but also more perceptive to your proffered extensions. It's a 'foot in the door' tactic to alleviate consumer skepticism. For example, suppose that you are new to Amazon's services. It's most likely the case that for your first or second purchases, you'll be 'testing' the service's reliability. Once that trust is formed, only then will you give serious consideration to some of the marketed items Amazon displays at checkout or within one of their e-newsletters.

As it concerns hotel e-newsletters, would you deem a golf e-blast to be as efficacious when read by a known spa customer or a golf customer? My bet's on the latter and the only way to discern between the two psychographics is via past data on spending habits. Amazon does this expertly with emails and cookie-based browser widgets coded from a shopper's past purchases.

"But it doesn't hurt to advertise with the spa customers," shouts the cynical hotelier. This is a double-edged sword. True, targeting spa people will raise awareness for your golf program and compel a few to spend. But, it might also compel them to ignore future e-newsletters as there's no personal value in the current edition, so much so that when a spa-specific advertisement comes their way, it's already in the trash.

Taking another look at airlines and how they treat their loyal customers, there are many other cross comparisons for hotels. Instead of increased mileage accumulation, how about increased complimentary

F&B? Priority luggage equates to priority check-in and check-out. Waived baggage fees or service charges should hopefully get you thinking about waived Internet fees, free spa treatments or rounds of golf. How about a dedicated phone line for specific services or for catered offers to certain classes of guests? Use your imagination.

The idea behind customized loyalty requires a full shift in mentality towards valuing everyone as having elite status, or at least the potential of becoming loyal, elite guests. You need to ask lots of questioning and note taking when it's a guest's first time with you. Motivate them to complete an online survey prior to arrival so you have a better idea (and a record) of what they want. Keep in mind that people hate being over-questioned to the point of interrogation, so counter this by explaining your long-term motivations for this program and how much you value their personal preferences.

Obviously with all this data collection comes a need for lengthy software upgrades. Rest assured, your dollars and time spent will translate into heightened loyalty. Return guests are cheaper than new guests after all. Augmented data collection systems will help you maintain your current clientele and get them talking about how much they are valued at your property, continuing the marketing efforts for new consumers on your behalf. Treat customers like friends and the sky's the limit.

Cvent: A Group Sales Automation Tool

Reggie Aggarwal, Founder and CEO of Cvent, speaks in a slow deliberate fashion. When asked to describe his approach to business, he replies, "Running scared always, and the paranoid survive." Perhaps those hotel managers who do not embrace his computerized group RFP system are the ones who should be scared.

In 2008, Cvent solicited about $60 million worth of meeting RFPs on behalf of prospective meeting planners to hotels in their system (meeting value defined as guest room sales plus ancillary charges). In 2011, Cvent's throughput reached nearly $4 billion. For perspective, Reggie estimates this to be about 10% of the total worldwide group meeting business. Impressive, yet with lots of room for growth!

Reggie accomplishes this with a staff of 850 that helps manage 500,000 events in 50 countries. These numbers led to a further $136 million investment, which according to the Wall Street Journal, is the biggest US software deal since 2007 and the largest in the history of the events technology industry.

But it wasn't always this way. On 9/11, Mr. Aggarwal's business was a typical, budding dot-com with 126 employees and very limited revenue. When the bubble burst and reality hit, his immediate goal was survival, leading him to shed 80% of Cvent's staff. As he puts it, "Sometimes you need to be dumped in cold water to wake up." Looking retrospectively, he thinks this allowed him to effectively get back to fundamentals.

Reggie claims success has come from a focus on corporate culture. With over 90% of all senior managers having been with Cvent for 10 or more years, his team thrives on a culture that maintains its innovation and entrepreneurial spirit. Reggie calls this 'core energy'. His concern is that the outer organizational rings might start losing their core energy, and in doing so, Cvent becomes just a 'job', something he wants to avoid at all costs.

Cvent's mission is to make it easy for meeting and event planners to do their jobs. Cvent offers four products: an event management solution, a strategic meetings management offering, a web surveys tool and the Cvent Supplier Network—a free online marketplace connecting event planners with venues. The latter is of particular interest. By offering the Cvent Supplier Network to planners for free, Cvent becomes nearly irresistible. After all, why canvass five hotels separately when one single RFP issued and managed online will provide all of the information necessary to make a final decision? Moreover, the Cvent Supplier Network has meetings-specific search criteria and the ability to make apples-to-apples comparisons of RFPs received from venues. For example, while both respectable in their categories, a Four Seasons and a Four Points should probably not be directly compared in an event search.

For the hotel, Cvent offers a wide variety of opportunities via the Cvent Supplier Network, from basic listings through to special promotional programs designed to raise the awareness of the property in front of targeted meeting planners. All of this is priced in accordance with the level of participation that each property seeks. Since a lot of the materials you use to respond to RFPs are boilerplate, the use of the Cvent system allows sales teams to focus on the differentiating elements unique to the proposed meeting.

A great modern tool indeed, but thinking that participation in Cvent is the panacea to building your property's meeting 'funnel' is somewhat naïve. According to several hotels that I spoke to, and corroborated by Cvent personnel, Cvent success requires a three-part strategy.

First, make sure your hotel is in Cvent and the information is completed in all aspects of the Cvent web site (also known as forming a rich profile). "Hotels need to be where their customers are," as Reggie says. Second, Cvent encourages hotels to respond to RFPs quickly. It makes no sense to do all the work to get an inquiry, only to see the request languish. How fast is adequate? In the Internet world, 24 hours is the target response time. Your sales staff should manage accordingly. Third, depending upon your business needs, you might consider some of the promotional packages offered by Cvent. This element of the strategy should be tailored to the individual property, and from my perspective, rationalized along with other marketing programs such as Google Adwords.

With all of this automation, I asked Reggie if a property still needed a sales team and could manage the Cvent system without them. He was adamant that the Cvent Supplier Network was never meant to replace a sales team or to change the relationships between planners and suppliers. Rather, it's a complement for your current efforts and an extra avenue to get your property in front of highly qualified prospective planners. Sales staff are still needed to close the sale. Importantly, with Cvent improving the qualifications of prospective customers, your sales team will be more focused on finalizing deals, thereby improving their close ratios.

Reggie's vision is, "To be the Microsoft Outlook of the industry." To me, his vision is sound. Perhaps a more appropriate metaphor is that Cvent is transforming into the sole OTA of the meeting planner channel. And he's well along the way to accomplishing this goal.

B4Checkin Internet Booking Engine: An Interview with Saar Fabrikant

The first Internet booking engines were somewhat crude, clunky and expensive. Hoteliers had to load room inventory onto the system independently as they didn't properly link to the property's internal PMS. Luckily, those days are long gone, and most Internet booking systems offer two-way interfaces. There are numerous providers of Internet booking engines; a field currently dominated by two excellent products: TravelClick's iHotelier and Sabre's Synexis. Both are widely available, offering a myriad of add-ons and back-end systems designed to enhance connectivity and rooms inventory management.

But, just when you thought this was a two-horse race, a number of new entries have come into the market. One of them deserving your attention is a Canadian-based upstart called B4Checkin. I had an opportunity to spend some time with the company's Founder and CEO, Saar Fabrikant, to talk about their positioning in the industry.

1. **Tell me a little bit about the history of booking hotel inventory over the Internet.**

    According to a survey by the Hotel Association of Canada, and parallel activity by AH&LA, nearly three-quarters of all hotel reservations are made online. This is either through an OTA like Expedia or on the hotel or hotel brand's web site. This is a stark contrast to 10-15 years ago when the telephone was the dominant channel.

    By using the Internet, the online booker can easily compare services, facilities and prices for a variety of hotels. They can also access an OTA to get this information in one place.

    In order for properties to take advantage of the online travel booker, it's necessary to have a searchable, aesthetically-pleasing, and functional web site with booking capabilities. This will allow the property to meet the guest's information needs and to make a reservation.

    These hotels require a 'booking engine' application to be attached to their web site to permit people to book rooms in real time. One advantage of booking directly with the hotel is the use of the hotel's full cancellation policy as well as not needing a deposit, as is the case with most OTAs.

Based on these increasing trends, it's important that hotels have a robust and functional booking engine to capture the reservations of the modern traveler.

2. When you first looked at starting your venture, what was the status of these booking interfaces.

B4Checkin was started as a custom solution for the Canadian hotel management firm, Centennial Hotels & Suites. They used Visual One as their PMS. It was determined after they used the product for 18 months that we met all performance criteria. The 'stand alone' non-interfaced version was developed next and we started to actively market the product. The next PMS we became certified with was Micros 'Opera'. With the addition of the Micros interface, we learned that interfaces were standardized through HTNG (Hotel Technology Next Generation) and that PMS vendors would not allow us to develop these interfaces unless they were initiated by existing or potential customers.

3. What was the unique niche that you wanted to exploit?

The simple situation where hotels were buying PMS packages, including reservation systems, then they had to decide whether to incorporate a third party reservation system, third party email CRM solutions or third party feedback systems. We identified this as a 'unique niche market' that was underserviced by a 'one stop shop' software methodology instead of treating it as 'an extension' of any given PMS, which is where we fit in.

4. The leaders in this industry are Sabre's Synexis and TravelClick's iHotelier. How do you successfully compete against these 'big boys'?

The big boys are selling a 'canned' solution, similar to Microsoft Office, which was designed for the masses. They are both large companies that have a full suite of products. Both companies added products after being primarily GDS providers. Their pricing models are a percentage of revenue or a dollar per transaction fee.

This can penalize a hotel with a large ADR or a high number of transactions.

B4Checkin offers a more customizable solution that has similar features to the 'big boys'. With Version 2.0, B4Checkin is the first booking engine to allow the customer to choose from four design templates. This allows the hotel to have a truly customized look. B4Checkin also charges on a flat monthly fee model that allows hotels to save thousands of dollars as booking volume increases.

5. Why did you pick Halifax, Canada as the home for your business?

I moved from Israel to go to school in Halifax, met my business partner at a co-op term I did prior to graduation with his previous company. From there, we started a software development company, then project managed a PMS installation for a group of Canadian hotels and identified the niche that led to B4Checkin. The rest as they say is history.

6. What are your Company's expansion plans?

From a tech perspective, we're currently in development of our platform to the latest technology and adding various new products to encompass all our offerings under one platform, as well as a couple of new product developments. From a sales perspective we are planning to start looking at Europe and Asia as new markets for us.

7. How does your product go beyond those of your competition?

Because we see ourselves as an extension of any given PMS, our products offer interactions for all customers present in the PMS, regardless of how they made a reservation. Whereas all our products focus on increasing and maximizing revenues from the most cost effective channel of any hotel, as well as retaining customers loyalty and feedback. We are currently the only player in the marketplace that focuses on all these types of products as our core business.

8. What does the future hold for this business?

Distribution in general has become the main focus of hotel operations, which changed radically from a decade age. OTAs and distribution channels literally created the revenue manager position in the hotel world. I believe the hotel industry is going to have to redefine the reality of expensive distribution channels. We're going to continue to develop tools to increase even further and maximize the value of the direct channel.

Could This Be The Best Hotel Site Ever Built?
An Interview With Robert Simon

When you have $5 million and a clean slate, what type of web site would you build? And, what process would you undertake to deliver the ultimate Internet experience? These were some of the questions I asked Robert Simon, Director of Web Development for Four Seasons Hotels & Resorts, following the launch of their revolutionary new site.

Implemented in late 2011, Four Seasons once again set a new standard in web design, replacing a site that had served this luxury chain for seven years before. Unfazed by the task, Robert was the leader of a team that at times reached 100 members at its peak. Of note, the team average was 42 members, with approximately 80% of this staff compliment outsourced.

Robert's background is totally non-hospitality. Prior experience managing Home Depot's Canadian web presence as well as a stint with the Canadian arm of London-based Isobar Interactive helped usher Robert into a 14-hour interview session that ultimately resulted in the job offer at Four Seasons.

Whereas the task at hand might have seemed daunting, Robert explained his approach in this way. "I was impressed with the existing web site platform, as it had served the chain well, averaging 3 million unique visitors per month and representing a not insignificant 12% of total chain wide revenue. Where the site fell down was that it did not have an open architecture, and thus, the technology of the site was hampering the ability of the site to respond to the growing needs of the Internet consumer."

The 12-month process that spawned the site's development was quintessential Four Seasons. The core philosophy focused on the user experience. This commenced with a three month travel adventure with Robert meeting with over 100 stakeholders (GMs and owners), interviewing each one to understand their desires and needs for future growth. With this initiative setting the goals, prototype designs were tested with past guests through a series of focus groups undertaken in three centers: Philadelphia, Shanghai and Doha.

Once the overall design elements were selected, imagine the process of collecting the appropriate materials for the 91 individual properties that would comprise the site. For each individual property, the requirements of photography (both professional as well as guest-sourced through social networks such as Flickr and Instagram), property facts, descriptive text and local activities all had to be incorporated into the build out. At the same time, social media considerations were paramount, with immediate integration of influencer comments from Twitter, Facebook and TripAdvisor.

To accomplish this rather massive undertaking, a new layer of staff, called producers, was created within the Four Seasons web team. Producers were assigned to each of the properties to assist the local teams in securing the necessary materials to complete the content requirements. Of note, the content management system of the site now has the flexibility to allow local property staff to make updates. Or, alternately, these updates can be undertaken through the Four Seasons head office web team.

Robert offers this advice to those hoteliers interested in revitalizing their own Internet presence. "It's the people we service. When the iPhone first came out it wasn't the best phone on the market from a hardware perspective. But the one thing the iPhone did better than any other phone is that it got better every day because of the new services you could layer on top of it. When thinking about your digital impact on the business, you're really thinking about your services architecture between web, mobile and hotel. How you orchestrate those services and make them consumable for customers as well as your operations is how to innovate and win."

While the core site was launched and functional, Robert saw several critical tasks that were completed under the hood. Social media integration was expanded. Additional languages (primarily French, Russian, Chinese and Spanish) were considered for mirror pages where it was requested by the property teams. A superior 'luxury tablet' solution that could take full advantage of the unique imbedded capabilities of this technology platform was also developed, as was a mobile version.

If you have not yet experienced the Four Seasons site, you're in for a treat. Give it a spin and you'll come away as impressed as I am.

Conclusions

Among the first websites we built back in 1992 was for the Post Hotel in Lake Louise, Alberta, Canada. I remember presenting the completed site to the owners as we marveled at the small-sized photo rotator. I also recall a statement made with some skepticism of the potential for booking significant business over the Internet.

That was 20 years ago. Times have changed, almost laughably so. Websites are a de facto requirement for all properties. There probably isn't a hotel manager on earth who isn't familiar with basic website functionality and the overarching goal of SEO. The same is probably true for social media and the integration of social media elements into the property's website presence.

But what about mobile and tablet technology. Will having a fully-functional, mobile-equipped website continue to be as importance as a conventional website displayed on a large monitor? Will the advent of broadly available 4G smartphone networks spur irreversibly shift the balance? Will the network integration of data management tools give hoteliers the ability to manage their entire operations through tablet and mobile devices?

Stay tuned. Just as the past 20 years have brought about a revolution in hotel marketing, expect the same to occur over the next two decades.

Online Travel Agencies

The Hotel Elysée in New York City is small and refined, yet exceptionally guest-friendly. Consistent top-10 TripAdvisor ratings are a natural for this property, whose management team understands their guests' appreciation for value-added extras.

Introduction to Online Travel Agencies

If you haven't figured it out by now, I have a 'mild' grudge against online travel agencies (OTAs). My qualm is not with the companies themselves, as I believe they are brilliant marketers, programmers and business operators. My problem is with the gradual process by which they are reducing the hotel industry to a series of price points rather than features and services. I've made my opinion known online and received all kinds of responses, some supportive, some skeptical and others in complete disagreement.

My hope is that in reading the previous sections, you can now understand where I am coming from. Whether you sympathize with my position or not, I hope you can appreciate why I value guest services over price-oriented valuations. So, read the following passages that further explore my side of the argument and then come to your own conclusion.

Will Online Booking Sites Kill the Planning Committee?

My first 'Executive Planning Committee Meeting' was at the Toronto Four Seasons in 1984. New to the business at the time and as the ad agency account executive, I was told the invitation by the GM (at the time, Klaus Tenter, still a close friend) was quite the honor! Back then, out of respect, you addressed the GM as 'Mister,' which seemed quite old fashioned, even for the 80s.

Fast-forward thirty years. Remarkably, planning committee meetings have not really changed. The same management positions meet to review the same issues their predecessors discussed. Yet, look at the changes we have experienced: the Internet, revenue management, automated meeting RFPs, social media, online reviews, and a myriad of systems designed to improve management decision making.

Perhaps the biggest game changers have nothing to do with the systems designed to enhance the hotelier's success. Rather they are the ones that evaluate performance: online booking web sites—the OTAs. Aside from word of mouth recommendations, third-party sites like Expedia, Travelocity, Orbitz and the behemoth that is TripAdvisor are the premier research tools when seeking a new travel destination, all boasting user-generated reviews, which can make managers, cringe.

All a reader has to do is log on, pick out a hotel where they have online proof of a past visit (sometimes even this isn't required). Type to their heart's content, click submit and voila! Barring any expletives, the review is generally posted within two-three days. Typically showcased as a new comment at the top of the listing, it will have status at the top and most viewed portion of the page. Due to the efficient layout of these sites, it's hard for web users not to notice the latest critiques and a steady stream of inflammatory remarks may work to turn potential customers away for good.

Even when the issues are small, they all appear bloated by their online facades. For example, one person might rate a stay as two out of five stars with the sole reason listed as a shortage of towels. Granted this is a problem, but hardly a deal breaker. Reviewers sometimes mark down the quality of their rooms based on mutually exclusive issues such as the pricing of restaurants or the friendliness of staff. All it takes is one finicky little thing to go wrong and a five-diamond resort now looks like a cubic zirconium.

Is it really fair to label a place as a bad experience solely as a result of a ten-minute wait for the concierge? Should tech-savvy patrons, often with a narrow range of hotel experiences, really be entitled to the same level of influence as seasoned magazine travel writers? I think not. And yet with the preeminence of the Internet, these misinformed critics continue to rise in power.

And there's almost nothing managers can do outside of checking the review sites everyday and responding to complaints after the fact. Unfortunately, in most cases reviews are permanent. Unless all operations are immaculate, users always seem to find something wrong to debase an otherwise sound excursion. My agency's hospitality clients are pleading with me, 'How do we address our TripAdvisor ratings?' Excluding a multimillion-dollar renovation, it all boils down to guest services.

Based on an independent analysis of over 1,000 different TripAdvisor comments for properties rated in the four or five diamond level by AAA, we found that over 90% of all commentary, either positive or negative, related to service issues. (Note that we used TripAdvisor for this research rather than digging into the reviews from individual OTAs, so the results might be different with, say, Expedia.) This brings us back to the hotel planning committee meeting: why has this meeting failed to adequately address the service issues critical to the property's success?

Nowadays, mid-level hotel managers, at least those in the planning committee, are few and far between. For instance, the room division manager might have under his/her direction: an executive housekeeper, engineering and maintenance manager, front desk manager and reservations manager. Each of these team leaders might also have several line managers reporting to them. With so many layers, the transmission of critical information often gets muddled as it moves up and down the totem pole, hampering the decision-making process. Thus, to address guest service issues, you have to first address the lines of internal communication.

Alas, every hotel manager I know is swamped with work. Throughout North America, the past decade has crunched middle management ranks. There are now fewer assistant managers and more work for everyone else. Schedules are often staggered, further hindering exchanges about service quality. The result: those attending planning committee meetings often have less time to evaluate how their teams' performances.

It's time for hoteliers to use technology to fight technology. To survive in this new era of speedy information dispersal, managers must fully embrace smartphones, social media and web-based monitoring systems—all potent tools for heightened communications. With any luck, over a short period of several months or so, these kinds of upgrades will work wonders to create an effective means towards more positive reviews. After all, the majority of people only view the most recent comments, so if you improve today, there'll be greener pastures tomorrow.

Would the Real Hotel Rating
Agency Please Stand Up?

In the pre-Internet years, hotel ratings were easy to understand. The American Automobile Association (AAA) awarded a 'Diamond Rating' and Forbes (Mobil pre-2009) used their 'Star Rating,' both on a scale of one to five. There are several other prominent organizations but for simplicity, let's focus on the two most pervasive authorities.

AAA and Forbes use qualified inspectors who follow a comprehensive and rigorous scorecard. They examine everything from scuffmarks on the edge of doors and dust on the drapes to the proficiency of guest services in every minute detail. Performance is justly weighted according to its significance; that is, a scuffmark will result in a much smaller deduction than a waiter neglecting to serve you at the restaurant. The inspectors show up unannounced and their results are shared with the property at the end of their appraisal; advanced notice given for any rating changes. By and large, the system is honest and egalitarian with the same technical criteria applied across the globe.

Hoteliers look towards their annual audit with a mix of anticipation, worry and dread. A decline in a rating level, let's say from 5-diamond to 4-diamond, could mean instant shame, an inability to rationalize the current ADR, reduced occupancy or certainly a lot of explaining to property ownership. A move up the totem pole is usually cause for celebration, often reflective of a sweeping renovation or steadfast dedication to service improvements.

With the rise of Internet review sites, this long-established ritual has just about gone the way of the proverbial dodo bird. Properties still have their ranks assigned to them by AAA and Mobil, but who really uses these systems as a primary resource? Which consumer demographics still anticipate the yearly rankings? Most importantly, how does this impact reservation volume?

I conducted some directional research on this topic in the Fall of 2010. Let me stress that this study was carried out amongst a limited database of one hundred respondents; by no means corroborated with an absolute degree of significance but a hunch nonetheless. The research consisted of a telephone survey amongst American adults in their 30s, split equally between male and female. To qualify, a valid passport was required and respondents had to have made a leisure trip via airplane within the past year. (Note that AAA is generally coined the 'king of car travel' and this study in no way reflected the critical importance AAA plays in helping American navigate the Interstate road network.)

The data was startling. Some 57% of interviewees were aware of the AAA Hotel Rating, but only 19% said they used this scale as a factor in their verdict to stay at a given property. The same query for Mobil/Forbes generated such abysmal metrics that I dare not repeat them here. However, our answers for TripAdvisor were the exact opposite. Of those questioned, 99% were aware of the site and 86% said they utilized its reviews and rating average as a part of their decision-making process.

It took AAA some 94 years to build a reputation as an honorable arbiter for destinations worldwide. Yet, in just over 10 years, TripAdvisor and its ilk have become the foremost bastion of the modern consumer. Their assessments are not the work of official evaluators, but of any individual who has previously stayed at the property. The reviews may be honest and 'at the speed of the Internet', but they may also be fraudulent schlock from a disgruntled ex-employee; and who's to be the wiser.

In September 2010, a band of 420 hotels and restaurants publicly considered taking TripAdvisor to court for their leniency towards defamatory posts. (In this book, you will also find an article on insurance protection now available to cover a property for damages resulting from this type of action.) The site now has tighter restrictions on who can post, but this nothing insofar as regulating how performance criteria are weighted. One key illustration of this is people marking down a five star resort for being overpriced. Oftentimes I've found these complaints to be written out of misinterpretation and spite; a guest thinking prices would be equivalent to a three star property then becoming disgruntled when they assess the real costs.

So what can you do? To start, we would never advocate apathy towards the traditional rating systems as we suspect they may still be beneficial for older patrons and group business solicitation. But the OTAs are here to stay and their clout will be a hot topic with property ownership for decades to come. With this in mind, there are some definite calls to action you can take to mitigate this dilemma.

First, scrutinize every detail of your online reviews. Were the criticisms written from a constructive point of view or merely inflammatory? Nevertheless, there's something to be learned from every opinion, even the unfair ones. If you get a negative report, post an honest and forthright response on the corresponding OTA. Stay calm and never debase your opponents. Above all, don't try to argue with the guest. It won't work.

Next, heighten internal communications. This does not just apply to the planning committee level, but right down to the direct line staff. Everyone must be in the know when something is done right, and especially when something is done wrong.

Third, be proactive. Encourage guests to write up their experiences on the OTA web sites. Consider linking these from your computerized evaluation feedback forms.

If you follow these three steps, you may still get some bad reviews. But, there's light at the end of the tunnel. Whether the write-ups are impartial or not is up for grabs; experience suggests that people have a tendency to exaggerate both the positives and negatives. The average traveler understands this. If they see a ratio of ten or twenty excellent reports to one less-than-favorable response, that one scathing eyesore will not become the deciding factor.

This 'law of the majority' applies with one volatile caveat: the most recent comments are shown at the top. This means that if you slip up, it'll find its way to the most viewable part of the site within a matter of days. On the contrary, if you work to steadily improve your operations, then this will also reverberate online. The guest sees and the guest knows. It's a consumer-driven market, and as long as you understand that principle, you'll be fine.

Hotel Reviews Aren't About the Numbers

Do you remember in school how jealous you felt when you got a 'B+' on your English test, while your friend got an 'A-'? Now that we are all grown up, hopefully, we can safely look back at how insignificant one grade was in the grand scheme of things. Apparently the lesson hasn't been fully learned. Many still look at their hotel review scores as if it were a college GPA.

Statistical methods must first be recognized. Is it really important if your property's star rating on a review web site goes from 4.6 to 4.3 within a two-week span? Why are property GMs micromanaging these tiny fluctuations? They're statistically irrelevant. In school, real performance changes were denoted by evaluating your report card handed out at the end of each semester. Much the same way, you can't judge your hotel on a review-by-review basis.

A caveat would be a significant jump, or decline, in rating aggregates. The engineer/statistics student in me reasons that a shift of +/-0.6% or greater probably would be deemed statistically worthy of note. But how often does a variation like this occur within a two-week or even a month-long span? Ratings typically move a tenth to two-tenths of a percent at a time. You'd be mistaken to fret over a drop of this size. Numerical micromanagement represents another risk of the Internet, as we're confounded with more metrics than we know how to handle.

It's a double-edged sword though. The solution is not to study the numbers with close scrutiny, but what the guests are saying. Alas, this isn't baseball; you can't fall back on something as thoroughly delineated as sabermetrics. Embrace the chatter and respond to deficiencies, rather than worrying about rating points.

One of the merits of online review sites is that they give guests an anonymous platform to be voice their criticism. Drawbacks aside, this system allows guests to be as sincere and forthcoming as possible. It affords them an outlet for their concerns, allowing you to gain new perspective on aspects of your performance that may not be wholly satisfactory. Before the proliferation of the OTAs, one can only imagine how many guests would stay silent over their particular dislikes, denying the hotels a chance to improve.

Word of mouth may be a powerful behind-the-scenes motivator, but word of mouse is open to the public, available for you to study and hopefully learn from. These web sites are your opportunity to gain new insights and constructive criticism about all parts of your operations. As well, replying to individual commentators is a great way to broadcast how willing you are to accept outside advice; further encouraging honest feedback. But all your response efforts will be negligible if you don't take your guests' suggestions to heart and develop a plan of action to correct your mistakes.

Evaluate quality from qualitative data then look for commonalities. Grab a pad of paper and take notes on each and every comment. After a couple dozen, you may start to notice some trends. What are the most frequent criticisms? Was the front desk staff regarded as friendly and cooperative? Housekeeping issues? Room service? Was restaurant food beyond what was expected or just adequate? How did the customer perceive your value equation?

A small number of reviews will undoubtedly be written with a very hurtful slant. Don't be frazzled, or worse, antagonistic. Every evaluation is an opportunity to learn, even if that wasn't the intent. Also, keep in mind the 'heat of the moment' frame. Online review sites allow people to vent their frustration before they've had time to cool down and consolidate their dissatisfaction into a rational, cohesive prose.

When you assess such negative remarks against the average and the long-run of events, you'll find it very similar to that one 'D' you got on a trigonometry exam back in grade eleven; the pain long gone and forgotten. Ditto for baseless diatribes against your property. Moreover, don't discredit the entire online community based on a few rotten eggs. The average poster is here to help, but only if you can be bothered to listen.

The key is to value the long-term over the short-term. Read reviews, group commonalities and develop your own quarterly scorecard for measuring qualitative performance over the past three months. Then put this scorecard up against previous metric surveys or past critiques. Is the situation improving? Are specific complaints less prominent or absent all together in the latest series of posts? The benefit of scorecards is that you can track particulars over a broad period of time; enough breadth for major trends to noticeably shift.

The other crucial tactic is to glance over the reviews of your key competitive set, keeping a lookout for occurrences where they are praised relative to where you are shammed. If their restaurant's food presentation is lauded while yours is merely pedestrian, then you best have a meeting with your F&B director and executive chef to address the discrepancy.

Look at this again from a guest services perspective. Most individuals arrive at your hotel with given expectations set by what they see on your illustrious website homepage and what others have said both in person and online. Such guests will be more obliged to grant you a positive grade if you meet or exceed their standards.

It's when you slip, however, that your online reviews will falter. Your staff jumbled a restaurant reservation. Front desk was near oblivious to a guest's needs. The room wasn't clean. A visitor's requests go unfulfilled. Take advantage of your hotel reviews to investigate and hone your guest service abilities.

I advocate that improving your overall rating aggregate is more dependent on guest service than on large-scale issues that require significant capital investment. Do most guests perceive the differences between a $2 million and a $5 million spa? It isn't something they can gauge, nor are they looking for it. More likely, would a guest notice when restaurant service is bad or when hotel staff is rude?

Do yourself a favor, read through all the Internet review chatter. Address the guests' issues, not the ratings. You'll know when you succeed because problems will disappear from the latest posts, or better yet, a recurring customer might even praise you for your conscious improvements. Regardless, hotel review sites are here to stay. The sooner you start paying attention to what people are writing, the sooner you will see your ratings improve.

No Defense for the OTAs

Are OTAs converting your customers into theirs? As you know by now, I believe this to be true. But there are still many hoteliers who think the opposite, and they're not without proof. Neither are the OTAs, who are interested in their own self-preservation.

One such rationale is what's called a 'billboard' effect. The concept: your hotel is prominently positioned on one of the OTAs for potential customers to find. This visual mention raises awareness for your property name. People might click through to your web site and they might even make a booking there. But, does anyone really think this happens with frequency?

Look at the OTA contracts then examine issues of channel conflicts. Realistically, the only reason an individual might purchase on your web site instead of the OTA is because the inventory on that particular OTAs' site is either not the right room or bed type or the desired dates weren't available. It's all but impossible for the price on your web site to be less than the OTA. If it was, you'd probably be in violation of your OTA contract.

Frankly, I just don't buy it. The self-serving arguments put forward by the OTAs are just that. Rightfully so, these OTAs are businesses designed to build their own corporate revenue, like any other well-oiled organization. They have exceptional advertising plans, often brilliant creative, expertly-produced booking engines and they have worked hard to establish their own branding and loyal followers. The power of their marketing programs can outgun even the largest hotel chain. So, let's call it what it is:

1. **OTA customers are not your customers.** You don't have them on your database for repeat marketing opportunities and they aren't a part of your loyalty marketing program. The motivation and drive for customers to choose your property through an OTA may not be the same as those for someone who came directly through your web site, a traditional travel agency recommendation, or word of mouth referral. OTA consumers most probably have less loyalty to you and a different set of expectations.

2. **OTA commissions are high.** Traditional travel agents are generally 10%, while OTAs are often 25-30%. In days where every dollar is precious, this commission level is a grave concern, especially for independent hotels where there's no corporate backbone to lean against. You can't equate marketing fees levied by a chain to this as chains give back to the individual property through extensive branding campaigns compounded over years of marketing activities.

3. **OTAs level the playing field.** More than that, they scorch the earth! All that work you did in branding and creating points of differentiation for your property go by the wayside. Your hotel's display within the OTA site is compressed into the exact same physical space as everyone else on the site. Our brains don't process text the same way we do color photography and themed menu displays (like what appears on a hotel's own web site). As such, there's not enough visual distinction for customers to remember or differentiate your property's distinct brand from the next twenty hotels on the list.

4. **OTAs' primary goal is to secure reservations.** The hotel a consumer selects is not really their primary concern. It's a large-scale volume business, whether your boutique property is selling or not. They want your inventory—even at a higher price—so they can sell rooms and hotel-air packages. That's how they make their money. Anytime a consumer clicks through and books through a hotel web site, it counts as a loss to them. In fact, everything about the OTAs' web sites is designed to motivate you to book through them.

5. **OTAs are still all about price.** Despite what might be stated to the contrary, the OTAs generate customers primarily on the basis of providing the broadest distribution at the lowest price. Just look at most OTA advertising strategies. They focus on offering the customer the best price, not necessarily the best travel experience, which is what should be touted by your property and brand.

6. **OTAs intrinsically have an easier to use web site than you do.** Why? Simple: they book the entire trip, air, hotel and car rental,

while you only manage hotel bookings. Remember, unless your guests are driving, your web site requires more work than the OTA to complete the booking.

Ultimately, the decision about how you maximize your return on inventory is in your control. Your revenue manager will help guide you insofar as the appropriate balance of channel opportunities. But beware: an independent property's success lies in cultivating its own core of loyal users and supporters. The odds of you finding these loyal guests in an OTA storehouse are somewhat remote.

OTA Debate: Is the Industry at Stake?

Since launching my campaign to raise awareness for some of the possible negative effects of the proliferating OTAs, I've received quite the backlash from fellow hoteliers. Despite the belief that the OTAs are in fact beneficial to the industry, there hasn't really been any significant proof to solidify this argument. OTA sympathizers all seem to have the British 'Stay Calm, Carry On' attitude. However much I try to view this issue through a bipartisan lens, there just hasn't been enough evidence to mollify my concerns.

The much-quoted STR report presented at the Hotel Data Conference in 2011 found that in the prior year OTAs accounted for 9.8% of rooms booked with property-direct sales amounting to 51.6%, brand.com 17%, CRS/voice 13.7% and GDS 7.9%. From this ratio alone, the OTAs' share seems rather benign. But let's apply some channel logic just to be sure. Direct property bookings are mostly group sales, wholesale and preferred contracts. This is business not considered 'up for grabs' from a consumer marketing standpoint. When we subtract this from chunk from the pie, the OTA share doubles to roughly 20%.

Look at the numbers again. Now imagine losing one fifth of your FIT customer base. These consumers are booking through the OTAs and are primarily, albeit subconsciously, loyal to them, not necessarily your hotel. Remember that the customers who come through an OTA have forgone all of your other marketing channels in favor of their location and price based services. Aside of the marginal click-through, these consumers' go-to for reservations is, first and foremost, an OTA website.

Furthermore, assuming that a conversion of OTA customers back into hotel customers can be accomplished while on property is naïve. Most FITs are looking to explore new places, and an OTA web site—which combines transportation and accommodations in a single booking interface, along with oftentimes cheaper prices—is fairly hard to resist. Unless such guests are utterly enchanted by their entire stay, someone who finds your property through an OTA will likely go through this channel again to find their next vacation. The OTAs' interfaces make it far too easy to seek out the 'next best thing' instead of prompting their clients to return to previously visited hotspots.

And after each trip when their friends ask them about where they stayed, I wonder how often the response is, "Oh, just some place I found online," or "I found this great site that let me get 4 star hotels for the price of a 2 star." This mentality shift is just the tip of the iceberg.

To give you a little perspective, my hardliner stance against the OTAs has come out of eight years of brand management for Procter & Gamble and PepsiCo, where wide-scale marketing campaigns were germane to the whole process. Bar none, television advertising, when well executed, delivered customers. Despite any television ad stigma that has arisen in the past decade, this medium still has far reach and the union of colorful visuals and sharp dialogue is undeniably pervasive.

The OTAs know this and are broadcasting some very sticky material to grow their market share. Conversely, hoteliers' use of this critical medium has nosedived in recent years—we're being out-advertised! My experiences working in numerous product categories predicate that voice share will eventually match market share; it's only a matter of time.

Another cause for alarm: Query any list of the Top 100 Worldwide Brands and you'll be hard-pressed to find a single hotel brand. True, the OTAs are not there either, but hotels have a one hundred year head start, so one would think they'd have some major equity already in their brands.

A large part of this problem may be that the hospitality industry is chock-full of new brand introductions from the major chain, each trying to wedge into an eclectic niche and out-decorate or out-boutique their competitors. There are now so many variations and sub-iterations of Starwood, Hilton, Intercontinental and the other major chains; it's dizzying to keep track of them all. And all are more or less missing the point—build your core brand first then diversify.

I wouldn't be surprised if the OTAs are featured on these world brand lists soon, but I cannot say the same for the major hotel brands, especially after they've become so diluted. How are customers supposed to identify with one hotel or another when they're marred in confusion? Just food for thought if you're considering any sort of brand segmentation in the near future.

This all said, we can debate the OTA issue ad nauseum, but it won't solve anything. It's the 'global warming' issue within the hospitality industry. Everyone knows we need to fight back and soon, but whoever acts independently will certainly become the loser.

With hotel GMs and revenue managers driven by a need to deliver short-term room and income targets, I fear this problem can't be solved at the individual property level simply by implementing a new pricing strategy. The charge has to be led by the corporate head offices at the major chains. And their actions will reverberate throughout the industry and even trickle down to benefit the independents.

So, my challenge to the big five in hotels (if they happen to be reading): stop being interior decorators. Have your core brand stand for something and tell the world through mainstream multimedia campaigns, not just one-off ads in *Travel & Leisure* or *Condé Nast Traveler* (both are outstanding publications, but by themselves insufficient to move core brand value indices). Invest in your business to build your brand's equity. Above all, be innovative and mange your channels, rather than having your channels manage you.

Is RoomKey the Game Changer We've Been Waiting For?

January 2012 was marked by the launch of what was touted as the panacea for our industry—a counterattack to the online travel agency onslaught that has so dramatically shifted the hospitality power structure. I am referring of course to RoomKey, the new OTA managed by the hotels. It's a very good try, but not enough to get a consumer to switch away from their current favorites.

For those who don't know, I encourage you to spend a few minutes touring this web site. Launched by a consortium of six major hotel chains including Choice, Hilton, Hyatt, Intercontinental, Wyndham and Marriott, the site allows visitors to search by destination to easily find a given property. Once a location and property is selected, the site refers a visitor directly to the selected hotel's official web site. This transfer is seamless to the user, and lo and behold, reservations are made directly with the property, thus avoiding the significant commissions OTAs proscribe.

RoomKey's aesthetics are sophisticated, clean and quite welcoming. The performance of the site is also exemplary. Try as I might, it completed searches quickly and flawlessly, delivering accurate results, even in locations I thought were obscure. Immediate results allow you to search by star rating or price. Links to Google Maps in the same interface allow for easy understanding of micro-location details. A terrific feature allows for instant email to a user's traveling companions of details on a prospective property. The question remains, why would a consumer go to this web site in lieu of their current favorite OTA? Frankly, at least at this stage, there's no reason to do so. Here's why:

1. **RoomKey is all about hotels and does not complete the journey**. Airlines? Car Rentals? Attractions? Restaurants? Stores? Sorry, but RoomKey is accommodations only. The OTAs cover the entire trip and that is a significant consumer advantage. Most travel planning starts not just with the hotel, but with the physical movement component, whether it be plane, train or automobile. Unless you're driving your own car or are privy to preordained business arrangements, you're likely to first search by airline for available

dates, and then browse accommodations that fit. It's usually the airline that has the least price flexibility, and so the leisure traveler first books the flight, then the hotel room, and lastly the car rental, dinner reservations or events. Does anyone expect a consumer to book their airline ticket through one of the other OTAs then mosey over to RoomKey for their hotel room booking (let alone go to a third site for their car rental)?

2. **RoomKey lacks completeness.** With inventory limited to the participating hotel chains, RoomKey is highly exclusionary. In many places, the smaller chains, independents and non-participants provide useful accommodation alternates. Without them involved, RoomKey is only a partial search tool. The OTAs have almost a decade leg up in terms of property input. And going beyond hotels, the OTAs offer a complete travel experience, with widgets that include everything from weather to travel advisories, from packing tips to essential travel tools.

3. **The OTAs have gone beyond the basics to include promotions, last minute offers and package deals**. In contrast, RoomKey's approach is straight up, no-nonsense, and just the rooms. For business, this is spot on. Business customers want a room, with location as the key decision factor. Leisure consumers, however, have a wider degree of flexibility. They're more prone to influences like a shiny deal or package. RoomKey doesn't offer any promotional activity, except for those that might be 'buried' within the participants' linked web sites.

4. **RoomKey has a major user convenience issue.** Inherent in the design of RoomKey, the interface efficiently pushes the user to the individual property web site for each booking. In doing so, there's no thorough storage of customer profiles, as this data resides with the booking property. While this is terrific for the hotel, it's counterintuitive for the user. Each time a booking is made, the consumer has to reenter all of his or her information, creating a new profile with each of the chains. If users were interested in only one hotel chain, they would already be booking with that company directly.

5. **What logic is there for the hotel chains to promote RoomKey?** I'm still scratching my head on this one. If I were the CEO of a hotel chain, I wouldn't see the logic of putting funds into promoting or advertising RoomKey, not unless all partners were equal financial contributors. That might indeed build a sizeable war chest. But for what purpose? It still doesn't help the one critical factor that the major hotels are facing—lack of brand awareness. Creating RoomKey as yet an additional brand to support and promote only serves to further dilute and complicate the branding challenges already being faced by the majors.

6. **The OTAs have a massive head start.** Is this a case of too little, too late? Perhaps. Look at the total dollars spent by the OTAs over the past five years. Look at the Alexa traffic ratings and you'll see a very tall mountain for the hotels to climb. In social media the OTAs are well ahead with tens of thousands of Facebook fans and Twitter followers. I'm afraid RoomKey doesn't have the legs to help customers make the switch. It'll take some very serious monetary efforts to bring RoomKey up to a standard the OTAs have developed organically over the past decade. Plus, one of the most important features of the OTAs is each hotel's inherent credibility through its numerous critiques. RoomKey will have to do some sizeable front-end promotions to get travelers to kick-start the review process.

Despite these drawbacks, I would very much like RoomKey to succeed. But unless it adds a lot more functionality, I'm afraid that it may be a hotel search tool for those sophisticated travelers who never use OTAs, and who go to the airlines then search hotels separately. If all properties were involved, it would be a terrific product for that narrowcast requirement. An OTA blocker? I would call it, is it currently stands, a speed bump.

Library Hotel Collection: Value-Added Charm, Real Luxury and TripAdvisor Gold

A business trip to New York City prompted me to try a new hotel. Based upon impressive TripAdvisor scores, I decided to eschew my traditional stay in one of the larger, well-known properties. TripAdvisor's ratings consistently ranked the four boutique-style Manhattan properties of the Library Hotel Collection (formerly HK Hotels) among its top ten locally. This feat immediately caught my eye, particularly given the hundreds of accommodation options available. I was determined to see if I could learn more that would shed some light on this incredible success.

At first glance, the web sites for the four properties were non-descript. What drew me in was a discussion on the home page regarding the value these hotels offered. The value-added services offered included breakfast, free WiFi, all-day coffee, newspaper, sports club membership and an evening reception with wine, all included in the price. While the text was small, and the details seemingly repetitive, in an era where 'the innkeeper lives to add pennies for everything', I was intrigued.

I selected The Elysée, located on 54th Street near Madison Avenue and close to several meetings I had that day. The property is small and narrow with 100 rooms and suites in a fifteen story structure; one so closely wedged between two office towers that it clearly had to be constructed before either one of them reached fruition.

Just a regular guest upon arrival at 3PM, I was greeted warmly by one of two doormen. The front desk had three staff on duty (surprising given the time of day and property size) and all seemed eager to welcome me. The room was in excellent condition, with a small but well-appointed bathroom. Everything worked perfectly; plants were real and the furniture clearly not out of some made-for-hotel catalog. In all, the room delivered more of the feeling you'd get from a small European boutique property.

Probably most impressive was the second-floor Club Room. Here, breakfast was served, as were all of the complimentary F&B services. The room was sectioned into be a library and a living room. This multi-purpose facility allowed The Elysée to deliver all of these value-added services in a cost-effective manner. Lensed differently, the luxury service here was being offered on a self-serve model.

My trip to The Elysée raises some very interesting questions regarding the travelers' appreciation for what we generically consider 5-star service criteria. Clearly, one of the critical ranking components within the TripAdvisor ranking is value, so there is an immediate survey bias for this as one of the core criteria. But ask yourself the question: Is value an important component to your guests? There are few, if any, hoteliers who would say no to this question. Henry Kallan, CEO of Library Hotel Collection, has gotten it right, at least from the guests' standpoint. He clearly understands the 'what counts' factors for success.

In conversation with a guest while waiting for the elevator, she remarked, "This property feels like home. Friendly staff, comfortable rooms, and no one asking me to sign for a few bucks everywhere I turn." Maybe we can all learn something from this in terms of how well-executed guest services relates to online appraisals.

Conclusions

Despite my hellfire and brimstone prophecies, the OTAs are here to stay. Although I'd love for them to change their formatting to better highlight features versus pricing, with their current adoption rate amongst properties, I doubt they'll be willing to change in a way that might decrease their reign of power.

It's hard for hotels to change as well. I have to agree that the old adage of 'go where the customers are' demands OTA compliance. Few hotels can rightfully deny the benefits of opting in to these prevailing channels. Even with their exorbitant commission rates, you need their revenue stream. But this says nothing about provisions for the near future. Don't be an ostrich and keep up your tunnel vision when it comes to your revenue streams. Sit back and assess all factors on a long-term basis, much like our venerable llama!

How are you going to distinguish your brand in the face of such commoditization? How will your property be unique? What strategy marketing plans can you implement now to increase your brand awareness so that you are not reliant on cash flow from the OTAs?

Again, I believe that the answer lies in guest service. And for improving this aspect of your operations, the OTAs have significant value. It's a double-edged sword though. People will always complain for the sake of complaining, but reading between the lines are nuggets of constructive criticism.

Ask yourself what guests consider most important when they express themselves online. Your job is to extrapolate these insights from OTA reviews, then improve the effectiveness of your guest services accordingly. Flawless operations combined with strategic marketing will surely drive new business and customer loyalty to a point where the OTAs are no longer vital to revenue.

Free WiFi

Don't let the exterior of Tallahassee's Hotel Duval fool you! The lobby and the variety of rooms will delight your sense with an eclectic combination of design elements.

Introduction to Free WiFi

Along with my strong feelings for how online travel agencies are affecting the hospitality industry, I've also stated my case for why offering free WiFi on property is important for organic growth. It may seem like a no-brainer, but there is still some strong opposition to this idea. Since starting my campaign midway through 2011, I've read articles in support of my argument, yet there has not been much action by hotels.

I consider the case for free WiFi to be deeply related to my qualms against the OTAs. It has to do with a generational shift. For the longest time, the baby boomers held court over market trends and demands. However, this is rapidly changing as the baby boomers continue to get older and the Internet dominates our social interactions.

Young people nowadays are tech savvy and heavily reliant on a connection to the World Wide Web. They have been raised in an era of convenience—both in terms of speedy hotel reservations through an OTA and easy Internet access via wireless systems. As I'll soon explain, free WiFi is becoming an expectation, rather than a bonus, and while it is important to provide extra value to your guests, you have to meet their expectations first.

The difference here is that installing free WiFi networks, and thus fixing the problem, can be done on the cheap. Much like my recommendation for how to deal with the OTAs, read through my explanation and form your own opinion.

Let Freedom Ring: Free WiFi is a Basic Right, Not a Profit Center

I am well aware that the concept of free WiFi Internet in hotel rooms is an aspiration of every hotel manager. However, based on my stay at the Hilton Hotel in downtown Toronto, I don't believe that such managers truly grasp how fundamental it is to provide this service.

As a P&G Alumni, I was delighted that the corporation's global reunion was being held in my hometown, using none other than the first-rate conference facilities at the Hilton. Even though I am a local, it's still a grueling commute to get downtown early in the morning. The last thing I want to do after standing and socializing for fourteen hours straight is drive back to my house in the suburbs, only to repeat the process the following day.

So I get a guestroom for the evening. When I arrive, everything is in order. It's clean, chicly decorated with a business desk, ergonomic chair, plasma TV, comfy bed and reading chair. This is a beautiful room, worthy of the property's 4-star rating in AAA. My plan was to unwind and answer emails until my eyes caved in. Problem: there's no WiFi. So now I have the options of going down to the lobby and using their free wireless, or sitting upright at the desk and plugging in their Ethernet cable which doesn't reach the bed. Only the in-room Internet is nearly $15 per day, and seeing as how I only had about an hour's worth of memos in me, that would make it the costliest hour of web surfing I've had to endure all year.

It's not the actual cost that annoys me. A sum of $15 is paltry. But the mere fact that they would force an additional payment is, frankly, insulting. I'm in the business world, and in case you've been living under a rock for the past decade, all of my colleagues use a little thing called the World Wide Web; fairly often too. In fact, most of us can't live without it these days. It's an essential business service. So, to me, a fee for in-room Internet is equivalent to charging a bottle of water to a dehydrated Bedouin after emerging from a month-long trek in the desert.

Weary and unkempt, I changed back out of my PJs, threw on some street clothes and marched down to the lobby for some good old free WiFi. Note that the Hilton lobby's WiFi was password protected, which

I liked for two reasons. A password implies a basic level of security, giving me partial relief that my computer won't be hacked. And to obtain the password, I had to visit the front desk, which I deemed the perfect opportunity to instruct the hotel staff about the towering significance of having free WiFi in every room.

"We're looking into it," the front desk manager scoffed. Sorry to burst your bubble, sir, but looking into it just doesn't cut it. As a traveler primarily for business, I am adamant about having wireless service in my room for the simple reason that it makes me more effective at my job. It lets me relax my feet and work right up until I nod off. The room was superbly furbished, but the lack of free in-room WiFi was a deal breaker. Would I recommend this property to my business colleagues? Until this qualm is rectified—doubtful.

I find this to be a rather bogus situation because free WiFi is a straightforward issue to fix. I say 'straightforward' and not 'easy' because there is nothing easy about installing secured server access into 600 suites or more all at once. But it is straightforward nonetheless. It's not like the hotel management has been tasked with executing a long-run rebranding strategy. For IT upgrades like this, I'd wager there's a well-defined procedure to follow. Whatever costs are incurred will be effortlessly recovered through heightened customer loyalty.

You go to Starbucks and pay $5 for a designer coffee and you get free WiFi. You go to a luxury hotel and pay $250+ for a designer room and you get an additional bill for 15 bucks. What's wrong with this picture? Does this mean Starbucks knows more about guest service than hoteliers do?

I'm not naïve enough to enter this diatribe without knowing all too well about the legacy Internet contracts that have many hotels in a stranglehold. Too often was the case where hotel management agreed to usage surcharges that would now be deemed archaic, goaded into binding long-term agreements by lucratively cheap installation fees. This is a cost properties must eat, not forward to the consumer as a method to ensure short-term profitability. By comparison, you have metered contracts with the local utilities. Does this mean you charge guests for electricity and water separately? It's 2012; start thinking of the Internet the same way.

A 2011 United Nations report has deemed that disconnecting people from the Internet is a violation of human rights and a breach of international law. Is it going too far to suggest that any property that fails to provide complimentary WiFi is in violation of guests' rights?

In retrospect, I don't feel angry with the Hilton for their failure to provide this essential business service. I feel sorry for them because I'm certain they're losing customers every day over this very curable grievance. And if your hotel doesn't have free WiFi in every room, then I feel sorry for you too.

Let Freedom Ring Part Two:
Reasons and Solutions

The bottom line with free in-room WiFi is that consumer behavior now has some very lofty standards when it comes to web surfing. Internet connectivity is a necessity for many, if not the majority, of travelers. They want it readily accessible and fast.

So when a property charges for this service, it's not a matter of cost, it's a matter of undermining consumer expectations. People won't understand hotel legacy contracts, nor will they care. All they see is an additional bill for something that should be a part of the room fee, like heating and air conditioning. That's how consumers view the Internet these days—a utility—and you'd be wise to treat it as such.

A caveat to mention before we delve into some nitty-gritty is the distinction between regular Internet access and WiFi. The former is wired, and the latter is wireless. I advocate that providing wired in-room Internet is an insufficient tactic, whether it's free or not (although free is always better). Most smartphones and tablets run solely off wireless Internet. Given their widespread adoption, it would be smart to cater to these devices. There's also the comfort factor. Ethernet cables can only reach so far, but WiFi can be picked up from a desk, bed, washroom or perhaps while dining at the hotel restaurant.

Needless to say, I've received quite the backlash for writing on this issue, beginning with the outright denial that there's a problem. To clarify: free WiFi is not a make-or-break feature. True, some travelers look for places that specifically offer this service, but for argument's sake, let's ignore this social media savvy and rapidly growing populace. For 'regular' guests, free WiFi will not be the single factor to dissuade them from returning or not, but it will exacerbate how other grievances feel.

On the flip side, when you do offer this service, it'll imbue your guests with the sense that you empathize with the modern traveler—one little feature to amplify positive feelings about your hotel. Compared to refurnishing rooms or upgrading facilities, this is a very cheap endorsement to buy. From a social media perspective, when the Internet is served on a silver platter, it's an open invitation for guests to sing your praises online.

The next set of disbelievers contended that I didn't provide enough numerical evidence to justify web services as a primary issue for guests. I implore you to do your own Google search if you're still skeptical. Offhand, I found the May 16, 2011 issue of *Business Travel News* for support. In the magazine, they ranked hotel traveler services according to importance (I) and performance (P). The winner was clean, comfortable rooms (I = 5.6, P = 5.0), but the close runner-up was in-room high speed Internet access (I = 5.4, P = 4.8). In-room wireless connectivity ranked sixth behind good value for price, adequate number of staff at the front desk and proper lighting at the desk and chair for working.

Consulting the late 2011 edition of *Condé Nast Traveler's* 'What Matters Now?' some interesting statistics were offered about American affluent travel trends derived from over two thousand surveys completed in April 2011. When prompted about complimentary WiFi connections, 82% of respondents agreed that this is an expectation, not a bonus. This percentage is up from 69% in 2009 and is now the top affirmation in its set.

This is a very similar situation to how people reacted when airlines started charging an additional fee for checked bags. Travelers adapted and began to ration their luggage. They packed a check bag only when necessary and they pushed the limits for what was acceptable as a carry on, both in size and weight. In the end, this still worked out great for the airlines. Less overall luggage meant they saved on fuel costs, and were able to earn a little extra in the process. When it comes to hotels, I have observed a likewise rationing, but unlike the airlines, consumers have a lot more options to circumvent additional fees.

A fair number of guests will only pay for in-room Internet access if it's essential. If they only need the World Wide Web for a few simple tasks, they'll likely work off their smartphone's 3G or 4G data plan. For groups, I've noted that one person might bite the bullet with the Internet surcharge, and then everybody else in his or her party will go in rotation to use that one authorized computer.

Or, many guests will seek out places offsite with free WiFi, and while they're at it, they'll probably eat out, too. Many smartphones can easily be equipped with applications that aid in the search for free Internet hubs, and restaurants for that matter. This is serious. Do yourself a favor and don't let Internet obstinacy become a detriment to your F&B sales. Your guests have options, and they will exercise them wherever possible.

Alas, even though you might wholly appreciate the need for free in-room WiFi, sometimes it just isn't in the cards. As such, I've thought up three alternatives that will adequately appease your consumers. All of which I've based off hotels and reward programs that already employ such tactics with excellent results.

- **Tiered Plan***:* Make your WiFi free only for suites or premium rooms. The waived fee becomes an additive perk, helping to validate a more expensive purchase and giving travelers another incentive to upgrade.
- **Package Deal:** Offer your Internet services as a part of a larger amenity bundle which might also include free breakfasts or spa discounts. Get creative with this one. Think of it as a lifestyle package, encompassing a variety of features that make your brand exceptional. Guests will spend more time and money at your hotel, making their experiences all the more enjoyable.
- **Enhanced Web Portals:** In addition to being an Internet gateway, these innovative systems can integrate hotel amenities such as laundry, dry cleaning and room service. The portal companies will handle the upkeep costs to satisfy guests with free access in exchange for advertisements; an easy tradeoff. During initial negotiations, you could even ask one of these companies to help install thorough WiFi networks. They'll likely be receptive to the idea because it'll translate to more Internet and advertising traffic.

Let Freedom Ring Part Three:
A Final Word

No matter how hard I preach, real change is often slow. Capital-intensive projects take time. So, let's first discuss the difference between an expectation and a value-added service. The former is one you meet in order to keep your guests content. The latter is one that actually makes them happy. In this day and age, with the dirge of OTAs always ready to serve up your competition, only meeting expectations won't suffice. Time conquers all, and what is nowadays perceived as additive will soon regress to an assumed service.

Back in the mid-90s when the World Wide Web had yet to reach maturity, Internet access at a hotel was value-added. It wasn't anywhere near the norm, and thus, sure to impress, even when offered at a hefty daily surcharge. Within a decade urban properties without basic Internet service exuded a rustic and archaic aura while in-room access and wireless became the new paid-for extras.

By 2012, however, both these 'extras' segued into expectations. That's the speed of the world we now live in. To help me compute all this pandemonium, I like to apply the banal Spanish expression, "Mi casa es su casa." Whatever the average middle-class suburbanite presumes as standard living amenities is what you must provide for free. Twenty years ago, that laundry list would include heating, air conditioning, basic cable and a functional bathroom, but now, wireless is on it as well.

As we've seen with the resounding uproar against SOPA and PIPA bills in early 2012, the Internet has a nagging way of demanding freedom of speech as well as freedom of cost. Charging $15 (or more) per day for Internet access is outright insulting. You can argue all day and night about how you've been ensnared by a lawyer-proof legacy contact, but do you honestly think the customer gives an iota about all this behind-the-curtains nonsense? Frankly, your costs have nothing to do with your rates. Remember it is market factors that dictate a successful rate structure.

Guests expect free Internet and they're going to get it whether you have it or not. So, you have two options. Adapt and keep your guests satisfied. Or, ignore all this and let your guests wander down the street to the neighborhood Starbucks. Not only will you look bad for lacking quality service, but your F&B will suffer. And it's not just Starbucks that's doing it right, but other major food chains, trains and airport lounges are all conforming to this new standard.

In order for hotels to fully get in line, there needs to be a fundamental change in outlook. There have been many studies published over the past few years highlighting how important free WiFi is for guest satisfaction. Whenever I read these papers, I see the phrase, "The majority of hoteliers now realize free WiFi a great feature for business travelers," or, "Hoteliers now believe the Internet is most important feature to offer leisure guests." Your spa and gym are features, but the Internet is a necessity. If you recognize WiFi as such, you'll have no problem adapting to any future technological upgrades.

I cannot stress how important this mindset shift really is, particularly when considering the next generation of travelers. I'm talking about the millennials—the kids who've been ushered into a world without knowing what it was like before wireless connectivity. As sad as it may seem, the baby boomers (myself included) can only dictate the market for so long. You need to grow your popularity amongst the next generation if you are planning to stay afloat long-term. To many teens and young adults, a lack of free Internet is surefire method to destroy your chances of earning their loyalty.

One final note on loyalty programs. Many already offer free in-room Internet connectivity as a part of their package. But why would someone new join a loyalty program if the hotel in question hasn't made a good impression with their essential services? Is heating and air conditioning a part of your loyalty program, too? Guests will not purchase your loyalty program just to avoid inflated daily Internet fees. They'll buy in because they're impressed by your basic service offerings, which just so happen to include free in-room WiFi.

But enough of my fatidic diatribe; let's look again to solutions. When it comes to legacy contracts, it's best to rip the BandAid off fast and clean. Scan through the original agreement and you're sure to find some sort of buyout fee. Bite the bullet and prevent yourself from slow loss of all your customers over such a trivial matter. The beauty here is that if you do this now, there's still time to advertise that you are now offering free WiFi. But this window is rapidly closing. When you finally sneak out of your legacy contract two years from now and try to advertise such a feat, no doubt you'll be hearing snide laughter from all around.

Conclusion: Lessons Learned from the Movie *The Dictator*

When a movie like *The Dictator* starts to mock WiFi charges, it's time for an industry change. I had the pleasure of seeing Sasha Baron Cohen's latest movie recently and thoroughly enjoyed it for what it is—a slapstick piece of risible nonsense. Yes, it's crude, racist and misogynistic. And yes, the jokes require an IQ of no greater than 80 to process. But I was never expecting some grand contribution to the dramatic arts. If you can switch off reality for an hour and a half, then you'll be laughing nonstop.

The story of *The Dictator* portrays the eccentric tyrant, Admiral General Aladeen, of the fictional rogue North African state, Wadiya, who travels to New York City for peace talks at the United Nations. Most of the humor in this raunchy 'fish out of water' tale plays around with common stereotypes held for Muammar Gaddafi, Kim Jong-Il and their ilk as well as terrorists like Osama Bin Laden.

Between talks of secret nuclear programs and anti-Western and anti-Semitic remarks, Aladeen still had time to insult the hotel industry. When he first arrives in New York City, amidst unpacking in his 85 luxurious suites, Aladeen inquires about connecting to the Internet. His chief advisor promptly replies that it'll be an additional 20 dollars, at which point the Wadiyan dictator scoffs and compares this surcharge to his own malevolent actions.

Forgive me, as I cannot remember the exact line, but this gag thrown at hotels sent an uproar of laughter throughout the theatre. For the joke to hit its mark, it had to poke fun at something almost universally understood. And what's understood is that an additional hotel fee for Internet access is highway robbery.

Now this is a problem. If it's universally understood that there will be surcharge for Internet access, then a guest will likely make alternate preparations before arrival to avoid the needless fee. They'll download all necessary files and emails beforehand, or they'll map out the closest free WiFi carrier. Either way, it's a revenue loss.

But this can also work to your advantage. If the expectation is to be charged for Internet connectivity, then imagine a visitor's surprise when you offer it for free!

I contend that offering free wireless Internet is the only way to go. Even today and with *The Dictator* as proof, free WiFi is still an excellent opportunity to impress guests with superior service additives.

Examples of Hotel Excellence

From the tranquility of this hotel, you'd never guess that the COMO Metropolitan is in the heart of Bangkok. The attention to detail and commitment to personal service exemplifies the esteemed Asian approach to guest service.

Introduction to Examples of Excellence:
Five Strategic Examples of Strategic Marketing

Over the course of this last section, I will draw from the collective wisdom of the intelligent and experienced community of hoteliers that I've come to know and befriend over the years. This should serve as inspiration for your future endeavors by perhaps touching on specific aspects that affect your hotel or resort operations. Learn from the best and apply what works. Here are some short examples of marketing that works:

1. **Embrace Your Local Constituency**. Built on a verdant 220-acre property just outside of Los Angeles, Ojai Valley Inn & Spa is dedicated to being a community leader. Their 'Arts & Leisure' program includes special events throughout the year that emphasize the wellness-lifestyle standards of a 5-diamond resort as well as a strong neighborhood orientation. The itinerary includes guest speaker luncheons with authors and film actors, tea tastings, movie screenings, art classes, vintner dinners with guest chefs and wine tastings. In this way, the Inn helps bring together both guests and locals to events that may not otherwise come to this small Californian town. On top of all this, profits from the events are donated to local charities. This program has been scaled down since its original inception, but its fundamentals are without question brilliant.

2. **Create an Event to Increase Property Profile.** The Cranberry Golf Resort is a lakefront vacation destination north of Toronto with an interesting predicament. One of their goals is to attract the business crowd, but there's a nearby conference center many times their size. Moreover, none of the participating small to midsized companies can afford high caliber speakers on their own; they have to cluster at a large venue.

   The solution is differentiation. The resort organizes yearly leadership symposiums for groups of companies, giving them full access to the resort's amenities, F&B and golf course. Not only does this event yield modest profits, but it is quite literally the ultimate 'sampling' amongst key decision makers, and augers well for further corporate business.

3. **Turbo-Charge an Existing Event.** The Westminster Kennel Club Dog Show is one of the longest running sporting events in the world. Held each year at Madison Square Garden in Manhattan, the show attracts over 2,000 dogs along with their trainers and handlers, as well as tens of thousands of fans. And located directly across the street from all this excitement is New York's Hotel Pennsylvania.

   Everyone at the hotel eagerly anticipates the event, and management has reciprocated their love with welcome dog treats, an onsite spa for dogs (Spaw!) and even a Doggie Concierge. With this sort of pampering and a location that can't be beat, why would a dog and its owner want to stay anywhere else? As for the regular guests, they love the dogs, too! Every year, the hotel's efforts turn into a bigger and bigger success. Ask yourself, are there any local events that your hotel could better cater to?

4. **Segment Planning: Going Beyond FIT to ES.** The global slowdown of 2008-2010 hit the FIT segment hard, particularly in resort destinations. Windtower Lodge & Suites in Canmore, Alberta, solved this challenge admirably by reassessing their room inventory. Many of their suites include a full kitchen, living area and laundry facilities, so they concluded that the property was well suited for long-term guests. Using their web site as a primary marketing tool, Windtower repositioned itself as able to handle both FIT and extended stays.

5. **Extending Your Brand Into All That You Do.** COMO Hotels and Resorts operate eight luxury hotels throughout the world; locations range from downtown Bangkok and Parrot Cay in Turks & Caicos to the remote Himalayan Kingdom of Bhutan. All properties exude an aura of well-being and COMO applies this core philosophy to all facets of the organization, bringing a unique sense of balance to their business approach. For their guests, this is palpable upon entry.

And the same oasis of calm one feels while at one of their destinations is translated with perfection to their social media, electronic newsletters and printed material. It's this marriage of outstanding guest services with the subtler qualities of their marketing efforts that bolster exceptional repeat stays and strong sales conversion rates.

Notice that these programs were creative solutions and they did not rely on a price discount to achieve success. Each activity builds the property's brand reputation; something especially important to help fight the commoditization of the hotel industry.

In looking at your own marketing program, examine your property's situation and features. See what guest benefits can be derived from talking about your key points of distinction in fresh, new ways. Then start talking about them. Now that's marketing excellence!

COMO's Luxury Philosophy: An Interview With Commercial Director Simon Kerr

I had the opportunity to sit down with Simon Kerr from COMO Hotels and Resorts in early 2011; a brand I've had the pleasure to work with extensively over the past few years. Simon is the commercial director based out of London and a dear friend of mine.

Tell us a little bit about your background. Why COMO Hotels and Resorts?

I have been with COMO Hotels and Resorts for just over five years now. My responsibilities cover all commercial aspects of our business. My background prior to joining COMO has always been in the hospitality industry. After training in Hotel Management, I specialized in Sales & Marketing and my career has included time with InterContinental, Hilton and Marriott International at the world famous Grosvenor House Hotel on London's Park Lane.

I was drawn to a career with COMO because of the vision of the company. Our owner, Mrs. Ong's passion for both hotels and holistic wellness has created unique properties and guest experiences in wonderful locations around the world. My days are full of variety and can cover discussions ranging from trekking in Bhutan, to Yoga Retreats in Bali, private home rentals in The Caribbean and exclusive events at the world famous Met Bar in London.

What was the genesis of the Company?

The company was started 20 years ago with the opening of The Halkin in London and has grown to now offer eight properties in locations ranging from the Turks & Caicos Islands, London, The Maldives, Bhutan, Bangkok and Bali.

Tell us about the COMO philosophy.

The COMO Team is encouraged to push boundaries and ensure that our guests are constantly met with the best in hospitality, both within the hotel and in the destinations they are privileged to be set in. This relates directly to the core principles of the COMO brand. Design, culture, adventure, cuisine and wellness all ensure that our guests are familiar with the standards and service we offer. Yet each hotel infuses personal touches, reflective of the unique destination.

Who are your key competitors, and how do you differentiate the COMO brand?

Due to the unique nature and philosophy behind COMO, we believe that there are no direct competitors to our brand. However, we would look towards brands such as Aman Resorts, Six Senses and Four Seasons, who share some similarities in certain areas of our business.

How has COMO embraced technology such as social media?

Frequent and honest two-way dialogue with the guests and fans of COMO is essential for our business to grow. Now with platforms such as Facebook, Twitter and TripAdvisor, this conversation is fast and dynamic. Companies utilizing social media will all benefit tremendously in the future. We have a social media manager for the company, who actively manages our Facebook and Twitter platforms. This includes monitoring what people are saying about us on the web so we can start up an instant conversation. Our general managers all closely monitor what is being said by our guests on TripAdvisor and again, ensure that comments receive timely feedback.

Explain the rationale behind your departure from Leading Hotels of the World. What has the impact been on your business?

We worked for a number of years with a few representation companies including Leading Hotels of the World, Design Hotels and Small Luxury Hotels. All were excellent platforms from which we could supplement our own promotional work. As the company grew, however, it became important that we spoke directly to consumers and the travel community about the core brand values of COMO, along with giving them the opportunity to find and book our hotels directly on both the

GDS and Internet. It is also important that our clients are able to find us all in the same place—so guests who enjoy the COMO experience in one location can then easily learn about our other properties. We now have our own COMO GDS chain code (CV), a dynamic web booking platform and are investing resources into building the COMO brand reputation.

COMO recently announced a new hotel in Thailand. Tell us about it.

Point Yamu is due to open in late 2012. Positioned on the northeast side of Phuket and overlooking the stunning Phang Nga Bay, the resort will offer 125 stylish guest rooms, suites and villas, along with exceptional cuisine, a COMO Shambhala Retreat and inventive activities for our adventurous guests.

Do you have any plans for a COMO property in the United States?

Not currently, but our Owners are always looking at opportunities that may fit the COMO brand.

What does the future hold for the super-luxury resort segment?

The growth of experiential travel and guests looking for a truly authentic experience means that luxury resorts will have to up their game beyond the gates. This encompasses greater interaction with local communities, proof of environmental and sustainability programs, unique cultural and adventure experiences, and an atmosphere where guests feel there is a learning element from the memories they part with.

Checking-In on Luxury Caribbean Travel: An Interview With Sir Royston Hopkin

Spice Island Beach Resort is a benchmark for Grenadian tourism and a key influencer of Caribbean luxury as a whole. Leading this prestigious property is chairman and CEO, Sir Royston Hopkin. His property is an upscale hideaway nestled along the palm-studded Grand Anse Beach on the island of Grenada. Hopkin's expertise on luxury Caribbean travel is bar none exemplary as is his knowledge on emerging trends.

Tell us a little bit about this five-star paradise called Spice Island Beach Resort.

Spice Island Beach Resort is, in essence, exactly what Grenada's hospitality is all about. Grenada is the opposite of a mass-market destination, where the emphasis is on boutique properties instead of the high-rises found elsewhere. Our guests choose Grenada because they want a culturally authentic experience without the crowds one would find at other destinations. Spice Island Beach Resort delivers unparalleled luxury and privacy accented by world-class service and a gourmet culinary program incorporating many of the local spices and vegetables for which Grenada is renowned.

Grenada was ravaged in 2004 by Hurricane Ivan. What was the impact on the property?

Like much of Grenada, Spice Island Beach Resort was devastated by Hurricane Ivan. Most of our rooftops were compromised and we sustained extensive damage to our restaurant, spa and lobby. But it was a blessing in disguise as it led to a complete redesign of the resort. One year and $12 million later, Spice Island Beach Resort was reborn as a modern facility steeped in Caribbean decor with a timeless sense of class and elegance that has been described as poetic. It was a challenging period to say the least, but we emerged as a more environmentally-conscious property better suited to the needs of today's affluent traveler.

With the property fully restored, how has the business responded?

We could not have hoped for a stronger response when we reopened our doors in December 2005. Our enlarged Cinnamon and Saffron Suites, which each took the place of two suites from the original design, became immediately popular and sold out prior to our reopening. Guests who had stayed with us prior and came back post renovations were absolutely speechless. As well, journalists we had hosted for our inauguration have been using Spice Island Beach Resort as a benchmark from which to rate other luxury products ever since.

What has the impact of the 2008-2009 recession been on Spice Island, Grenada and Caribbean tourism overall?

Tourism took a big hit during the recession across the board. It was felt in Grenada, throughout the Caribbean and virtually all tourist destinations around the globe. Unfortunately, the Caribbean had been hit particularly hard as many competing regions throughout the world have stepped up their marketing efforts, while the Caribbean has remained fragmented. And while tourism has improved gradually since the onset of the recession, we have still not come together as a region to effectively promote the Caribbean brand and are being outpaced by emerging destinations. As conditions improve, this failure will continue to impact all of us until our collective governments join the private sector in promoting the Caribbean as one unified region.

Has the premium segment been especially hard hit, or has it suffered less?

While one might reason that the premium segment would suffer less than the tourism market in general, since affluent consumers were still able to afford luxury products, this is actually far more complicated than it would appear. One of the most challenging consequences of the recession was the reduction in airlift faced not only by Grenada, but most Caribbean countries. Fewer planes means less capacity, which takes its toll on hotel occupancy across all segments, including luxury. Airlift has been a major challenge for quite some time. Fewer first-class seats have limited the number of affluent guests we're able to attract to Grenada. The demand is still there, but without the airlift, we're in the same position as the budget-oriented resorts.

Do you see a difference between the luxury travel demands of North Americans versus Europeans?

There is a fundamental difference between the travel demands of North Americans versus Europeans, though this is not unique to the luxury segment. Aside from the obvious difference, Europeans tend to stay for longer periods than North Americans, who often indulge in weekend getaways and are more inclined to stay at all-inclusive properties. In contrast, Europeans often feel restricted by all-inclusive meal plans as they prefer to sample the culinary offerings of their destination, which is one of our biggest draws in Grenada. Additionally, European clientele tend to be extremely environmentally conscious and are less likely to stay at a property that does not take steps to minimize its carbon footprint.

As the leader in Grenada's tourism industry, how have you helped mould the future of tourism for the Island?

As the saying goes, you make the best of what you're given. Grenada is a unique destination within the overall fabric of the Caribbean. Instead of harping on our challenges, such as airlift, we've turned the negatives into positives. We don't have the infrastructure to attract the millions of arrivals received by some of our neighbors. That's okay because our customers are very different from those of mass-market destinations. As a prominent figure in Grenada's tourism industry, I've long been a proponent of the philosophy that less is more. Less crowds, means more privacy. Less development means more natural beauty. Less reliance on expensive foreign imports means a thriving agricultural industry that augments the cultural authenticity of the Spice Island. By building on our strengths, we've carved our own niche within Caribbean tourism that has enabled us to achieve growth in quality rather than quantity.

What is your vision for luxury tourism in the Caribbean?

Luxury tourism is the key to sustainability for the Caribbean. In order for this to happen, we need to invest in our infrastructure and establish a policy-driven strategic approach to a consolidated regional marketing program for the region. Only then will we raise our profile within the increasingly competitive global market and attract a more upscale breed of traveler.

Once we can achieve this, everything else will fall into place. We'll have more clout in our negotiations with airlines. By focusing on the quality of our tourism product instead of playing the numbers game, we'll protect our natural resources for future generations. We'll always have value-oriented properties to cater to the budget market, but I envision a Caribbean where hotels compete based on service instead of price. Then we'll be able to focus not merely on filling rooms, but on the needs of each individual guest. If we can achieve this, the rewards will be numerous.

An Interview with Kathleen Doheny of Kensington Tours

Kensington Tours is a worldwide tour operator specializing in custom-designed group tours for a more personal and rewarding experience. Their phenomenal growth stems from adroit use of electronic communications. For hoteliers who do not know them well or who have never heard of them, here is an opportunity to learn more about how you can participate in their success.

With private vehicles and experienced local guides at a ratio of one for every two travelers, Kensington delivers a flexible and memorable adventure with unmatched value for the upscale traveler. I had the opportunity to sit down with their VP of Marketing, Kathleen Doheny, and ask her a few questions about what makes Kensington Tours so extraordinary.

How long have you been with Kensington Tours?

Since October 2007, when the company was very small and there were five of us in a tiny office. I was originally hired to start up Kensington Cares, the company's charitable initiative. Since then, I have also taken on marketing as a responsibility.

What is your current role?

I'm the Vice President of Marketing, which includes oversight of our online and offline marketing initiatives as well as advertising, PR, CRM, collateral production and coop marketing initiatives.

Tell us a little bit about Kensington Tours?

Kensington Tours is the inspiration of explorer and Royal Geographic Society Fellow Jeff Willner. A veteran of global expeditions to over 70 countries, he has crisscrossed the continents to experience the extraordinary. Jeff started Kensington to provide the globally curious with a better alternative to ubiquitous but limiting 'packaged tours' also known as 'group tours'.

Jeff is a graduate of Wharton, has worked for McKinsey & Company and is a former CEO of a software company. He was determined to put his business and tech-savvy together to make private guided travel more accessible and more affordable to those who wanted to discover the world their own way.

How do you differentiate Kensington from other tour operators?

Most of today's tour operators are experts in group departures, which include preset itineraries, pre-selected hotels and a less flexible pace. Kensington Tours is proficient at designing tailor-made tours, customized to each client's particular tastes, pace, budget and travel style. Kensington's team is made up of experience destination experts who have lived and worked in the destination they represent. You'll never talk to a call center at Kensington.

Additionally, providing unbeatable value for your travel dollar is the hallmark of Kensington Tours. It's a commitment we take seriously. We benchmark our tours against luxury operators—on average our custom tours are 20-30% less. But don't take our word for it; the editors of National Geographic Adventure Magazine have said, "Luxury without the high price tag is the guiding principle on Kensington's tours."

What are the advantages of private guided tours?

Lingering longer to watch the lion cubs play, skipping the last Italian duomo to explore an out of the way artisan studio only your guide knows about, or choosing value-wise hotels for the first half of your trip so you can indulge yourself on the homestretch. These are the sorts of freedoms and flexibilities only possible on a custom tour. Whether you are travelling as a couple, with your family or a group of friends, a private tour ensures you have an itinerary to match your travel style, your passions, your pace and your pocketbook. The result is an experience that is more personal, more rewarding and frankly, a lot more fun.

What is a typical Kensington guest profile?

Kensington is currently focused on the North American market. Our clients tend to range from value-conscious premium level clients to those looking for the best amenities, the top properties and everything luxury level. Honeymooners, families exploring the world (including more and more multi-generational families), couples travelling alone or with friends—these are just a taste of what our typical consumer looks like. Clients are looking for control and flexibility with no group restraints. They want a genuine cultural experience, the ability to dig deeper into the culture and connect more through a knowledgeable local guide.

How many hotel properties does Kensington work with?

We have thousands of hotels at our fingers tips, readily accessible via very sophisticated proprietary software to make sure we can meet the expectations of the many different needs of our clients. That said, our experts certainly have favorite properties that they recommend for a variety of reasons—luxury, value, location, hidden gem, favorite boutique property, great circuit value, family amenities, the list goes on. As one of the leading FIT tour operators, we work closely with many properties and property groups.

What are you looking for in your hotel selection?

Properties with distinction, and that doesn't just mean luxury! We have a wide range of client needs like value, location, luxury, family amenities, hidden gem allure—some not necessarily overlapping. Crucial to Kensington is a property that recognizes the value of a great FIT partner, and where appropriate, a collection of properties that offer great 'circuit' pricing and options, as well as properties eager for innovative coop marketing opportunities by harnessing our impressive database of premium and luxury level travelers.

We look for properties that want to build a long term-partnership and demonstrate this credo by treating our clients right, even when the inevitable hiccups happen. Our destination experts are loyal to properties they know they can trust 100% of the time, and reward these properties with volume.

How can a hotel that meets these criteria reach you?

Our product development team is the best place to start. They work closely with our destination experts to negotiate rates and contracts for the properties that are a good fit for Kensington. Depending on the destination, we work both direct and through DMC partners.

Miami in Tallahassee? The Boutique Hotel Duval Draws Its Inspiration

Hotel Duval is a boutique luxury property located in downtown Tallahassee, Florida; the state's capital city along the Floridian Panhandle. It has been completely renovated within the past two years on the site of the former Duval Hotel, which opened in 1951. Every room and floor is uniquely decorated with many tech-savvy features and style.

I visited Tallahassee for business back in July 2011 and was captivated by how well they understand the finer points of the hospitality business. Since then, I've kept in touch with Hotel Duval's General Manager, Marc Bauer, and too the chance to ask him a few questions.

Give me a brief history of the property. When was its most recent incarnation as an Autograph property? How would you describe this 'Miami in Tallahassee' approach?

The hotel opened as Hotel Duval in October of 2009 and subsequently became a member of the prestigious Autograph Collection in July of 2010.

It was not necessarily a 'Miami in Tallahassee' approach, but rather an amalgamation of design and service elements from a number of excellent and very different boutique hotels. Inspiration was drawn from such notable hotels as the Gansevoort in Manhattan, the El San Juan Hotel, the W and many others. The goal was to incorporate some of the great aspects of these fine properties and refine them in the context of our own business model.

At the same time, we had to be sensitive to the community and make sure the model was one the community would embrace. Without the support of the Tallahassee community, Hotel Duval would clearly not have experienced the unprecedented success we have enjoyed.

Tell me about the senior management team. When did you start with the property, and your prior experiences?

I arrived at Hotel Duval in September of 2008 to help guide them through one last weekend prior to closing for renovation. The General Contractor was technically staged to begin the renovation and we had to open for one final weekend to accommodate a full house of reservation commitments for Parent's Weekend. Needless to say, it was an interesting experience.

Fast forward to the present. The real beauty of our management team is that many of them are experiencing their respective roles for the first time. I wasn't all that caught up on titles, experience and prior positions when I assembled the leadership team. I was more interested in people who had energy, passion and natural leadership skills. That's 75% of the battle. I knew I could instill the hospitality piece.

What that philosophy has brought to the table is a fresh perspective and experiences outside the hotel realm. It has been like looking at a hotel through a different lens—exciting to say the least. For me, it has been a bit of a renaissance as I'm surrounded by a team of free-thinkers who use their creative energy to create memorable moments and constantly position the hotel for success. I think you can feel the energy of youth throughout the hotel; it is palpable.

When you arrived at Hotel Duvel, what were the challenges that you saw? How did you address them?

I hate to sound trite and cliché, but I didn't accept the position because I saw challenges, only opportunity. True, this project in this market had some inherent risk as it was the first of its kind. However, if done right the reward far outweighed the risk. For all of us who were stakeholders in some way in Tallahassee, it was our opportunity to put a signature on something that the entire community would buy into and could be proud of. When you have that kind of personal and professional commitment, it makes the job of being successful that much easier.

From ownership on down to line level, I truly felt confident that we had put all the right pieces in the right places. From there, we just had to execute on all levels and execute we did.

Can you elaborate on your staff training methods? What are the motivators? What are your core principles that drive your recruitment and training practices? Who manages the training program?

This is where I give a lot of credit to my wife Pam Bauer. Rarely do you find a husband and wife team working in the same building. However, early on she took on a corporate role that we created called Brand Affinity Director. Her role was to help develop key training and affinity programs for both our valued associates and clients alike. She was also directly involved in the selection process for our initial team; many of whom are still on board after two years in an employment climate that was generally regarded as transient based on the influence of the universities. And finally, she brought a 'cheerleading' quality that I think helped solidify this group as a team.

Since that time, Pam has transitioned to the role of director of sales that is more aligned with her previous hotel background. In the process, she imparted that enthusiasm to one of our great interns who has grown into a management role and is an important asset to the process. Succession management is alive and well at Hotel Duval.

I also would be remiss if I didn't give a great deal of credit to our management team. Not only were they hungry to make this property a success, they embraced the ongoing training element as a way of life. To this day, each department still meets monthly to review training initiatives and every day we learn.

There are inherent benefits to being a stand-alone boutique property. We can write and rewrite the book as many times as we want without having to fly the ideas up the bureaucratic flagpole to vet them out for approval. If what we do is not in the best interest of the guest and the business, we go back to the drawing board and refine it.

Finally, I give a lot of credit to the Shula's corporate team. They provided incredible resources and support both in pre—and post-opening. I have a great deal of respect for their business model, many of their ideas we've adopted as a part of our own operating philosophy.

As for the recruitment piece, I have always preached that retention breeds recruitment. Never was that philosophy as true as Hotel Duval. Our turnover is some of the lowest I have ever encountered in my career. The plan was simple: create an atmosphere that was fun to work in, empower them implicitly to make decisions, reward them for performance, show them you care, do things as a family that may be a little 'outside the normal box' of other companies, and make sure they truly feel like they are stakeholders.

From there, we bred 175 advocates of working at Hotel Duval. We can hardly keep up with applicant flow. On the rare times that we have an open position, we have carte blanche of qualified candidates.

It also helps to have some of the best boutique hospitality schools in the Dedman School at Florida State and Florida A&M University feeding you talent. They have become pipelines of talent to the hotel. I think both institutions and their student bodies respect what we do and how we do it and in turn, they are an important part of our community outreach program.

How has the hotel performed? I do not want trade secrets, but how does ADR, OCC or RevPAR compare to your comp set? In other words, is this plan paying off?

The hotel has performed beyond my wildest expectations and the pro forma expectations of the five-year plan. Tallahassee is a 55 percent to 60 percent occupancy town. I am not shy to share the numbers and say that the hotel is on pace to finish somewhere just south of 85 percent occupancy in its second full year of operating. Hotel Duval consistently leads the market comp set in all matrices and even gives some of our sister properties in the Autograph Collection in destinations with greater potential a run for their money.

In short, I would definitely say the plan is paying off. As a small company, we have created a name for ourselves that is paying off with other opportunities. Again, I give every bit of that credit to the great team we have assembled.

What are your future goals? How do you plan to maintain your excellence in a period of continued pressure on government spending?

While we never want to take our eye off the golden goose that is Hotel Duval, the future goal would include plans to take the operating model to other locations for future growth. In the meantime, instead of writing a business plan each year, we write a 'reinvention plan.'

I would be lying if I said the downsizing of government doesn't have an adverse effect on spending everywhere in this Capital City. However, we have diversified our markets in such a manner that we don't have all our eggs in one basket. As one segment shrinks we attack other segments that much more aggressively.

Our biggest opportunity in the coming years is to continue to grow while our occupancies remain strong. It's a revenue shell game that we have been refining since opening. Year one, we simply had to build base at any cost. Year two, we had a better understanding of who we are and who our customer is. Year three, we aim to strike a better balance between the market segments to maximize rate and revenue opportunities. Each year we get a little bit better at what we do. Looking into the crystal ball, I see growth in Tallahassee in the coming years and along with it improvements in the economy. Those two factors will also help our rate opportunity.

Anything else?

I think a great deal of our success is due to the fact we have truly mastered the art of earned media, in some cases by default. As a stand-alone hotel of 117 rooms, we simply don't have a war chest of advertising dollars. Therefore, we have had to constantly invent creative ways to point the spotlight on ourselves via earned media opportunities and through strategic partnerships. This helped leverage the dollars we do have to spend to let us to go the distance.

In closing, I still believe that if you build and then rebuild a better mousetrap the guests will continue to come. After 25 years in the hotel industry, one thing I have come to learn is that the basic core principals still work. Those core principals to me all revolve around relationship building. If you galvanize relationships with associates they will deliver great customer service. If you galvanize relationships with your guest constituency, they will come back again and again. This success of this hotel and our delivery is all about relationships.

An Interview with William MacKay
of Four Seasons Hotel Hong Kong

It's not every day you get an opportunity to speak to the GM of one of the world's finest hotels. The Four Seasons Hong Kong is one such property, and William MacKay is not only the General Manager but also the Regional Manager for several Four Seasons properties. I had the opportunity to spend some time on property in the Fall of 2011 and the best I can describe it is a 'jewel box', as everything was gem-perfect. The property has received accolades from pretty much every critical source. In my conversation with William, I wanted to discover how this property maintains this incredibly high level of excellence.

Can you give a brief description of Four Seasons Hong Kong? What's its relationship with other Four Seasons properties in Asia? Is it the flagship hotel of the region?

Four Seasons Hotel Hong Kong opened in September 2005 as a new and purpose-built hotel in the heart of Hong Kong's financial district as part of the IFC Complex. It opened as the second property Four Seasons would manage in the Hong Kong, with the original Regent Hotel Hong Kong managed by Four Seasons until 2003, on the Kowloon Peninsula.

While we don't designate any single Four Seasons hotel as a 'flagship', we certainly believe that, as a Forbes 5-star hotel with a 5-star spa, ideally located in a major gateway city, the Four Seasons Hong Kong enjoys a high profile, and is representative of Four Seasons' commitment to excellence. In 2010, the hotel became the only hotel in the world to house two Michelin 3-star restaurants, with the Cantonese restaurant Lung King Heen being awarded three stars in Michelin's inaugural guide the previous year, and Caprice, the French restaurant was honored with two Michelin stars that same year.

What's your background with Four Seasons? What was your career path been with them?

I actually started my career in the kitchen of the Connaught Hotel in London in 1973 as a management trainee. I've been with Four Seasons since 1982 when I was employed at the Four Seasons Clift Hotel in San Francisco. I had the good fortune (although I didn't quite see it that way at the time) to work as Director of Food and Beverage with an extraordinarily intense and hands-on General Manager, Stan Bromley, who was a relentless taskmaster but a remarkable hotelier who possessed an unusual combination of creativity and attention to detail.

Since then, I've been fortunate to travel all over the world with the company and work in a wide variety of different properties in Toronto, Seattle, Tokyo, London, Milan and Palm Beach before my last posting in Beverly Hills. Quality companies attract quality people, and the caliber of the colleagues with whom I have been able to work, and our shared commitment to excellence, is the main reason that I am still with Four Seasons after so many years.

I moved to Hong Kong to open our new hotel in 2003 and have been here ever since. As a Regional Vice President, I now oversee three other operating properties in the region in addition to Hong Kong, as well as three properties in Mainland China that are under construction and in pre-opening—Guangzhou, Shenzhen and Suzhou.

Most of us are well acquainted with the superior quality of the Four Seasons brand. Can you elaborate on how the brand has been translated to Hong Kong and an Asian setting?

Four Seasons was already well established in Asia before our Hong Kong property opened, and people sometimes forget that Four Seasons used to manage the Regent, Hong Kong in its heyday. Any brand only comes to life through the experience of the guest, which is a combination of location, product, atmosphere, and, above all, service, which obviously depends more on people than anything else. Today's guests are less homogenous than ever, with widely differing tastes and preferences. The same guests may also be looking for different experiences depending on their situation; a businessperson who cares most about quick and accurate service during the week may be looking for a more indulgent or memorable experience of the destination at the weekend.

Our job is to be sensitive to the individual situation and expectations of each guest. At the same time, we reflect the authentic character of Hong Kong in the experience that our guests enjoy. Hotels are becoming increasingly about lifestyle, and the whole area of design is becoming increasingly important. However, the most significant elements of the guest experience—and the hardest to get right—are still delivered by our people. We continue to believe that it's the individual resourcefulness, skill and sensitivity of each member of our staff that is our greatest point of difference.

As in every destination where Four Seasons has opened, we try to combine the best of Four Seasons technical knowledge and with the talent and personality of our local staff, who are hired primarily based on attitude. In Hong Kong, we were very lucky that over 40 veterans of the old Regent (including our Chinese Executive Chef, Chan Yan Tak) rejoined us for the opening of the Four Seasons. By nature Hong Kongers are extraordinarily hard working and responsible, with great pride and integrity, which makes them an ideal fit for a demanding values-based organization like Four Seasons. The team we have here in Hong Kong is second to none.

Were there any physical modifications integral to this process? What distinguishes FSHK from other Four Seasons properties?

There are always some trade-offs in the construction of any building, but very few compromises had to be made in the construction of the Four Seasons in Hong Kong. Isadore Sharp always said that every new hotel should be the best yet, incorporating what we learned from all the projects that went before. In Hong Kong, the law stipulates that only 5% of the available floor area can be used for the back of house. In order to provide adequate employee facilities, this was insufficient and we were able to have this adjusted on appeal to 8.5%. We are very fortunate in Hong Kong to be in a vibrant market, where the owners (Sun Hung Kai properties and Henderson Land) built the hotel to a very high level of quality throughout. The hotel has a sense of space and airiness that is highly unusual in Hong Kong.

Are there any significant differences in customer expectations between guests arriving at FSHK and properties in other parts of the world? How have you adapted to exceed guest expectations?

Without a doubt! Asia has a deserved reputation for having the best service in the world; guests, who are resigned to a weary acceptance of poor service in many parts of the world, come to Asia with much higher expectations. Although basic service steps and accuracy in execution are important, great service is about an added level of sensitivity and intuition, not only adapting us to the individual needs and situation of the guests, but also being one step ahead of them.

A guest coming to Hong Kong on business will have very different expectations compared with a family going on vacation in Bali. Hong Kong is a fast-paced, dynamic city, with the majority of the transient population travelling through the city on business. Their wants are different to a honeymoon couple in the Seychelles, whose priority is more likely to be relaxation and romance. Having said that, we also have a significant mix of leisure guests who might be in town on a layover and do have time on their hands and a mind to explore the cultural depth of the city. We have to be able to recognize each guest independently of the next and anticipate and prepare for every need.

One of the recent introductions, in fact by Four Seasons around the world, is a 15-minute room service menu—implemented in various hotels that feel the need may be there—Hong Kong is one of those places and we've recognized that need and placed a menu in every room to accommodate guests who are time-poor. Teamwork and communication are a crucial element of exceeding expectations—without this, we would not be able meet or anticipate guests' needs.

What's your style of management? How do you feel that it has positively affected your staff and the guest experience?

I am a great believer in the importance of alignment, and put a lot of emphasis on collaboratively establishing clear goals that are a reasonable stretch, and then giving everyone all the means, encouragement and help (as well as the space) possible to help ensure that goals are achieved. I strongly believe that nobody comes to work wanting to do a bad job, and that the job of managers is to nurture the passion that lives in people. I'm not so naïve as to believe that people do not occasionally need an extra push, but sadly, many managers are unintentional passion-killers who deprive their people of the autonomy they need to feel responsible for the achievement of agreed results. Management is ultimately about getting things done, and woe betides any manager who forgets it.

I am frankly relentless in my own mind about giving first priority to employees and guests; I am continually involved with our associates on an individual basis, celebrating successes and trying to nurture a positive atmosphere of good humor and openness in which every colleague feels free to act in the best interest of the guests, and understands the critical importance of their individual contribution. At the same time, I am pushing, nudging and cajoling for excellence all the time in every aspect of the guest's experience, and frankly sniffing around looking for areas where we may have an opportunity to improve!

Many of our guests, especially in this part of the world, also expect a very high level of recognition. I spend a great deal of time involved in the individual coaching and mentoring of our young managers; besides giving me great personal satisfaction, the quick and constant improvement of their personal management performance is critical to our success and theirs.

This involvement with guests and employees takes a lot of time, and involves a significant trade-off; it means consciously keeping my 'bureaucratic involvement' in administrative process to a minimum, which sounds easy, but is not. Every administrative function is 'owned' by someone seeking validation for their work through the visible and direct involvement of the general manager, which can make me a challenge for other stakeholders to deal with!

No matter how many hours one works, it's just not possible to please everyone all of the time. I am sometimes complimented on how quickly I react to guest or employee-related issues, or issues of strategic direction, but also criticized for my slower responsiveness to some administrative issues that I see as ancillary to driving guest satisfaction or contributing to our business success, even if they are important to other stakeholders! I like to think that I do a good job flying at high and low altitudes, but try not to spend too much time at 15,000 feet!

Our hotel in Hong Kong is also a larger hotel than most Four Seasons properties, so I need to be sure that processes are working and communication is extensive, organized and clear so that nothing falls between the cracks because information wasn't shared. The role of any manager evolves as one becomes responsible for more, and the job becomes less about technical skill than it becomes about leading and coaching a team, connecting to the outside world, and striking a balance between the needs of multiple stakeholders, both direct and indirect.

Isadore Sharp always said that you have to focus on doing the things that only you can do, but multiple stakeholders increasingly feel entitled to first call on a general manager's time. The immediate access that technology affords is in many ways a fabulous gift, but it also makes it harder to focus thoughtfully on the strategic side of the business and manage one's time, when so many stakeholders expect immediate personal attention from a general manager—often to issues that our structure is frankly designed to handle by specialists elsewhere in the organization.

By definition, a general manager directly taking a reservation from a travel partner (important though it may be) or responding to a guest complaint personally is involved at a very tactical level, that many management gurus would think inappropriate (if not fatal) in a business of our size and complexity; and yet this level of attention is one of our greatest points of difference. In the end, one has to delegate a lot, but there is a real art to 'handing people off' to the appropriate people without offending them, and it's one that I have yet to master! Nobody wants to feel they are 'being delegated,' yet effective delegation lies at the heart of effective time management for any manager of a significant number of people. It's a conundrum for the leader of any "high-touch" service business that can never be resolved! In the end, I am reconciled to the fact that this is a 'life' more than a 'job,' And technology has made it increasingly so.

When I stayed at the hotel, I noticed that you have a Director of Guest Services and a whole department dedicated to this task. What was the impetus for this? What are this department's responsibilities?

We have a team of five in guest relations, led by a manager. The team was established as the hotel opened and determined as a necessity for a big and busy hotel operation in a fast-paced environment, to ensure we are able to constantly personalize guests' stays, especially for our most regular patrons, not only in Hong Kong, but also of Four Seasons worldwide. We now record guest preferences on a global basis, but the effort put into recording preferences is obviously meaningless if we don't execute properly.

As much as every single one of us in the hotel needs to see ourselves as members of an integrated guest services team, the guest relations team are also particularly focused on the needs of our highest paying (and thus most profitable) guests. Their responsibilities can most broadly be defined as 'making sure that the guest gets what the guest should get.' However, guests have widely differing needs and preferences, and it is the job of the guest relation's team to proactively ensure that we are aware of specific needs and preferences, and then ensure that we deliver on these needs one hundred percent of the time. As much as this may be about creating individualized experiences, and 'surprising and delighting' people, it is just as much about making sure that we deliver one hundred percent execution on delivery of the basics.

Putting Champagne in a room for an anniversary couple will have a lot less impact if they are mistakenly assigned a twin bedded room! With two Michelin three-starred restaurants, for example, that are almost invariably full, it is the job of the guest relations team to 'go the extra mile' by finding out ahead of time whether rack-paying and suite guests need reservations for Lung King Heen or Caprice, so as to avoid hassles over wait-listing or non-availability of a table, after they have arrived. Ultimately, this all takes time and translates into a need for proper staffing. The more senior the executive, the more last minute their schedule is likely to be. These people are often our most profitable guests, with the lowest threshold of tolerance for any shortcoming in service delivery.

How has your Guest Relation's Team improved the hotel operations thus far? How do you quantify the work that they do?

The guest relation's team plays a fundamental role in ensuring that guests feel well looked after. Their work is quantifiable, as is the entire staff body's work, by seeing contented guests willing to pay a premium to stay here, and longing to return! More now than ever, guests want to write about their stay, whether to me, via our web site or on social media platforms to share with the world—there is no greater feeling of pride for the staff, than when they see their names mentioned in thanks, so this equally helps us to know they are doing a great job.

How does the Guest Services Department integrate with other services such as the front desk and F&B? Where does it fit into the chain of command?

Any successful team needs a strong sense of accountability to each other, and any business needs a structure of some sort, but the idea of a "chain of command" within a hotel is simplistic and frankly outmoded. John Wayne would have made an awful hotelier! Great service demands a team approach, where everyone is focused on a seamless experience for individual guests.

The guests relation's team technically fall within the rooms division and report directly to the director of rooms, but they are continually interacting with every area of the hotel, initiating and following-up on detailed guest requirements. They are physically adjacent to the front office, so have a very close relationship with the front desk. However, it's important that we be staffed well enough at the front desk that the guest relation's team doesn't become routinely sucked into the routine work of the front desk.

To end, could you comment on where you feel the hotel industry is headed? What advice would you give to other hoteliers?

With the explosive growth of outbound travel from the developing world, especially Mainland China, hotels that continue to deliver a warm welcome, quality service and distinctive experiences in desirable locations have a great future. A company like Four Seasons, specializing in only one premium segment of the market has a great advantage over companies trying to juggle multiple brands at multiple price-points.

However, there is another dilemma we need to reconcile around the idea of what guests want to be consistent across a brand and what they expect to be locally authentic. Clients are better educated and better travelled all the time. At the same time, guests want to identify with, and be rewarded by, brands that offer them the assurance of consistently excellent quality of product and service. The trick of combining authenticity and a sense of place with the brand consistency that guests demand is something I believe Four Seasons has become extraordinarily good at over many years; it's part of our DNA.

The way in which people incorporate technology into their everyday life is also changing rapidly, and hoteliers will need to react to the technological innovation that becomes expected by the guest, without over-complicating things beyond what guests want. In particular, the way in which consumers acquire information and choose to buy travel is also evolving all the time, and hoteliers will need to stay closely attuned to changes in consumer buying behavior and continually innovate around the needs of customers if they are to prosper. In other words, work hard, but stand back occasionally and keep your ear to the ground!

Is There a Villa in Your Future? An Interview with Debbie Misajon of Epic Hideaways

Debbie Misajon is the founder and managing director of Epic Hideaways—a villa rental company specializing in destination luxury properties. She brings over 25 years of experience and a passion for traveling the world to every location offered and personal recommendation. I had the opportunity to interview Debbie and ask a few questions about some of the more exceptional aspects of Epic Hideaways.

Tell us about yourself. Where does Epic Hideaways fit into the picture?

My background has been in the luxury hotel arena working with Four Seasons, Leading Hotels of the World's Prima Hotels, and Aman Resorts. I also launched a successful villa company in Hawaii about a decade ago. After years of working with the best and learning from the best, I wanted to create something through which I could blend my hotel and villa background. So, I developed Epic Hideaways, offering top resort villas and private homes in epic destinations.

I have a passion for transformative, experiential travel. There's nothing more fulfilling than meeting a client by phone, creating an experience of their annual holiday or getaway, and receiving positive feedback at the end of it all. I'm happiest when I can personally meet guests at check-in, and then see them off at departure and witness their transformation firsthand. Just yesterday I shared in the joy of a guest's son as he walked up to the house having surfed his first wave. Epic!

The web site is a showcase of unique places and properties, an offering of what can be had for travelers who want the opportunity to live, if only temporarily, in a destination. For those who aren't entirely ready to let go of resort amenities, Epic is collaborating with a number of luxury hotel companies that have developed villas, including Aman Resorts, Alila Hotels, Trisara and many others under negotiation.

Just how large is the private villa industry? Can you give us some figures on the revenue and growth of this segment?

It's a growing market, indicated not only by the prolific number of businesses in the private homes segment of the industry, but also by the number of resorts with developing villa components. According to a 2010 survey by Radius Global Market Research, there are more than 6 million vacation properties in the Unites States and Europe that are rented to travelers every year. These vacation rentals generated more than $85 billion in rental income in 2010.

Many resort companies recognize the growing interest in villas demonstrated by the number of properties offering one or more luxury villas on site like Amanresorts, Alila or Ojai Valley Inn. It's a trend you just can't ignore. Resort villa sales are very different from traditional hotel sales with unique configurations, owners' needs to meet, and owners' uses to be worked around. You must have intimate knowledge of the villas you represent.

Who are your customers? Is it just the 'Lifestyles of the Rich and Famous' crowd?

Laughing! Private villa customers definitely include the 'Lifestyles of the Rich and Famous' crowd. However; villas have crossed into the mainstream. Today's private villa renters are a family, group of friends, special interest group, or destination wedding.

The typical Epic client is a family on an annual holiday, immersing themselves in a culture or experiential travel. They might live inland at home, and want to experience the beachfront lifestyle for two weeks, shop locally and feel like a part of a community. On the other hand, we have had celebrities and high net worth individuals who simply want to get away from the demands of their daily lives. They don't want to walk through the lobby and be gawked at, have paparazzi publish photos of their spa faces as they return to their suite, or be bothered while on holiday. This makes a private villa highly desirable, as many of these properties are located on exceptionally private estates. Epic Hideaways will organize the pre-arrival provisions, in-residence spa treatments, private chefs on demand, and cater to their desire to spend quality time alone and out of the frenzy.

What are the economics of a typical villa rental? What does it cost and what is included?

The costs are dictated by the guest's lifestyle, whether they are recreating their home or stepping it up. However, in general it is less expensive to rent a villa than multiple hotel rooms, dining in a restaurant every night and paying resort amenity fees. For example, a family of four may opt for a beachfront piece of real estate for their annual holiday because they don't live that lifestyle at home. They might require daily housekeeping and desire a swimming pool, but more importantly they hope to craft a meaningful experience for their family through personalized activities, which might include fly fishing instruction, surfing lessons, volunteering at an orphanage or clearing local hiking trails of invasive plants.

In this case, opting for a private villa home will pencil out more economically than booking several hotel suites. Preparing their meals in the home, doing laundry rather than sending it out, and buying juice by the quart rather than at spending $8 per glass are all examples of money saved through the villa experience.

Pricing will vary by country. Typically, the house is the only thing included in the US. However, in Asia and in Europe, you will find that the pricing includes housekeeping staff, security and a chef; it varies. That's why it's so important to work with an industry expert.

You also sell villas. Is there much turn over, or is this just a side business to rentals?

It's a natural side business. Guests spend two weeks of their time in a neighborhood and find they like it. Or, they like the destination and want to have a place of their own. Epic works with several real estate agents who focus on second homes in the best holiday destinations.

What makes Epic Hideaways special? Tell us about the Epic philosophy?

Epic Hideaways has a passion to transform what amounts to just two weeks of time off into a meaningful experience in a humble, residential setting. After years of working with the finest providers of service and product, I wanted to share what I've learned and come to love.

Reserving a villa home or resort villa with Epic Hideaways offers a number of advantages. With 25 years of travel knowledge, we offer our clients the best professional experience in accommodations. Because I'm on a first name basis with villa owners, management teams, and general managers of featured properties, your reservation receives the attention it deserves, insuring that all the details are tailored exclusively for your villa vacation. Whether you're staying for a quick getaway or your annual holiday, planning is always essential.

Who are your key competitors, and how do you differentiate Epic villas?

Epic doesn't compete with the behemoths or the large operators who cast massive SEO webs. This is because we rely on long-term relationships within the travel industry, taking the time to create an epic holiday; from finding the right villa, the ideal activities, the best providers, to the honed chef and even locating the right philanthropic programs (see: voluntourism). Anyone can rent a villa; the difference is in the making of the unique experience.

Do you have any plans to expand Epic beyond your Pacific Rim expertise, and if so, what regions are you considering?

My passion for Asia has lent itself to launching with a number of properties in the region. The resort properties of Trisara, Alila and Aman Resorts were natural fits for Epic Hideaways, largely given that a hefty part of my employed professional career was with Aman, and that both Trisara and Alila are headed by former Aman Resorts colleagues of mine. We work very closely with a former LHW General Manager in Italy representing the finest properties of his product line in Italy. We are beginning to receive interest in representation from many luxury properties in the US, Latin America and Spain, so growth is inevitable. Epic won't grow in number of villas represented simply for growth's sake; it will grow because the properties and destinations offer an Epic experience.

What does the future hold for the super-luxury villa segment?

It seems to be a growth area with the increasing numbers of Indian, Chinese and Latin American travelers we are seeing combined with the trends of generational and experiential travel. All said, the villa market is poised to accommodate these new travelers and trends.

An Interview with Gloria Ah Sam, Spa Director at Ojai Valley Inn & Spa

Gloria Ah Sam is the Spa Director at Ojai Valley Inn & Spa, a 5-Diamond resort nestled within the pastoral mountains of Southern California. As a destination spa, Spa Ojai has received numerous accolades for its unique treatments that blend new age aesthetics with locally sourced, organic produce as well as traditions from the Chumash, Ojai Valley's indigenous people. Spa Ojai fashions itself as a 'spa university' where, although the treatments are the main draw, there's also an organic restaurant, Café Verde, and an Artist's Cottage and Apothecary with holistic classes for guests to improve their wellbeing through self-discovery.

Tell us a little bit about your background. When did you join Spa Ojai and why?

Gracious hospitality has been in my career path beginning in the late seventies when I was a flight attendant. Back in the days of intense customer service training and fierce competition, passenger complaints were not taken lightly and there was always someone waiting in line to fill your position. When the US government deregulated the airline industry in 1978 only airlines who earned customer loyalty survived. This is something I have never forgotten.

After a 15 year airline career, I decided to 'stay grounded' and I discovered an interest in the skin care, hair care and beauty business. I worked in luxury retail for six years before landing a position as the Retail/Front Desk Director for the first Aveda Lifestyle Salon and Spa in the state of Hawaii. This was my first hands-on experience combining spa and salon operations with the 'front of the house'. Within a year, I was the General Manager overseeing the entire operations. I later moved on to manager of the Abhasa Spa at the Royal Hawaiian Resort, and then spent three and a half years as the Spa Director at Halekulani.

The move to Ojai Valley Inn & Spa in March of 2009 completes a career goal of mine to offer complete wellness experiences in a luxury environment.

Please give readers a brief overview of the Spa Ojai operation, insofar as overall facilities, treatments and services.

The Spa Ojai Village consists of a 31,000 square-foot spa facility, two spa pools, fully-equipped workout room, Mind and Body class studio, nail salon, Spa Boutique, Café Verde and an Artist's Cottage and Apothecary. We also feature a communal sauna experience called Kuyam. Inspired from traditional healing cultures, this treatment combines essential oil infused clay therapy, dry heat therapy and inhalation therapy. The men and women's locker areas are well appointed with guest amenities, steam rooms, saunas, whirlpools and relaxation areas.

We offer a full range of treatments in our spa menu of services. We feature seasonal inspired ingredients representing the bounty of Ojai Valley. Mind and Body classes are scheduled throughout each day including such classes as yoga, meditation, spinning, boot camp, body hoops, daily walks and water aerobics. Classes in watercolor, silk scarf painting or basic drawing provide ways for our guests to unleash their creativity and have fun with paints, colored pencils or pastels. Create a personal Mandala and receive feedback on the universal meaning of color, symbol, number and placement to provide insight into one's deeper motivations. Craft a unique blend of essential oils as your very own signature fragrance in our Apothecary.

Can you tell us about some of Spa Ojai's awards and the reasons it is continually honored with these accolades?

Spa Ojai is recognized as a benchmark facility for its architecture and design, its art program, Kuyam experience, seasonal treatments and Apothecary. We don't simply offer a spa treatment, but offer options for our guests to embrace a wellness-balanced experience. Consumers as well as industry experts continue to recognize not only our points of difference, but the personal attentiveness each guests receives while in our care.

Sampling of accolades include: Forbes 4-Star Spa, Spa Magazine Best Spa Cuisine, SpaFinder Best Spa with Golf, Ojai Valley News Reader's Choice-Best Spa in Ojai, Venture County Star Reader's Choice-Best Day Spa, Travel + Leisure Magazine Top 10 Hotel Spas in the United

States, Condé Nast Traveler Magazine Top 25 North American Resort Spas, Shape Magazine #1 Spa, USA Today 10 Best Spas.

Can you give us some examples of key differentiators between Spa Ojai and competitors?

We create memorable experiences with heartfelt intentions and perform extraordinary services. We nurture our associates and core values that perpetuates a culture of respect, professional behavior and passion for everything we do.

How you have applied learning from worldwide examples of exceptional spa programs and services?

We find inspiration in our team's diversity and training certifications from various schools in the United States, India, Bali and Europe. We work with our vendor partners to stay abreast with product and new equipment development. Our ISPA membership and marketing research help keep us connected to the pulse of a worldwide health and wellness industries.

What are the economics of a large-scale hotel-spa operation? What are some of the unique aspects you face operating as part of Ojai Valley Inn & Spa, versus an independent entity?

Being associated with a 5-diamond resort gives us an unbelievable amount of support from other departments at the Inn including engineering, housekeeping, uniforms, central reservations, public relations and our sales and marketing team. We have 24-hour access to these various departments to assist us in maintaining our facility as well as promoting and selling our treatments and programs.

Recently, Spa Ojai has been noted as having among the best cuisine of any spa in the country. Tell us more about the philosophy behind your restaurant, Café Verde.

It's a dream come true to be located in the heart of such a thriving agriculture center. Locally grown and often organically grown produce is available year-round. In addition, our Executive Chef has a garden on property where he grows a variety of tasty sensations including heirloom tomatoes. Café Verde compliments the Spa Village by offering freshly squeezed juices and nutritional packed smoothies. The philosophy behind Café Verde is to serve fresh, organic when available, locally grown when available and seasonally inspired, flavorsome cuisine.

It seems as if every hotel or resort has a spa of some sort. Where is the spa industry heading? Has the industry reached a point of saturation?

The number one reason a person visits a spa is to reduce stress. Spa treatments are no longer viewed by the majority of consumers as a simple pampering experience. In today's fast-paced environment, I believe that people worldwide will continue to seek ways in which to reduce stress. Day Spas are more plentiful than ever and can be found in even the smallest of communities. Providing a complete menu of spa services in a luxury hotel or resort is expected and appreciated by the guests we serve.

Spa goers are become more sophisticated and experienced. Spas that do not connect with their guests will not survive. Spas that do not deliver professional, quality services will not survive. Spas that are not managed properly will not survive.

What does the future hold for Spa Ojai?

Anything and everything is possible. Our business has made a healthy recovery since the downturn of the economy in 2009. We listen to our guests and have responded with menu changes, a resent 'facelift' renovation, new Mind and Body classes, creative value priced packages, loyalty programs and creative art class options. We honor our past traditions while keeping our hearts and minds open to new products, innovations and trends. We stay focused on why we do what we do and our goal remains the same—to deliver extraordinary guest services and memorable experience for all guests, each and every day.

How ARC The.Hotel in Ottawa, Canada, Sets Itself Apart

With 112 rooms, ARC The.Hotel is a boutique property ideally located for leisure and local business in Canada's capital city of Ottawa, Ontario. What's most appealing about the property is its distinguished quality of guest services. The staff is particularly friendly and ceaselessly helpful. Here's my discussion with General Manager, Colin Morrison, digging down to the roots of their success.

How did you get into the hotel business?

My introduction to the industry was somewhat accidental. I was raised in Montreal and involved in Scouting as a teen. In 1972, my father also started a steakhouse as a hobby in the Laurentians area in Northern Canada. I had gained an interest in hospitality through my dad, but wasn't thinking of it as a career.

Through Scouting I had the opportunity to meet Reg Groome, then the vice president of Hilton Canada. I remember having a conversation with Mr. Groome in his office in Montreal's Queen Elizabeth Hotel and asking him, "If I was interested in hospitality as a career, what would I have to do to earn this office?" That conversation started a mentorship that spanned several years. My first 'official' hotel job was with Hilton Hotels in their Management Training Program at the Queen Elizabeth. That was back in 1982 when I was fresh out of university with a business degree, and I haven't looked back since.

I have seen the TripAdvisor recounts. Guests love the property. What's the secret?

There is no specific 'special sauce' for it. ARC The.Hotel offers more than a bed, bath and a meal. You can get that anywhere; we offer a unique experience in Ottawa. The experience is one of being pampered—from the greeting at the door to a glass of sparkling wine and Belgian chocolate as you check in; from the signature cocktails in the Lounge and inspired menu creations in our dining room to the daily turndown service featuring Granny Smith apples on your bedside and chocolates on your pillow. In short, we care, and to that end, I respond to every TripAdvisor review of the hotel.

When you stay at the ARC, it does not feel like a standard, traditional mid-range property. How do you maintain this feeling?

In addition to the unexpected creature comforts, the feeling is created by the team who work tirelessly to maintain the experience. The selection process for new team members is also quite different. Our questions focus more on the individual and less on what they have done in the past. It's more of a conversation than an inquisition. We are looking for a personality that is outgoing and friendly but calm when faced with pressure. We can train the job skills, but not the personality.

How do you stay innovative with your Food & Beverage programs?

We are very fortunate to have a young talented chef who is dialed into the Ottawa food scene. He has established personal relationships with local farmers and producers to ensure only the best products arrive at our loading dock. Fresh ingredients and a progressive culinary team can achieve fantastic results. Equally important to the F&B experience is a service team who are passionate about the product and colorful in their presentation. Their ability to verbalize the menu is very important in creating the desired experience regardless of the time of day that our guests are dining.

With new staff joining each year, how do you imbue the spirit of guest service excellence?

In addition to the hiring process, we request that new team members experience the hotel as a guest. This allows the incumbents to see the hotel through the guests' eyes, and experience the service as a guest would. They are generally 'wowed' by the experience, which makes a lasting impression. I have found that while this approach can be expensive, the benefits far outweigh the costs. An orientation program and position shadowing are also employed to ensure continuity to current standards. At the end of the 'training period' there is a one-on-one with the Department Head, and when time allows, the GM. We ask the new team member to be critical of their training and identify the areas where the training fell short, providing a venue for continued improvement.

What lessons can you give other mid-range properties striving for improvement?

A hotel is a business first. We all need to make the right business decisions to ensure the financial success of the operation, all while never losing sight of the guest experience. We all offer a clean room, a comfortable bed, and a hot shower. What is it your property does differently from your competitors? Determine what your point of differentiation is, then focus on it. Talk about it to your team to get their buy-in. Talk about it with your guests to get their buy-in. Talk about it in public and create a buzz. Embrace social media and tell them about it. Make it your passion. You'll be amazed by what follows. Energy flows where your attention goes.

Kingsbrae Arms, Building a Reputation Despite Its Off-the-Radar Location

I first heard about Kingsbrae Arms through my relationship with Relais & Chateaux. Located in St. Andrews By-the-Sea in New Brunswick, Canada, just north of the border with Maine, I was perhaps most intrigued to visit because I spent much of my childhood in Saint John, less than a half hour's drive north.

Revisiting the land of my youth in the summer of 2010, my wife and I made an effort to stay here and experience this quaint, eight-room inn firsthand. Almost immediately we were captivated with its charm and exceptional service. Since then, I've kept in touch with owner Harry Chancey and was given a chance to interview him about how they've developed their standard of excellence.

Tell me a little bit about Kingsbrae Arms, one of Canada's incredible gems.

In 1897, a prominent Nova Scotia businessman built Kingsbrae Arms as a summer 'cottage' for his family, high on the ridge overlooking the town and harbor. By the mid-1990s the house had fallen into disrepair. The current owners saw its potential, renovated and opened to the public in 1996. Two years later, Kingsbrae Arms became one of only 14 members of Relais & Chateaux in Canada, one of 11 Mobil (Now Forbes) four-star properties in Canada, and the first five-star inn awarded by the Canada Grading Authority.

Through the years, our house has hosted a number of prominent guests from around the world including all the premiers of Canada. Kingsbrae Garden, one of Canada's finest horticultural gardens, lies just next door. Currently, our guests experience the very fine cuisine of Provence-native Chef Guillaume Delaune who has created a fusion between his Mediterranean training and the products of the Bay of Fundy. The calm and picturesque setting of Kingsbrae Arms transports guests to less hurried times without the anxiety of present global concerns.

When you enter Kingsbrae Arms, you feel as if you're entering someone's home, rather than a hotel. How do you maintain this feeling?

The key is in the unobtrusive yet high-quality service, the personal attention paid by staff to each guest (just as staff in one of the country houses of older days might have done), and the perfect mixture of friendliness and respect. Our staff open the door to guests when they arrive and greet them by name throughout their stay. No matter who or where you are, a personalized service becomes an intrinsic part of a memorable experience.

The physical plant and the food and wine alone do not necessarily qualify as memorable without the personal component. We remember individual tastes. Guests are free to wander in and out of the garden, borrow a book or CD from the library, ask for travel planning assistance, or just be left alone. We train our staff in how to read body language. This is a big factor for every tiny interaction, even the customary, "How is everything?" that so many establishments, particularly restaurants, employ with zero, if not negative results, especially when table conversation is interrupted by this plea from a server.

I have seen the TripAdvisor recounts. You seem to make guests create new levels of excellence in their descriptions. What's the secret?

We've been delighted with the OTA submissions this year. The secret: dedicated work from our professional service and kitchen staff, as well as the goals expressed in the previous question.

You ensure that food and wine is part of the guest experience. Yet, many hoteliers have moved away from this art. Your thoughts?

There are certainly challenges to maintaining excellence in food and wine. Nonetheless, we believe that it forms an integral part of the experience we wish our guests to have. As M.F.K. Fisher said, "There is communion of more than our bodies when bread is broken and wine is drunk." The Bay of Fundy is rich in produce from land and sea, and Chef Guillaume Delaune is an expert at crafting local foods into his superb menus. Fine wines just naturally go with them. We move toward our food and wine program, not retreat from it, because we are so confident in our product created by the kitchen and presented by our service staff.

Recently, a New York Times article saw an individual travel from New York to Kingsbrae for one her 'last wish' food experiences. Tell us about that.

We have all read Anna Stoessinger's article. We were so touched, it's hard to know what to say. It is a rare privilege to be part of a story of such courage and zest for life. When she told us her intention at the end of her visit, we felt incredibly honored that she had chosen us. It was incredibly gratifying.

"It had been a long time since I had experienced such satisfying fullness. There was comfort and exuberance, a familiar feeling like a long embrace, a coming in from the cold. It's about love and memory and the capacity to conquer even the worst hours with something warm and wonderful," says Stoessinger. This description of hers confirmed our hopes that our tiny operation might just be making a difference in people's lives. We think of Anna often, and wish her all the best.

How do you stay innovative in F&B given the inherent costs of doing so?

You find, hire, and keep a fantastic chef, then give him the tools needed to exceed everyone's expectations.

What is your greatest staffing challenge?

Finding, hiring, and keeping fantastic service staff! The greatest challenges in doing so are the ridiculous and unreasonable expectations of many young people who intern here or are graduates of so-called hospitality schools. Their work ethic is often marred by a sense of entitlement and incredulity when they find out that the performance of excellent service means everything from the sublime to the disgusting.

Guest interaction is of course a top priority, but a plugged toilet has to be plunged from time to time.

With new staff each year, how do you imbue your spirit of guest service excellence?

It comes primarily from the example and ongoing training provided by owners and returning staff, including familiarization with Relais & Chateaux standards. Many incoming staff have fine dining or hotel experience, of course. We try to pass along the Relais & Chateaux concept of 'l'âme et l'esprit', our own particular identity, and the challenge to exceed guest expectations.

What lessons can you give other hoteliers in striving for improvement?

As to striving for improvement (not to teach anyone else their business!), first have a clear picture of just what kind of hotel you wish to be, then be that to the utmost possible. Our ideal was to be a small, seasonal inn, with five-star hospitality and cuisine. So that defined to some extent the amenities and markets suitable for us. After that, the devil's in the details, so to speak. We constantly seek feedback from guests, watch new trends and products in the trade, and look for the best marketing strategies and partners. But most of all, we put great care into even the smallest details of house, service and kitchen.

What has been your greatest achievement?

The greatest achievement, I think, has been to create a bridge between the remote, rustic and unspoiled beauty of Atlantic Canada, and the exquisite comfort and cuisine of Relais & Chateaux. Admittedly, our region is not top of mind for luxury travelers, but through the years we have built both reputation and clientele. We think the remote and the exquisite elements of our property are a wonderful combination!

An Interview with John Halpin, General Manager of COMO Shambhala Estate

COMO Shambhala Estate is located to the north of Uma Ubud, Bali, about one and a half hours north by car service from the Denpasar International Airport. With just forty rooms (including villas), this resort is truly dedicated to the well-being of its guests.

Having spent several nights at the property, I was awestruck by both its remarkable beauty and its commitment to exceptional guest service. Staff is particularly friendly and ceaselessly helpful. I had the opportunity to talk with John Halpin, the GM, to explore the essence of the fantastic COMO experience.

How did you get into the hotel business?

When I turned 13 years old, I asked my parents to sign a permit allowing me to work in a local restaurant outside of school hours. In the summers, I'd work at a family friend's restaurant in Cape Cod. After high school, I went to The Culinary Institute of America and worked my way through most sections in the kitchen. Later I went back to school and earned another degree from Florida International University in Miami, and was recruited by Hilton Hotels to work as a Food and Beverage Outlet Manager at The Waldorf-Astoria in New York City.

When was COMO Shambhala Estate built and what is the property's history?

COMO Shambhala Estate was formerly known as Begawan Giri, which was built by Bradley and Debbie Gardner. It first opened in 1998 in its extraordinary 23-acre (9.3 hectare) location, flanked by jungle-covered riverbanks on three sides, a brisk 15 minutes away from Ubud. In 2004, COMO Hotels & Resorts assumed management and ownership. The Estate is a haven of peace and quiet, and is privy to beautiful natural surroundings. The Estate easily manifested into the flagship of COMO group wellness brand—COMO Shambhala.

Substantial health facilities were added along with five new villa accommodations. Experts in wellness, yoga, Pilates and master therapists all contribute to this unique property, offering extraordinary services and holistic therapies. All staff work together to devise a personalized holistic experience for each guest. Well-being packages are tailored to each individual's personal requirements, including fitness, detoxification, stress management, or just time out from the world's many rigors. Specific treatments are paired with a daily activities schedule, which can include morning yoga, exhilarating walks, hydrotherapy, or pilates sessions as well as our healthful and delicious COMO Shambhala cuisine.

Tell me a little bit about the COMO brand philosophy and how you apply it to the COMO Shambhala Estate?

COMO Hotels & Resorts offers customized luxury travel experiences. The five pillars of the COMO brand really do all culminate here at COMO Shambhala Estate. The combination of wellness, culture, adventure, design, and cuisine drives all our programs, fully customizable for each guest to make their stay as enjoyable as possible.

COMO services begin right from the moment the guest steps off the airplane. Can you elaborate on the steps you take to ensure the guest takes their mind off of work and gets down to the serious business of relaxation?

The COMO experience starts with a personalized airport pick up by our driver who can also facilitate 'fast track' custom/visa immigration for our guests. This continues with a greeting from your butler upon arrival at the Estate with our COMO Shambhala Invigorate scented hand towels and drinks. You'll then have a pre-arranged personal consultation with an Ayurvedic Doctor, Fitness Professional, or a Nutritionist to better understand your goals and helping you make the most of your stay by planning activities, holistic therapies, Asian inspired treatments, exercise training, cuisine, or just some down time. Each guest is assigned personal assistant who will (in their friendly Balinese way) ease you along every aspect of your vacation. Of course, if one just wants to enjoy the healthful tone and natural surroundings, The Estate is readily available for a simple relaxing holiday.

COMO has a second property, Uma Ubud, about 15 minutes away, which you also manage. How do you split your duties between the two, and what are the advantages and disadvantages of this joint management program?

I am very lucky to have great managers looking after all of the various departments and taking care of our guests. Between the two properties we employ 400 people! Being the manager for both can be a challenge, but the value of having a team of dedicated and qualified managers cannot be underestimated.

The main differences between Uma Ubud and COMO Shambhala Estate are that at Uma, we encourage our guests to explore the cultural and adventurous sides of experiential travel. Uma is within walking distance to the town, with art galleries, local markets, temples and rice fields at our doorstep. Uma guests get to enjoy commonalities with elements of wellness weaved into the overall experience. Pursuits such a, healthy menu choices, daily yoga classes, morning rice field walks and a team of local expert guides to make sure you experience the 'Best of Ubud', are all at hand.

At COMO Shambhala Estate, our focus is more on you and your well-being, and the environment there is very conducive to self-focus. Both Uma and The Estate have different themes and designs, but the overall feel still lets you know that you are staying with COMO. The most difficult thing for me is making sure that each property gets my equal attention.

Just over five years ago, Bali suffered through a horrific terrorist act that claimed the lives of many Australians visiting the country. Has this incident been forgotten, or is it still impacting business growth?

The most horrific terrorist attack in Bali was in 2002. There was another smaller incident again in 2005. It was so sad to see an island known for welcoming tourists to its shores suffer so much. Innocence was taken away from the Balinese. It seems ironic, but the attacks have in fact made Bali a safer place to visit. Geographically Bali is easy to get to from Australia, Hong Kong, Singapore, and Thailand. Tourist arrival numbers for Bali keep growing year on year.

In terms of staffing, it appears that you rely mostly upon the local talent pool. Do you find enough qualified people to meet all jobs, and what training programs do you have to maintain this human asset?

Bali has wonderful talent! We have promoted some of our Balinese staff and you can find Balinese working at Parrot Cay, The Metropolitan London, and Cocoa Island. We have a full time training manager working with us, and programs to develop our team to prepare them for bigger and better things. We have activities and programs that help our teams embrace COMO's philosophies. Staff yoga classes and environmental programs, as well as community outreach programs, are all part of working with COMO. Of course, some of our experts are internationally sourced, such as our group executive chef Amanda Gale and Dr. Deepak, our Ayurvedic expert, as well as certain specialized therapists and nutritionists. We combine an Asian Balinese spirit with international expertise; the best of both worlds.

How do you compare your product with key competitors such as the Four Seasons Resort in Ubud?

Well, if you just compare rooms and occupancy, I am sure we could categorize Four Seasons and other hotels on Bali as our competitors. COMO is something completely different though. At Uma Ubud, we encourage our guests to go out and explore the local village life, see a Balinese dance, visit a temple, and take walks along the terraced rice paddy fields. At COMO Shambhala Estate, we encourage our guests to focus on themselves purposefully. This differentiation really sets us apart and is what COMO is known for, garnering an ever-growing fan base.

What is your geographic customer mix, and have you experienced any new trends in this?

We really have guests from all over the world. The economy in Australia and the strength of the Australian Dollar has shown a big increase in Australian guests for the past few years. Chinese visitors are also increasing. Guest from other major Asian hubs such as Singapore and Hong Kong, Japan, the UK, and USA markets are stable at both properties.

With the average guests staying three or more days, and rarely leaving the Estate, how do you stay innovative with your Food & Beverage programs?

The food we offer at The Estate is very honest and thoughtfully sourced. Our group executive chef, Amanda Gale, has gone to great pains to create menus that are healthy and delicious. One of the things we really want to share with our guests is that healthful cuisine can be innovative AND fully appetizing. The Estate's award winning wellness concept includes the cuisine and advocates enzyme-rich, nutritious menus with a strong focus on organic ingredients and simple, natural preparations. Ingredients are locally sourced, some from our own vegetable gardens and fruit bearing trees, and delivered from field to table with minimum delay.

With new staff joining each year, how do you imbue the COMO philosophy of guest service excellence?

We have a great program to induct newcomers to our group and our brand. We also make sure we select the right people from the beginning. The island of Bali has some very good hotel schools and many of the graduates have had training abroad. This really helps us source great teams. We do not have much staff turnover, other than those who we promote to our other properties around the world. As COMO has grown, the group always looks internally and creates opportunities for its team members. The philosophy is simple—you need great staff to feel great so they can in turn make your guests feel great!

What lessons can you give other properties striving to achieve service excellence?

It is never a one-man show. All of the team needs be on the same wavelength. It is vital that everyone is accountable and able to adjust the service levels to suit the individual guest. Serving people is a very intimate relationship. Like any relationship, there needs to be a certain level of trust. It's imperative that you trust your team and share a clear vision of expectations from the brand and guests.

What has been your greatest achievement?

In 1998, I stayed as a guest at COMO Shambhala Estate and it was the greatest hotel experience I ever had (at the time). I never thought that ten years later I would be the GM here. There are many miles ahead of me and I plan to keep looking ahead rather than looking at my past achievements. What makes me smile is that I never dreamed, as a little boy growing up in suburban Massachusetts, that my career would take me to places like Bali and Bhutan. For now, I'm going to keep looking ahead, not back!

Exploring True Blue Bay Resort in Grenada with Owner Russ Fielden

Do you really need a beach? That was the first question I asked Russ Fielden, owner and operator of True Blue Bay Resort in Grenada while on a recent visit. In the past 14 years, Russ, along with his wife Magdalena, have proven that a successful Caribbean resort need not have the classic sand beach centerpiece to be successful, provided that the hotel team treats this deficit as an opportunity.

Today, True Blue Bay Resort is considered one of the most prosperous lodging properties in Grenada. With 50 rooms, thriving dive operations and yachting for families and business travelers, the hotel belittles its modest start up when Russ acquired the near-bankrupt True Blue Inn. Now operating with occupancies well above those of competitive properties, Russ credits Magdalena's creativity and the broadest array of guest offerings for their success.

But it wasn't easy or even planned! As Russ explains, "We went to look at a place in St. Patrick's (at the northern coast of Grenada and far from the bulk of the population who are congregated on the southern tip near the capital St. George's), and stopped in at True Blue Inn for lunch where we heard they were going out of business. We called the bank holding the loan and agreed to a mortgage arrangement. The bank even sold us the furnishings of the then seven-room property for an additional dollar! The idea was that if we survived the first year, the bank would agree to restructure the loan and expand the capital base."

Using a building-block approach, Russ encouraged Aquanauts Grenada, a leading dive operation to set up shop within the confines of the resort. Horizon Yacht Charters subsequently followed suit. Both operate as independent entities, yet they serve to synergistically support occupancies. Building upon this foundation, Russ encouraged a local spa operator, Le Conch, and a local car rental company, Indigo, to add outlets as well. This creative program bolstered True Blue Bay Resort's product offerings to its guests without adding significant overhead.

Having these operations all under one roof was a good start, but these 'creative connections' were simply not enough. As Russ explains, "With no beach, you get an automatic deduction of one star in the guide books. So, we had to dig deeper and create our own environment."

Here, Magdalena's artistic approach to guest rooms and common areas played a critical role. Using vivid Caribbean colors, the property glows in a palette of warm blue, orange, yellow and red pastels.

At first, your eyes have trouble focusing, but then the genius of the hues takes hold, allowing you to notice the fine details—custom ironwork, metal signage and unique use of decorative materials. When I visit, my room was decorated with rose petals arranged in decorative patterns throughout my suite. I find these additional touches to be most remarkable because the hotel is classified in the mid-price range and not at the premium level.

Not having a beach also forced Russ into developing a strong corporate business. Tying in with St. George's University (SGU), just a few minutes away, provided an additional source of rooms' generation. By establishing close relationships with the students and faculty, parents of students deliver 15% of total annual rooms' occupancy. I experienced this first hand as an evening welcome party for SGU students made the property's Dodgy Dock Restaurant standing room only. Russ estimates that 35% of total F&B revenue is generated by the SGU constituency.

The property's leisure business augments dive, yachting and spa with family and couples programs. All are as creative as the owners. Social media confirms True Blue Bay Resort as a kid's heaven with a wide variety of activities and a 'mini-beach' created by trucking in more than enough sand for young children to think they are on a beachfront property. Couples can also try cooking classes or partake in rum tastings.

If all of this sounds a little bit frenetic, it reflects Russ' active over passive approach. Russ encourages his guests to go see all that the island of Grenada has to offer. Unlike those resort operators who want to capture every guest dollar, he recognizes the wide variety of excellent cuisine available in local restaurants and the myriad of local, completely unaffiliated, attractions. With this sort of gusto, it's no surprise that Russ is the current president of the Grenada Hotel & Tourism Association (GHTA).

An Interview with Bob Moore, General Manager of Hilton Garden Inn Carlsbad Beach

Hilton Garden Inn Carlsbad Beach is situated along the brilliant Southern Californian coastline in Carlsbad, thirty minutes north of San Diego. With 161 rooms, the property is ideally located for leisure and local business. But what's most appealing about the property is its distinguished quality of guest services. The staff is particularly friendly and ceaselessly helpful. I had the opportunity to converse with Bob Moore, the General Manager, to look into the roots of their continued success.

Perhaps you can start by listing some the hotel's awards over the past decade.

We're proud to have won numerous awards including three times with J. D. Power for hotel guest satisfaction. We have worked hard and have achieved the highest quality assurance score from Hilton management twenty consecutive times.

I have seen the Trip Advisor recounts. Guests love the property. What's the secret?

We have a five star service mentality. We are all about creating memories for our guests and that is a large part of the culture we nurture in our team. We take advantage of every opportunity to engage our guests and try to find out information that will allow us to customize their experience while they are visiting our hotel. Further, we'll often ask how they heard about us and what helped them choose our hotel. As expected, many guests will say they found us through TripAdvisor. During our conversation, we'll politely ask that they post candid comments about their experience after they depart to help prospective travelers make an informed decision.

When you stay at HGI Carlsbad, it does not feel like the standard, traditional mid-range property. How do you maintain this feeling?

This feeling is based upon our approach, rather than the physical plant. Our rooms and furnishings conform to Garden Inn standards. However, our owners are very supportive of our somewhat untraditional methods. They've allowed us to develop and sustain many programs and service offerings that go beyond the minimum requirement for a Garden Inn. So, I would say the secret is to look at the property against world standards.

For example, we have custom sea creature plush toys created with our logo on them that we give to children upon check-in. We hire an external yoga instructor to hold complimentary classes overlooking the Pacific Ocean once a week. We send a thank you postcard to every one of our guests, and we send it a day prior to their departure so by the time they get home they already have our note. The most impactful program we offer, however, is our 'Movies on the Lawn' where, from Memorial Day to Labor Day, we set up an outdoor movie theater, equipped with fresh popcorn and reserved blanket seating. This goes on for four nights a week where we project animated movies on an 18-foot movie screen. It really allows the families to enjoy some quality time together in the evening hours.

The location is a critical factor in the property's success. Yet, you are not directly on the beach. How do you make the location work for you?

It certainly does help having the beach right across the road. However, I would not attest our overall success to the fact that we are a beachfront property. This location helps drive attention to our hotel. But getting awareness is less than half the battle; turning guests into raving fans is where we focus our attention and this is how we create the hotel's success stories and loyal base of support. It really is all about the team members; they are the ones who breathe life into a property and make it what it is, regardless of location.

How do you stay innovative with your family-oriented programs?

Some of our most impactful beliefs are 'Out-of-the-Box Thinking' and the idea of 'Reinventing Yourself' each and every day. After 11 years with the same property, I truly believe that this is how I've been able to avoid complacency. To this day, I'm still able to contribute fresh and new ideas to the property to keep us ahead of the curve. To do this successfully it takes an open mind for every facet of your operations. Just because something worked in the past does not mean that it cannot be improved or that an entirely different route might actually be more effective.

For example, once a quarter, I take a specific, successful aspect of the hotel operations and dissect it to its simplest form, and then reevaluate whether or not it merits changes. It's important to be humble during this process as well. Be open to the suggestions of others and don't shy away from collaboration; multiple brains focusing on one task will always produce more favorable results than one.

With new staff and interns joining each year, how do you imbue the spirit of guest service excellence?

It's all in the training. Whatever you put into your team members, you can expect the same in return. Hilton Corporate has armed all of their properties with some wonderful training programs that, when embraced, are able to guide all team members toward their full potential.

What lessons can you give other mid-range properties striving for improvement?

It's all about being part of the guest's experience and engaging all of your guests to have a better understanding of their wants and desires during their stay. This does not just apply to the frontline employees either; it all starts with the management of the hotel.

For example, our front office manager makes it a point to spend at least three hours daily working the front desk, the restaurant, or interacting with guests in the lobby area. He doesn't use his 'Desk Work' as an excuse to disregard immersion in the guest's experience. This creed pervades our entire management team, and it's noticed by the frontline staff who follow in kind.

Another motto we have here is, 'The smallest things make the biggest differences,' which for us means that it doesn't have to be a sizeable monetary cost or effort to create unique and memorable experiences for guests. All that's required is an open ear and a willingness to take those small steps to make your guests feel truly valued and validated.

What has been your greatest achievement?

The greatest reward for me is being able to watch the successes and the career growth in the individuals who have worked in a hotel that I have managed; being able to follow their careers from frontline employees with me, through the management ranks, and then on to the duties of GMs, DOS and VPs. Knowing that I played an integral role in their continued growth through hospitality and helped guide them to success gives me the utmost of joy. It helps me know that I've done my job well.

(Bob is now the General Manager of a sister property, the Hilton Carlsbad Oceanfront Resort and Spa, recently opened about a mile south of the Hilton Garden Inn Carlsbad Beach.)

A Taste of the Orient with COMO Metropolitan in Bangkok

While touring Southeast Asia with my wife, and after visiting Sydney, Bali and Singapore, my fourth stop was Bangkok. At just two meters above sea level, we were scheduled to reach the great Thailand capital at a time when flooding threatened to shut down the city. Taking our chances, we landed to sunny skies and friendly faces.

When we arrived at the COMO Metropolitan, we were greeted by the hotel's GM, James Low, who promptly exclaimed, "You brought the sun with you!" For the three days in the city, the water subsided and we were treated to an urban experience so vivacious I'd recommend a Bangkok visit to everyone. Whether in the near future or years from now, you have to see it to believe it. Readying for departure to the next destination, I had the chance to sit down with James Low to talk about his experiences at the COMO Metropolitan.

To start, can you give a brief description of COMO Metropolitan Bangkok? How did you come to join the COMO team?

A part of COMO Hotels & Resorts, the Metropolitan Bangkok, arguably the city's first design-driven hotel, is located on South Sathorn Road, enjoying a close proximity to Bangkok's famed urban nightlife as the style hub of the east. The 171 rooms and suites—defined by subtle and elegant contemporary design—all offer generous space, with comfort and luxury felt in telling detail; from refined 500 thread count cotton beddings and silk curtains, handmade mosaic and limestone bathroom, to the COMO Shambhala signature bathroom amenities.

The Met Bar, a stylish members-only bar lounge, serves a comprehensive selection of tailored Martini cocktails. Headline restaurant Nahm by David Thompson delivers indulgent authentic Thai cuisine, whilst Glow focuses on extraordinary organic, healthful cuisine. Relaxation is also available with a signature COMO Shambhala Urban Escape, comprising holistic Asian-inspired treatments, a gym, yoga studio and 20 meter outdoor pool.

Prior to my joining the COMO team as the pre-opening General Manager for the Metropolitan Bangkok, I was working for Hotel Properties Limited (owner of the Metropolitan Bangkok) for 12 years. My personal file was forwarded to Mrs. Christina Ong for consideration to head the Bangkok project and after an initial interview in Singapore, I came on board COMO. My hotel experience goes back 33 years with the Regent Kuala Lumpur (now under the Four Seasons banner), Merlin Hotels, Holiday Inn Johor Baru & Singapore, Mandarin Oriental Kuala Lumpur, Hyatt Saujana and Concorde Hotels.

How does COMO Metropolitan Bangkok integrate with the other COMO properties around the world?

Metropolitan Bangkok is able to extend the unique COMO experience in this vibrant city; an experience that encompasses the five pillars encapsulating the COMO hallmarks. These are: Design (Western contemporary classics juxtaposed with Eastern antiquities), Service (warm and natural Thai hospitality), Cuisine (Nahm by the award winning chef, David Thompson, and Glow for healthful, spa cuisine), Wellbeing (Como Shambhala Urban Escape spa), and Culture/ Adventure (promoting Thai art and performing arts in this lively city). Also, as the hub into Southeast Asia, Bangkok is able to offer a first-hand introduction of the COMO experience prior to our guests visiting sister properties in Bhutan, Bali, Cocoa Island in the Maldives, and soon-to-be Phuket.

Although the property has not been directly impacted, how has the flooding in Bangkok altered the hotel's business?

Hotel occupancies in the city plummeted after advisories against travel into Bangkok were posted by major governments. Meetings and events were noticeably affected as well as the regional leisure traffic out of Hong Kong, Singapore, Japan and Korea. However, we managed to accommodate some local residents whose homes were affected by the floods and we adjusted staff schedules to support those living in the more heavily affected suburban regions. Bangkok is such a unique destination we expect the numbers to return to normal once the waters subside.

How did the hotel adapt to the floods, both to ensure the safety of patrons and staff, and to continue to provide the best quality experience while in the city? Did you have any crisis management plans already in place?

We have a crisis management team on standby 24 hours a day and the team is certified in crisis management training. We also have in place an evacuation manual in the event of any emergencies in the hotel. The following are some of the preparations made to adapt to the flood situation in Bangkok:

- Seal all possible areas (up to two meters) in which flood water may seep in using the building walls, sand bags and drain plugs in case of water backwash
- Basement electrical appliances moved to higher grounds
- Switch off main electrical board when the water approaches the 1.8m height threshold and call the area electricity board to turn off supply in our area
- Ensure sufficient supply of essential items in hotel such as bottled water, food, gas, diesel, blankets and basic first aid
- Allocate an area to evacuate all guests for briefing and to act as an information center
- Have passenger trucks on standby for evacuation to the airport
- Activate a 24 hour news desk posted on our web site to update incoming guests and reservations with the latest information
- Ensure sufficient staff are available at the hotel to service our guests
- Containment of operations and services in the event of prolonged flooding

While visiting, I had a chance to experience one of your two-story penthouse suites—one of the finest accommodations in all of Bangkok. Do you have a separate marketing plan for such rooms?

No, we do not have a separate marketing plan for the four penthouse suites but we do have press releases sent out when necessary. As you experienced, the product is remarkable: you are greeted by the soaring expanse of an eight-meter high ceiling, and a floating staircase to your guest bedroom and private office. Once a guest has stayed in one of these suites, there is no going back to a single story product.

Each penthouse suite comes with its own personal butler. Do most people understand the advantages of a butler?

Unfortunately, most visitors do not make full use of our butlers' expertise, even though most COMO guests know the level of service they can expect as the butler program is available throughout the COMO group. The butlers onsite here at the Metropolitan are very humble and talented individuals, helping guests plan their days, arranging for other services or reservations, and acclimatizing visitors to Bangkok by introducing them local customs and languages.

The hotel's signature restaurant, Nahm, is led by the renowned chef, David Thompson. How did you leverage his recognition to market the property?

As the Metropolitan Bangkok is already in its eighth year of operation, PR opportunities were less readily available. David Thompson's Nahm gave the hotel plenty of opportunities to refresh the brand. David has a very strong following in the UK, US, Australia, Hong Kong and Singapore, and they were scores of media requests to cover Nahm in these major markets. We also took the opportunity to market a package entitled 'Tantalizing Thai' to promote our rooms together with a dining experience in Nahm plus a personalized signed copy of David's prominent cook book, *Thai Food*.

In Search of Hotel Excellence: Montage Beverly Hills

There are few markets so quintessentially related to luxury as Beverly Hills. Here, within a few blocks of the famous Rodeo Drive are several of the world's most recognized venues: Peninsula, Four Seasons, Bel Air, Regent, Beverly Hilton and Montage Beverly Hills.

Montage, a relative newcomer to this esteemed group, has quickly established its position. Is it the best of the group? That's a matter of personal opinion. While some guests will show a personal preference, all will agree that the Montage Beverly Hills is one incredible property. General Manager, Hermann Elger, is master of this house. I had an opportunity to ask him a few questions and learn about how he delivers service excellence to one of the most challenging guests in the world—celebrities.

Montage is one of the finest properties, catering to a demanding level of clientele. Tell me a little bit about how you maintain your guest service standards.

We train our employees to perform at high levels of service from the very beginning. This starts with modeling to them the same respect, humility, and courtesy that we hope they show our guests. From guest service manager to housekeeping coordinator, our entire team is assigned with the task of capturing as much information as possible about our guests. We log these 'Montage Moments' immediately to compile extensive guest records. This enables us to really engage our guests and appeal to their interests with future bespoke experiences.

We are committed to knowing our guests as we know they expect a high level of attention to detail and sense of urgency every time and for every request. We maintain our guest service standards by providing our team with the training to really take ownership of all guest requests, creating personalized gestures that exceed guest expectations and build lifelong memories. It's these emotional connections that truly keep our guests returning time after time.

Does having residences in the property create greater challenges for your team?

The residential component complements the guest experience. It has truly been designed for the special guest interested in the Montage lifestyle and all of the accompanying amenities. We have a dedicated Residential Manager who acts as concierge, personal assistant, and estate manager to our residents. This role is essential to communicate the unique preferences of our permanent guests to our operations team in such areas as housekeeping, laundry, or in room dining.

Our residents are like family to our team, often celebrating their most memorable or momentous experiences with us. It is extremely fulfilling to foster relationships with them over time, and they truly appreciate the high level of service and hospitality with which we welcome them home each day.

Tell me a little bit about the HR process: hiring, training and maintaining service excellence at all levels, from housekeeper to manager?

We exercise meticulous hiring and screening practices, a structured interview process, and we immerse new Associates in two full days of our training orientation upon arrival. They build a strong camaraderie there while learning our culture, etiquette, and methodology. While there, we empower them with the steps to resolve a guest complaint, truly listen to our guests, and create the unique surprises that can make a guest's visit truly memorable.

We maintain service at all levels through ongoing training and learning opportunities, and constant internal evaluations that all standards are being adhered to. Our Associates enjoy the sense of teamwork that our culture provides, the recognition of a job well done, and we experience an extremely low turnover rate. As such, it is an extremely competitive job market, with a ratio of 80 applicants to every 19 positions available.

Whenever possible, we encourage promotions from within and we train our growing leadership teams with ongoing learning opportunities largely based on 'The Seven Habits of Highly Effective People.' We search for talent, sincerity and a genuine desire to serve. An Associate who joins us armed with these attributes will become an expert in the Montage service culture very quickly.

What is your ratio of repeat guests to new customers? How do you nurture guest loyalty? Do you cross-sell other Montage properties and if so how?

Our ratio of repeat guests to new customers is approximately 60% repeat guests to 40% new guests. We nurture guest loyalty through recognition and a strong guest relations program. We have a great relationship with our sister properties and cross-sell whenever possible; it is highly encouraged.

There is quite a bit of group and repeat crossover to our client base, and our guests have come to enjoy the Montage experience at all three of our unique properties in our three very special destinations. Our sales team is encouraged to promote all three properties with joint participation on sales calls, in tradeshows, and client events. Our team always travels with each hotel's brochures and access to the occupancy and availability of our sister properties.

For example, we have previously offered room packages promoting our incredible 'City and Sea' properties together, coupling the serenity of Laguna Beach with the sophistication of Beverly Hills. Our guests are always delighted to learn that their most detailed preferences have been communicated between our properties prior to their arrival, whether it's greeting their children and pets by name or greeting them at the door with their favorite cocktail.

What role do local and community activities play in your property's development?

The local community has welcomed us with open arms and we thoroughly enjoy being involved; whether it's participation from our chefs in local events such as the prestigious Greystone Concours d'Elegance or through our associate-led volunteer community outreach program, Hearts of Montage which supports such initiatives as Clean the World, Race for the Cure, and the Wendy Walk. Personally, I participate as a member in Rotary Club of Beverly Hills, the Beverly

Hills Chamber of Commerce, and their Economic Development Council. We assign responsibility to our Associates of all levels to act as ambassadors in the community.

The 2008 recession affected all luxury hotels. Is the Montage Beverly Hills fully recovered from this period? What is your forecast for the future?

There is no denying that the recession affected the luxury market. We're on our way to a full recovery with a very optimistic forecast for the future. ADR and occupancies continue to grow. Beverly Hills is such a unique destination and we are encouraged by the continuously growing number of guests who visit us here at Montage. The needs of our guests dictate the changes that we've made in the last few years.

For example, we changed our previous restaurant to Scarpetta, bringing in celebrity chef Scott Conant and we partnered with The Macallan and Lalique to create a unique experience in £10 to feature hand-crafted cocktails and light fare in an intimate and refined setting.

How do you differentiate yourself from other luxury competitors such as Four Seasons and Peninsula?

We reinforce comfortable luxury, a warm and welcoming service without pretension. It's the grace and humility of our team that truly differentiates us from the competition. We welcome our guests as if we were welcoming them graciously into our very own homes.

Anything else you would like to add?

I frequently tell my team to avoid the 'if it's not broke, don't fix it' mentality. I encourage them to break it, fix it, and make it better. It is only by adapting this philosophy that we can eliminate the fear of making changes and truly become great.

Boutique Super-Luxury Lives Amidst Behemoth Luxury Brands: An Interview With David Mounteer, General Manager of The Hazelton Hotel in Toronto

The Hazelton Hotel is a very fascinating case study. Situated in the heart of the chic Toronto shopping enclave of Yorkville, this 62-room and 15-suite independent hotel opened in the summer of 2007 to instant applause and 5-star status. Since then, it has become a landmark for Canadian ultramodern hospitality as well as for its feature restaurant 'ONE' and for celebrity spotting, especially during the Toronto International Film Festival.

The Hazelton is also weathering a surge of new luxury brands to the city including the Thompson Hotel (opened June 2010), a Ritz-Carlton (opened February 2011), a Trump Tower (opened January 2012), Shangri-La (opening late summer 2012) and a new Four Seasons (also scheduled to open late summer 2012)—all of them substantially larger and able to leverage international corporate engines. Yet no one at the Hazelton is overly worried, especially David Mounteer, the GM, who believes that his hotel's biggest strength is its boutique status and its unique approach to luxury.

As General Manager, what approach to luxury do you and your team adopt?

People don't want the old-fashioned, 'white glove' version of luxury. Many high-end hotels are holding on to that concept and think that the 'white glove' treatment is what the consumer wants, even though the reality is quite different.

This modern iteration of super-luxury is less about formality and pretense. Instead, it draws on the warmth, comfort, and personable nature that guest services can offer. That's where the Hazelton excels.

Guest services here have embraced this approach. And furthermore, we have tailored every aspect of the hotel to fit this ideology—the room, the materials, the fabrics, the furniture, the art. It's extremely luxurious but also approachable and totally unpretentious, embodying a new niche in the marketplace.

At some of the hotels I've stayed at, I feel like I'm sleeping in an 'operating room'. The Hazelton delivers that rare balance between super-luxury, modern design, and personality—not just in terms of the building but in the services we offer as well.

Our team is dedicated to creating that 'coming home' feeling for visitors. Our guests are people who travel often. They've experienced luxury properties across the globe and they say that the Hazelton is where they feel most at home. That's exactly what modern luxury is about; it's about warmth.

In what way do you gear guest services toward the qualities of warmth and personality? Could you describe any specific stories that demonstrate the impact on guest experience?

When I visit New York City, I always indulge in a street hot dog with sauerkraut and spicy mustard. It's something special, and Manhattan is the only place in the world where I can get that feeling. To me, that's luxury—it's scarce. It's only in New York where I get that feeling and it has nothing to do with cost!

It's in this capacity that we strive to play to our guests needs and wants on a much deeper level than the competition. We empathize and enjoy the people who stay here.

Here is a parallel from a real experience on property. We have a guest who stays here who was born and raised in Montreal. He told one of the bell services team that he missed Schwartz's smoked meat sandwiches every time he came to Toronto. You can only get Schwartz's in Montreal. So, we FedEx Schwartz's smoked meat for him when he stays with us every few months or so. We even order their kosher pickles!

We have another client from Montreal; he stays here every few weeks. We could send him a bottle of champagne or something along those lines. But that wouldn't have a personal impact on his stay here. This client and I were talking at the hotel's bar one afternoon. He mentioned that despite his great satisfaction with his stay here, there was one minor flaw—he didn't have the ability to watch his favorite hockey team while in Toronto.

Without notifying him, I called the hotel's tech department and asked them what we could do. We called the cable company to remedy this problem, which they did. Then we informed this client that he could watch his favorite hockey team in his hotel room whenever he so pleased. I think it goes without saying that this type of very personalized service creates a far greater impact than sending a bottle of champagne to his room.

Considering that the Hazelton Hotel attracts many high profile guests, are there any privacy issues or personal requests that the staff find difficult to appease?

Catering to high profile guests is not easy, but it is fun. The Hazelton's approach to privacy and confidentiality is second to none in Toronto. The Hazelton attracts A-List Hollywood stars and top musicians, and we do our best to ensure their privacy. For starters, we create codenames for certain high profile guests to ensure that they receive the privacy they desire.

Often, these high profile guests make all sorts of eclectic requests. These types of guests tend to have erratic travel and work schedules, and it is our responsibility to ensure that they are always comfortable when they're with us. Such demands often come from a stressful place; they're under a lot of pressure, and the fulfillment of these demands helps alleviate that pressure.

Their presence, in fact, invigorates the staff and helps us perform to our best. I always find high profile guests to be a motivational boost. In many ways, high profile guests are far easier to please than our other guests. They are often more vocal about their wants and needs—many even come with a specific list of requirements. With most guests, you don't learn about what they want until they arrive or after they've left. You have to dig deep and listen; you have to observe very carefully. So in this sense, it's much easier with high profile clients.

Can you cite any specific examples of demands that high profile guests make?

One high profile guest from the music industry comes to stay with us two or three times a year. He is known to be a rather fastidious fellow when it comes to his accommodations. He has been known to simply walk out of hotels if they don't meet his expectations. But when he comes to Toronto, he will stay nowhere other than the Hazelton.

This particular guest likes cookies. He has a specific cookie recipe—oatmeal raisin cookies—and the recipe has to be carried out in a precise way. It's posted in the kitchen at all times whenever he stays with us. These cookies have to be ready to go at any time, whether it's 3 AM or 3 PM. The cost isn't too high, and it's an easy request to fulfill because the communication beforehand is explicit. In the end, we're happy to oblige; it's what we're here for.

How do you choose your team to meet the level of clientele that stays at the Hazelton? Is there is a specific HR philosophy by which you abide when considering applicants?

We have a great team; we know what we're looking for in people. We listen to candidates during interviews very carefully, and there are certain key elements that pique our interest. When considering new employees, we primarily look for the yearning motivation to take care of people. If a work applicant says in earnest, "I just love to take care of people," I'm pretty much sold at that point.

It's that essential quality we try to find in our employees, because that's what our industry is all about. You can teach a skill set, but it's far more difficult to foster a great attitude in people. Our HR philosophy is to seek not just a refined and experienced repertoire of expertise in a potential employee, but also a positive and motivated attitude.

How will you position your hotel amidst Toronto's recent influx of luxury hotels?

Increased competition is a double-edged sword. These new luxury hotels are great for the city; they'll bring even more people to Toronto every year. The Hazelton and these new luxury hotels will really put Toronto on the luxury destination map.

However, we are not nervous about these new competitors. We are confident that we have exceptional service. We plan on emphasizing and reemphasizing our position as a warm, modern super-luxury boutique hotel with paramount guest services—services that can't easily be replicated for a substantially larger hotel.

We have a unique philosophy, a unique staff and a unique property. If we stay true to our values then we will continue to thrive, regardless of the competition.

Conclusion

The Kingsbrae Arms is located in St. Andrews-by-the-Sea in Nova Scotia. A seasonal operation, patrons travel 10 hours just to enjoy the cuisine and the atmosphere of being in this idyllic country manor.

Are You An Ostrich or a Llama?

When you think of an ostrich, you probably visualize a large bird, with its 'head in the sand'. I'm well aware that ostriches don't actually stick their heads in the sand, but I'm using this allegory to demonstrate a point. In fact, an alternate dictionary meaning for an ostrich is 'a person who ignores unpleasant things'. Call someone an ostrich at your own risk!

Now imagine how this big bird might apply to a managerial setting. But, what about the venerable llama? This South American pack animal is mostly known for its soft coat which is woven into fleece clothing, but it is also sure-footed, reliable, patient, and actually quite friendly.

These two animals have come to represent two distinct approaches that apply to hotelier mindsets. Let's examine the character traits most likely associated with each of these. In doing so, I ask the question, "Are you an ostrich or a llama?" To see which moniker best suits your management style, answer the following questions about the way you conduct your business. Scoring is simple: gain one point for each 'Llama' statement you agree to, subtract one point for each 'Ostrich' statement you agree to. No cheating, though; neither animal is known for this particularly human characteristic!

Consider yourself a llama if:

- You have embraced tablet technology in your organization, or have a firm plan to do so (at a minimum) in sales, F&B, front desk and concierge departments.
- You manage your social media presence through continuous monitoring and pro-actively analyze means to optimize your response to guest demands.
- Your social media is not managed by your secretary on a 'when she has the time' basis, but is a truly defined function within your operation, either in-house or out-sourced.
- You eschew OTA programs, recognizing that customers garnered through this channel are forever lost to your brand.
- You rarely, if ever, use flash sales, recognizing the discounts offered undermine your loyal guests' paid rates.

- You read industry columns regularly and send key, relevant article links to members of your planning committee and senior team.
- Your property is committed to substantial energy savings, recycling and waste reduction.
- Your team is involved with at least one local/regional charity. This commitment transcends just sending used furniture and bedding when available. You have investigated and are donating excess food to your local food bank.
- You hold a bridal open house at least once every 4-6 weeks and actively pursue a continuous goal of holding more weddings than the previous year. To this end, you offer incentives to staff members who are able to secure wedding referrals.
- You encourage your chef to test at least one new dish on the menu each season.
- In the depths of your low season, you encourage all members of your staff to have their families spend at least one night on property to experience the product. You do not charge for this. At a minimum, you include breakfast in this experience.
- You not only read every major OTA review of your property, but also personally respond to all of them and circulate them as a means of improving guest services.
- You motivate your front desk personnel to capture the email addresses of all guests, and together you are working towards a goal of 100% compliance. Beyond email, you record preferences and any additional information into the profile section of your PMS.
- You encourage the hiring of interns and/or co-op students to augment staff, and while you might not pay interns a salary, you ensure that they get rewarded with complimentary rooms and other benefits.
- You have a crisis communications plan and review it with your team once every six months. You share this plan with both your PR and ad agencies.
- You see your entire team as guest service ambassadors, training and motivating accordingly.
- You are an active member of your local CVB, and contribute manpower and materials to assist in its success. (Add a bonus

point if you, personally, are currently a board or committee member.)

- You attended at least one of last year's AHMA, HITEC or major trade show. (Add a bonus point if you were a presenter!)
- You often lie awake at night worrying about how to make the property better for your employees and your guests.

Consider yourself an ostrich if:

- You insist that your sales and marketing teams develop a comprehensive marketing plan that includes detailed day-by-day sales forecasts for the entire year, recognizing that the day-by-day plan is mere conjecture to 'force' a final occupancy percentage.
- You have not yet totally embraced social media, because you are waiting for this 'fad' to fizzle out.
- You rarely answer your own telephone or promptly return emails, and you make it next to impossible for anyone, with the exception of your planning committee members, to speak directly with you.
- You refuse to empower your sales team to negotiate comprehensive rates for groups and/or weddings during peak periods because 'we'll fill up without them'.
- You still believe in rack rates, generally thinking that they can be increased by $10 to $20 each year independent of competitive and market conditions.
- You think that those scuff marks in the hallway will easily be managed by housekeeping and a little bit of elbow grease without involving your maintenance team, thereby hoping to save some money on minor repairs.
- You answer or scan your Blackberry or iPhone during most meetings in which you are present, and allow other members of your team to do the same.
- You see your entry-level positions as a cost, rather than seeing these candidates as potential planning committee members in the future.
- You rarely eat with your staff in the cafeteria and don't even know the menu. You think of the subsidized cafeteria as a cost,

rather than seeing it as an opportunity to improve your staff relationships.
- You don't speak at least a few sentences of another language to interact with foreign guests.
- You lie awake at night worrying how to make the bottom line closer to your owners' ever-demanding targets.

If you've been honest, it's rare get a result of 15 or more when this test is first completed. If you do, consider yourself an enlightened manager, well ahead of your peer group. A score of 8 to 14 shows that you have good promise and it recognizes your determination to improve. If you score below 7, remedial development action may be needed. Seek help from a coach, take some professional development courses at an hotelier college or pick up some additional literature in our field.

The world needs both great managers and great GMs. There are ample ways to further your career successfully, both by always thinking of the human factor and by applying a little ingenuity. Ostriches make good zoo animals and, according to many hotel chefs, great entrees. For the path to enlightened and empowered management, however, follow the llama.

Glossary of Terms

ADR: Average Daily Rate; a calculation of the total room revenue for a day divided by the number of rooms sold, generally excluding ancillary revenue, such as F&B, parking, etc.

Comp: Room given on a complementary basis. As a verb, "He was comped."

CMS: Content Management System; the 'back-end' of a modern website, allowing for revisions without directly involving a programmer.

DofM: Director of Marketing; can also be referred to as the Director of Sales and Marketing (DofSM).

ES: Extended Stay; a guest who utilizes a room for a period longer than 14 days, typically renting the accommodation on a monthly basis.

F&B: Food and Beverage; referring not only to the outlets, but as well, catering and room service.

FIT: Frequent Independent Traveler; as in leisure guests who are not part of a specific group, wholesaler or tour operator package.

GDS: Guest Distribution System; a computerized system generally utilized by airlines and hotels, and managed by traditional travel agents.

GM: General Manager. In some properties there are some variations, with a two-tiered senior management including a Managing Director and a Hotel Manager (other variations exist).

IT: Information Technology.

MOD: Manager on Duty; when the general manager is not in house, his/her replacement becomes the MOD.

OCC: Percentage Occupancy; the ratio of rooms in use to total rooms in house; often comped out of service rooms are not considered as in use.

OTA: Online Travel Agency; agencies operating primarily through the Internet.

PMS: Property Management System; the software used to internally manage and integrate rooms, revenues, ancillary services, etc.

POS: Point of Sale; being the data accumulated through cash registers/computers located throughout the property.

RevPAR: Revenue Per Available Room; calculated by taking the total revenue of the property and dividing it by the number of rooms times 365, or the number of days in the revenue period.

RevPOR: Revenue Per Occupied Room; calculated by taking the total revenue of a property and dividing it by the number of rooms occupied; generally more useful in analysis of properties with a high degree of ancillary revenue, such as a spa, food & beverage and a gold course.

RM: Revenue Manager; responsible for analyzing competitive rates and advising the general manager on setting room rates to maximize yield on occupancy.

SEO: Search Engine Optimization; the process of enhancing how a property is found when using search terms within Internet search engines.

VIP: Very Important Person. A person who is 'VIP'd' typically receives a special welcome amenity, upgrades and personalized reception from a key member of staff.

Acknowledgements

I'd like to extend a special thanks to everyone at LMA Communications Inc. who has worked (and survived!) with me over the years. Without your dedication to serving our clients, this book would not have been possible. Specifically, I'd like to thank my son and editor, Adam Mogelonsky and the book cover's graphic designer, Ryan Tong.

Next, my deepest thanks and admiration go out to all those I interviewed over the years in order to make this book whole. In alphabetical order by last name, this includes Reggie Aggarwal, Gloria Ah Sam, Renato Alesiani, Marc Bauer, Mike Braykovich, Harry Chancey, Kathleen Doheny, Hermann Elger, Saar Fabrikant, Russ Fielden, Adele Gutman, John Halpin, Sir Royston Hopkin, Simon Kerr, James Low, William MacKay, Debbie Misajon, Bob Moore, Colin Morrison, David Mounteer, Carley Roney, Shawn Seipler, Sandeep Sharma, Robert Simon, Kristin Stark and Felicia Yukich.

I would also like to thank several individuals whose names do not appear as an interviewee, but have nevertheless provided valuable insight. In alphabetical order by last name, this includes Howard Breen, Marshall Calder, William Callnin, Gordon Carncross, Janis Clapoff, Benedict Cummins, Anne Edwards, Kuno Fasel, Fred Grapstein, Glenn Haussman, (the late) Linda Jalbert, Chuck Kelley, Isadore Sharp, Ann Stork, Klaus Tenter and Jeff Weinstein.

Lastly, I'll like to especially thank my wife of 31 years, Maureen, who has put up with me all of this time, as well as my family, friends and clients who I've had the pleasure of knowing over the years. Life is a winding road and our time together has been a critical influence for me to write on the topic of hospitality.

Charitable Cause

All endeavors that we undertake should recognize that we are part of a global community, where others less fortunate than us deserve our support.

A portion of the proceeds of this book will be sent to CNIB, the Canadian National Institute for the Blind, a well-deserving organization that demonstrates their commitment to helping the sight-impaired.

Since its founding in 1918, CNIB has grown to become the primary resource for Canadians who are blind or partially sighted, with offices in communities across the country. It is proud to help thousands of Canadians see beyond vision loss every single day.

CNIB is a registered charity, passionately providing community-based support, knowledge and a national voice to ensure Canadians who are blind or partially sighted have the confidence, skills and opportunities to fully participate in life.

To do that, its dedicated specialists work with people of all ages in their own homes, communities or local CNIB offices—providing the personalized rehabilitation support they need to **see beyond vision loss**, build their independence and lead the lives they want.

In addition to community-based services, CNIB also works hand-in-hand with Canadians who are blind or partially sighted to advocate for a barrier-free society, and strives to eliminate avoidable sight loss with world-class research and by promoting the importance of vision health through public education.

Visit www.cnib.ca
1-800-563-2642 or 416-486-2500

About the Author

Larry is the founder and chief executive officer of LMA Communications Inc., a Toronto-based advertising and consulting agency that focuses on the hospitality industry. He earned an Honors Bachelor of Civil Engineering degree from Concordia University in Montreal, Quebec and a Masters of Business Administration from McMaster University in Hamilton, Ontario. He holds a Professional Engineering accreditation in the province of Ontario.

He commenced his marketing career with Procter & Gamble, working in their advertising department as a brand manager on many well-known product lines. Next, he moved to the service side of the business, spending several years at Bozell Palmer Bonner (at the time Bozell was one of the world's 'top ten' advertising agencies), shifting latterly as managing director of their retail/promotions division, Promotion Solutions Group. During his tenure at the agency, he created a hospitality and tourism team, which served Four Season Hotels & Resorts, Howard Johnson, and American Airlines.

It was the era of giant agency mergers, and Larry took the decision to hang his own shingle, founding LMA in January of 1991. As one of its first assignments, LMA was promptly charged with the role of strategic planning for Preferred Hotels and Resorts Worldwide. LMA conducted worldwide surveys and wrote the strategic program that is still in place today. In addition to Preferred, LMA increased its hospitality presence with hotel clients across North America, Asia and Europe.

Today, LMA works with hoteliers across the world, helping them solve marketing challenges and grow their businesses. Larry also serves as a mentor for LMA's young and diverse team members. His knowledge of hotel marketing has been demonstrated through the accumulation of more awards, over sixty at last count, at HSMAI (Hospitality Sales and Marketing Association Institute) than any other Canadian agency. This includes the only win of the coveted Platinum level award outside of the United States. LMA was also awarded 'Worldwide e-Marketing Agency of the Year' by TravelClick in 2007.

Currently, Larry is actively involved in several voluntary charitable board roles. He has lectured at the Cornell University Hotel School. He is one of the most frequently published writers in the field of hospitality marketing, with weekly contributions in five of the world's top industry publications. He is an associate of both G7 Hospitality and Cayuga Hospitality Advisors.

Larry lives in Toronto with Maureen, his wife of over 30 years and a 120-pound Bouvier des Flandres named Caesar. Maureen and their two children, Sam and Adam, are all active in the business.

You can follow all of Larry's hospitality writing on his blog at <u>www. larrymogelonsky.com</u>, you can subscribe to RSS feed, or subscribe to his weekly e-newsletter. Alternately, just email him at larry@ larrymogelonsky.com.

CPSIA information can be obtained at www.ICGtesting.com
Printed in the USA
LVOW11s1817130614

389977LV00002B/417/P